FREUD EGO

CLEMENT FREUD

ISIS

LARGE PRINT

Oxford

First published in Great Britain 2001
by BBC Worldwide Ltd.

Published in Large Print 2003 by ISIS Publishing Ltd,
7 Centremead, Osney Mead, Oxford OX2 0ES
by arrangement with BBC Worldwide Ltd.

British Library Cataloguing in Publication Data
Freud, Clement, 1924–
    Freud ego. – Large print ed.
    1. Freud, Clement, 1924–
    2. Politicians – Great Britain – Biography
    3. Television personalities – Great Britain – Biography
    4. Large type books
    I. Title
    941'.085'092

ISBN 0–7531–9798–7 (hb)
ISBN 0–7531–9799–5 (pb)

Printed and bound by Antony Rowe, Chippenham

FREUD EGO

For Jill.

(Whom I met on page 133, married on page 139)
without whom my life would have been quite unsuited
to an autobiography.
With love.

Contents

PROLOGUE

I was twelve years old; my prep school English master had given as homework: "Write your obituary in not less than three pages", and I came to school on Monday in my pink blazer bearing a black Maltese cross with my homework in my satchel.

I described the death in some detail (painful, slow, suffered with not much courage), wrote of Freud's impeccable late cut, his prowess as a wicket-keeper, the City firm he had founded and which made him one of the richest men of his day; I mentioned the yacht and the women who were noticeable by wearing black lipstick . . . and finished the piece with the belief that "his behaviour in later life meant that he will be little mourned, though missed by his cat".

On Tuesday Mr Millard, a serious schoolmaster whom I once tried to draw on the good news that had been brought from Ghent to Aix ("What was the news, sir? Had we beaten the Aussies?" "Shut up, Freud."), examined the class through his glasses, pursed his lips and said, "There was one obituary that made no mention of his school. Freud, you will stand outside the door and await the headmaster's attention."

I was going to be beaten. I had not hitherto been beaten, neither by my parents, who were not those sort of parents, nor at my previous school: a co-educational, nudist, lessons-are-optional, West Country progressive institution where the housemothers showed us illustrated books on the joys of sex before we went to bed. We would have preferred *The Railway Children*, but then it was not us, it was the school, that was progressive.

The headmaster of my prep school had a study on the first floor, and every half hour, or when he had nothing better to do, he would amble to the banisters and glance down at the doors to the classrooms below. Should there be a boy standing outside one, he was identified by name and summoned.

"Freud!" called the headmaster.

"Sir," I replied, making my way up the stairs.

"You have misbehaved and will be beaten."

"Sir," I replied.

"Pull down your trousers and bend over the desk . . . and your underpants, you stupid little boy."

"Sir," I replied, doing what I was bid.

The headmaster had a wicker basket full of canes. He picked one, thwacked it a few times on the pillow of an easy chair while he kept his eyes on me, and said, "As you are not a big boy, I will smack you with a gym shoe, across my knees."

He sat down and I moved from desk to chair, lowering myself where he indicated.

"Freud," he said, stroking my bare behind with the palm of his gnarled hand, "I believe that your

2

grandfather is opposed to corporal punishment; therefore I have decided not to beat you. Do you understand?"

"Yes, sir," I said. "May I pull up my trousers now?"

When people ask whether it is a help or a hindrance to have a famous grandfather, I admit that occasionally it is marginally helpful; I write "marginally" because after a caning you went to the bog and showed your friends the fearful weals on your bum. I had to tell them he had hit me so hard that the blood had congealed and my underpants were stuck and I couldn't lower them. No one believed me.

I wonder, is this where one starts an autobiography — the circumstances of one's first grope . . .?

CHAPTER
ONE

In which I say "Heil Hitler" to the Führer in Berlin, attend a progressive school in Devon where I play roulette and a non-progressive one where I learn to play cricket.

My parents met at Munich University, where my father studied architecture and my mother read classics. It was the year after the end of the First World War, in which my father had been an artillery officer in the Austro-Hungarian Army fighting the Italians. Twenty-five years later his son was an infantry officer in the British Army fighting the Italians. If you ask how this can be, both the Freuds and the Italians changed sides between the wars.

My father's family was distinguished; my mother's was rich. I know she got a dowry of a million — I am not sure a million what, but had it not been substantial I would not have got to hear about it. They married and set about having three children, then considered the proper number. We were born sixteen months apart, each given an archangel's name as the middle moniker. Stephen Gabriel was followed by Lucian Michael and then by me, Clement Raphael, on 24 April 1924. My father was one of six children, only three of whom had issue. Had it been otherwise, my share of grandfather's royalties would have been less. My mother had two sisters, each of whom had three children. She also had one brother, who after the war became a Catholic missionary, went to Palestine and was murdered on the Mount of Olives by mistake. A note and some money were left with the body, apologising for the mix-up. I read that he had married his childhood nanny, but the matter was never discussed at home.

After their marriage my parents bought a large apartment in the best part of Berlin. My father, who belonged to the Bauhaus school of architecture and designed houses for famous clients, had his office in our flat. When I was about three I built a Lego-type castle in the corridor outside his study; as he came past with an assistant, he looked at it and said, "That is an interesting construction." I spent the years before I went to school building interesting things in the corridor, hoping he would notice them. He did not.

My mother was very beautiful and fairly distant. When she came into the nursery she nodded to Stephen and me, and sat down with Lucian and whispered. They had secrets. I did not realise for many years that this is not what good mothers do.

My father had perfect taste. He knew how high pictures should be hung and would move them, unasked, in other people's homes. He also moved furniture and carpets and there were occasions, when he called on prospective clients, that they came to the reception room, saw what he was doing to it and went off to find another architect. He was a gourmand but in good shape: kind, generous, humorous, with a fund of

Viennese jokes that tended to revolve around food and the class system.

The man who says to the waiter: "The food was absolutely poisonous and the helpings much too small." The man who is asked whether he has enjoyed his dinner and says, "If the soup had been as hot as the champagne and the champagne as old as the chicken and the chicken as fat as the waitress it would have been all right." The aristocrat who is on a Vienna tram and the conductor, having sold him his ticket, recognises him.

"Count Bobby," he says. "I was your batman during the war. Don't you remember me?"

Count Bobby examines him through his monocle and says, "I remember you. How are things going?"

"Well, I am a tram conductor."

"OK, let me have another ticket."

On Sundays the family had lunch together and the fact that we had heard all his stories many times never dissuaded my father from telling them again, nor us from laughing. We children ate sparsely. My mother's brother-in-law was a paediatrician and had discovered that what was wrong with children was that they ate too much. As a consequence, we were always hungry. My uncle eventually divorced my aunt and emigrated to Shanghai, which could be why you see no fat Chinamen.

Religion did not figure in my family. I think my paternal grandfather was an atheist and, as far as I know, neither of my parents attended religious services. When I was sent to Derflingerstrasse infants' school in

7

Berlin at the age of six, my nanny left me at the door and I went in and met my teacher. After a few general questions, he asked, "What religion are you: Protestant or Catholic?"

I said I did not know.

"Where do you go to church?"

"I haven't been to church yet."

I was instructed to find out when I was collected for lunch, so asked my nanny whether I was a Catholic or Protestant and she said, "I don't know: I'll ask your mother tonight."

The next day on the way to school she told me about religion — "Your mother says you are Jewish" — and I told the teacher. When there were bible classes I was sent to a room where Herr Schindler tried to teach me the Hebrew alphabet, but God was not a subject that came into my life a lot.

My family arrived in England in the spring of 1933 . . . refugees from the Nazis before the habit had caught on. We were freaks. When my father designed his first house, in Sussex, the builder said, "You are Jewish. The only other Jew I have heard of was Jesus, so I will give you a discount." I doubt he is still doing that.

My parents took lodgings in Clarges Street, opposite the Ritz Hotel in London, and waited for a table to be sent on from Berlin. It was a specially designed table with a red marble top, circular, on a single tubular leg. The Freud fortune was secreted in that leg because there was a limit to the amount of money you could legally take out of the country; after the table arrived there was much relief.

8

While my father was gregarious and acquired friends who were peers, judges, doctors, builders and estate agents, my mother's friends tended to be refugee women of her age and station; women who also had to cope with bringing up children in a new country, a new language, a new set of manners . . . in Germany, for instance, it had been absolutely *verboten* to eat with one hand in your lap, cut your potatoes with a knife, not overtly wipe your mouth on a napkin before drinking from a glass.

Father's English was deliberately Austrian; Mother's was . . . well, became . . . rather good, though it started badly. I remember when we lived in Clarges Street she went to a dairy to buy cheese and the man behind the counter said, "We don't sell trees." Not understanding the social milieu, she went to a fishmonger in Shepherd Market to buy cod; the man said, "Cod, in Mayfair, never." She finished with a goodish accent and a vocabulary that excluded the colloquial. When we lived in St John's Wood, after a Sunday lunch party, one of our departing guests needed a taxi. My mother said she would phone the rank, and after a number of rings was heard to say, "Taxi, please, 32 St John's Wood Terrace." She listened, said thank you and put down the receiver, announcing, "He won't be long. He is just going to have a wank first." Unknown to her, the telephone had been answered by an obliging, inebriated, passer-by.

She told me that she hoped I was popular at school because Frau Koenig's son was at an establishment where they liked him so much that they had given him the name of a flower: "Isn't that sweet?" It transpired the boy was called Pansy.

Having never shopped before she came to England, she took to the Co-op, was passionate about her "divi" and in 1936 returned from one shopping expedition with five tickets for the Coronation of George VI . . . on which she also got a "divi". We went, had seats in the Mall and there was a vendor standing in front of us with a sign stating: "Real Viennese Frankfurters". I waved to the King and Queen in their coach — I who had waved at Hitler when we lived in Berlin and he had visited the Spanish Embassy next door. I had also said "Heil Hitler", which was cool. I didn't know who Hitler was, but everyone around me and my nanny said, "Heil Hitler" and I hated being different.

On arrival in England, the three Freud boys were sent to Dartington Hall, a recently opened co-educational school near Totnes in Devon, where the air was suffused with the smell of wild garlic and the natives spoke a language we could not understand. Stephen, serious, studious, with a slight nervous twitch, was then eleven and a half; Lucian, fearless, curly-haired, belligerent and artistic, was ten and a bit years old; I was coming up to my ninth birthday. We were not particularly close, having been nanny-reared and never taken anywhere other than together, which is a rotten way to bring up children. I was puny, a typical youngest son, sought attention, cried a lot.

We were scholars at Dartington — that is to say, my parents did not pay school fees because we were Sigmund Freud's grandsons, just the sort of folk parents wanted to have their children educated with; other scholars included the children of Bertrand Russell and Aldous Huxley. Fee-paying children tended to be the sons and daughters of parents who felt that having a child at school in Devon (while they lived in Yorkshire) was nearly as good as having no children at all. Barely a normal kid as far as the eye could see. Everyone had their own room, lessons were optional, and if you did not want to go to classes you could work on the school farm or in the pottery or pick up fallen leaves and get 4d an hour (for those too young to remember pounds, shillings and pence, 12 pence made a shilling, and 20 shillings a pound). One girl rode a horse outside the classrooms shouting, "Come on out — it's more fun than learning!"

There is a story told about Dartington at the time. A man rang the bell of the main school door . . . which was opened by a naked girl of about fifteen. He looked at her and said, "Oh, my God!" She said, "There is no God" and closed the door in his face. Nice manners were not part of the curriculum.

The food was good. Throughout my time at home prior to Dartington I had had steady hunger pains; thanks to that bloody uncle who had decreed that food was bad for us I had never had a second helping of anything. Now, in the school dining room, my eight-year fast (I was wet-nursed) was over. I particularly remember sausages, so peppery hot I could barely put them in my mouth, so delicious I was unable to leave them on my plate.

Let me get back to language. No one had told me — or, if they had, I did not take it on board — that in this new country to which we were going and where, after the arrival of the marble-topped table, we would live nearly as comfortably as we had in our house in Berlin and the one on a holiday island in the Baltic Sea, people would not speak a language I could understand. At first I thought they were doing it to make me angry, and I remember rushing into rooms in which I heard conversation, trying to catch them out. "Speak properly!" I shouted at them in German. "Speak so that I can understand."

What they were doing seemed rotten and unfriendly and, thankfully, after about a month they caved in and I understood them. There was a day when, at breakfast in the dining room, someone announced "a meeting" that afternoon and I said to Lucian, to whom I had got closer by default, that we should not miss that. We knew the word "eating" and this was not too different. We waited all afternoon at our table.

The three of us boarded in different houses: Stephen in one across the courtyard, Lucian in the one next to mine. In those first weeks Lucian would wake me early and we went to the farm where there were horses. Lucian threw stones at them and they galloped away.

"Why do you do that?"

"I love to see them galloping."

A master saw Lucian's action and tried to reason with him. Lucian ran off.

I settled into a sort of lifestyle during that first term: spent it eating a lot, getting beaten up (everyone could beat me up), having my pocket money taken by bigger children, stealing by slipping into other children's rooms and going through their pockets. I went to the cinema in Totnes where the price of seats was 3d but we went in a group — one of us paid 3d, went to the loo and opened the window, through which the rest of us climbed in for nothing. There were always two pictures, a major movie and a B-film, and the management had bought outright two films which they showed week and week about as their second feature. Thus did I learn English from Jessie Matthews in *Evergreen* and Tom Walls and Ralph Lynn in *Turkey Time*.

No one had taught me that you could leave a cinema before the film was over, so I saw those epics at least thirty times and came to love them, quoted from them, "There's something about a soldier which is fine fine fine." My accent was bad; I could not get the "th", which came out as "z" (as in "sumzink"), and throughout three years in what was supposed to be a seat of learning no one tried to do anything about polishing my accent.

In my second term I discovered drink. There was no great incentive to attend lessons, so I chose to help David Leach in the pottery for my 4d an hour. Leach discovered that I had a facility for making spouts for teapots, my fingers being the right size for that work, and several days a week I put in time winding rectangles of rolled brown clay around my little finger. When I had a shilling I took it to the Dartington cider works, for which I got a flagon of cider, which I drank.

I did not see a lot of Stephen, who was very unhappy at Dartington, but Lucian and I, having now become close, remained so. He took up riding, at which he excelled, having no fear. He also fought a lot. I think it was to do with being insufficiently fluent in English to counter insults, so he went for people: hit them, wrestled them to the ground, gave and got black eyes and bloody noses and I, who loved him a lot and had no other friends, stood on the perimeter of the fight crowd and cried.

But my life developed also. By the time of my tenth birthday I was making teapot spouts, drinking and staggering around the fields between school and pottery; I also read boys' comics: *Hotspur, Rover, Skipper, Adventure, Champion* and *Triumph*.

In my second year I took up gambling. On Saturdays an older boy called Bion Guy ran a roulette school in his bedroom; he had a wheel and a baize cloth and said, "*Faîtes vos jeux*" and "*Rien ne va plus*" and took maximum stakes of a halfpenny on a number. The wheel was less than totally true — must have had a ledge a fraction of a millimetre higher than the other ledges, causing the ball to favour the zero sector. With 6d pocket money, which I now knew how to keep, and the fourpences an hour I was comparatively flush — would risk a halfpenny on number 32 whenever I could get on and won one shilling and 5 pence ha'penny as often as I lost 6d. I noticed that I did not mind losing 6d and greatly enjoyed being able to push the boat out with my winnings: Crunchie bars cost 2d and I would take a girl called Sally Swing to the pictures and sit through *Turkey Time* yet again. I liked *Turkey Time* more each time I saw it, learnt more from the films and the comics than from such lessons I attended.

There was a very beautiful open-air theatre behind Dartington Hall and in my second year Paderewski came to give a concert. Paderewski was Prime Minister of Poland and a famous composer pianist; it was a huge feather in the organisers' cap to get him to play there. The art critics of the national papers were all coming to the event and it was decided that the occasion could be further enhanced if Sigmund Freud's youngest grandson would sit by the great man and turn the pages. I was delighted: my first time in the limelight.

My housemother ironed my best short trousers and found me a clean shirt and tie. I was introduced to the visiting party and given some sheet music to put in the rack over the Bechstein and at the appointed time Paderewski and I walked on to the stage. There was loud applause, I think mostly for him. He bowed and took his seat at the grand piano and I sat on the raised stool next to him, waving to some of my friends who were in the audience. He started to play and after a very short time he kicked me . . . which I considered a rotten thing to do bearing in mind the difference in our sizes and ages.

He said, "Turn" and, being a bright child, I realised he meant "Turn the page of what you have placed on the rack" and did so, wondering why no one had instructed me. I looked at the page. It contained rows of telephone wires with different birds sitting on them which I worked out must be music, of which I knew nothing.

We Freuds are a very unmusical family. In Vienna the Professor's house was a music-free zone. At home we had neither radio nor gramophone and, although in my first term at Dartington I had learnt to play "London's Burning" and "Three Blind Mice" on the recorder, I am tone dumb and in later life chose "Teach Yourself Spanish" on Linguaphone as my first record on *Desert Island Discs*.

I sat by Paderewski for over an hour, getting amiable kicks at regular intervals, and realised that, while sitting on a platform in front of a large audience was fun, music was not for me. I did, however, spend some of my birthday money the following term on a gramophone and the hit record of 1935, which was a song called "The Pig Got Up and Slowly Walked Away". (I played that second on *Desert Island Discs*.)

The one rigid rule at this progressive school was bedtime. At whenever it was, we had to be in our house, got swept into a bath — usually with a girl called Diana Petrov whose father had won a Nobel prize and who never spoke — then into the housemother's room for reading and looking at pictures, and finally bed. I slept badly then and still sleep badly now. I lay on my tummy and masturbated myself to sleep, never, as in later life, thinking of sex symbols as I did so (sixteen-year-old Livia Gollancz, daughter of the left-wing publisher Victor, swam in the outdoor pool naked, with huge tits and pubic hair and frightened me). I had this recurring nightmare which dated back to when I had first learnt arithmetic in Berlin. I was running along a road backwards and there was a huge steamroller with numbers on it coming for me; I would have to add and multiply and divide these before I could move away; I woke up sweating and screaming. The nightmare was called The Big Thing and ensured that no nanny my parents employed ever got a good night's sleep.

Our first holidays were spent in London, in the house in Clarges Street. We lived on the second floor and in the hall was a cigarette machine filled with Players Navy Cut cigarettes in packets of twenty. They cost 11½d — you put a shilling into the slot and pulled open a drawer containing the cigarettes on to which your halfpenny change had been stuck. It was Lucian who worked out that the technical sophistication of the machine enabled purchasers to obtain the fags by inserting a halfpenny, roughly the same size as a shilling coin, and discovered what I thought was perpetual motion — cornering the Clarges Street cigarette market with an initial investment of a halfpenny.

I don't think he smoked. He went out a lot, probably sold the cigarettes at a discount and did grown-up things. My role was to watch and encourage and not tell and lend him money when I had some; I do not remember getting any back.

After Clarges Street, going back to school was a pleasant change. The Dartington train left Paddington Station at around noon; we were locked into carriages (we were those sort of children) and, because we had a reputation for being those sort of children, the beginning-of-term train to Totnes was a red-letter day for the sex offenders of Britain, probably a close second to the Schoolboys' Exhibition at Earls Court. The pervs waited for us in the lavatories, which they did not lock, and one went in to find amiable men telling you not to be afraid. "Have some of your friends got big ones . . . like this?" one of them asked me.

Thinking back nearly seventy years, my years in Devon were almost entirely unacademic; also there were no organised games of any kind, though some of the masters played hockey and I watched that with interest and would like to have taken part. The Russian Ballet Joos had been accommodated at Dartington and I danced with them a lot; we were encouraged to do so and I was agile and they had a choreographer who was child-orientated. I remember dancing to the words:

Has a cow, has a cow, has a cow got common
  sense?
The answer to this question
In my book of indigestion
May be found, may be found, may be found in
  chapter three.

On reflection, it cannot have been "indigestion", but it sounded like it. Lucian rode, Stephen sulked and there was I dancing, also stealing chestnuts from the Elmhursts who owned the estate. I was caught stealing by Bill, the Devon yeoman whose land this was, who had married an American millionairess and built the whole shooting match. When I climbed down from the tree he was waiting, appeared angry, told me that I would have to pay him 3d for what I had taken. I said, "I'll owe you", which is what Dartingtonians always said. I still owe him.

When Stephen was thirteen, he wrote a letter home saying, "I am wasting my precious youth" and went to a public school, later getting an Exhibition to Cambridge. I realised that I would be unable to emulate my comic magazine heroes who left Greenfriars and became ace bicycle salesmen in Africa; no one had taught me how to multiply, and I asked to be sent to a proper school. Lucian stayed at Dartington longest, was finally requested not to return, the headmaster being unable to extend scholarship status to someone who only fought and rode and did what boys at co-educational schools do most of the time. He went on to be expelled from Bryanston, where they now boast of him as "an old boy who made good".

Dartington Hall School closed in the 1980s. Successive scandals — suicide, a murder, pregnancies and the headmaster posing in the nude for a naturist magazine — are what did it, and as there were not, being Dartington, a school magazine, an Old Dartingtonian association or famous ex-pupils proud of their alma mater, what remain are the music, the estate and the smell of wild garlic. It must have been quite a blow for sex offenders, not having that Great Western Railways train to Totnes three times a year.

My two and a half years at the Hall School, Hampstead were the happiest of my life: my green and salad days which I might not have appreciated as much had I not spent three years being "progressive" at Dartington. I was an orderly boy and the Hall was an orderly school. I liked discipline: the Hall held discipline high among virtues. I loved games. The Hall was into games.

I joined the Scouts and in time became deputy patrol leader of the Peewits; I joined the Ovalteenies, sang their song with tuneless vigour ("We are the Ovalteenies/ Happy girls and boys/ We run about/ And sing and shout/ And make a lot of noise." *Everyone* knew that song), and I learnt the Ovalteenies' secret code: your right forefinger to the side of your nose meant "Will you come home with me after school?" Doing it with your left finger to the left side of the nose conveyed "Someone is trying to find out our secrets." Thus one often went home with boys after school when one had intended to warn them of infiltrators.

For diversion we had Patsy Chases. A girl called Patsy waited outside the school entrance when we came out in the afternoons, ran away and we chased her. What we would have done had we caught her was not a subject to which we gave thought.

In the Scouts we had Saturday morning meetings on Hampstead Heath and indulged in a particularly violent exercise called "ankle tapping". It was as close to fighting as Scouts get, using our 6-foot-long staffs to try and tap an opponent's ankle before he tapped yours. Tapping was a euphemism; we limped home — those who did not have to go to hospital to have their ankles set. I collected cigarette cards of cricketers and footballers, swapped Hammond for Bradman with friends, of whom I had many: Sutton and Rickards and Cairns and Woodcock and Hunter and Frizzell, whose father was in skins — "which is furs, only you don't ever say furs, promise?"

I promised.

John Barnes was the big department store in Finchley Road, half a mile from the Hall; it supplied school uniforms, on which the headmaster got commission. Especially did he get commission on blazers. In my first term I played soccer, did well, got into the Second XI, but was told that I could not play in away games until I had bought a Second XI blazer. My poor parents did so. I played one game and was picked for the First XI . . . who had a different blazer and cap. Ditto rugby and cricket — never a selection for the first teams until the second-team equipment had been bought at John Barnes. I had blazers the way Imelda Marcos had shoes.

We sometimes went to the store after school, for they had a milk bar and we were into milk-shakes. My personal drink was milk and ice and honey whizzed up in the milk-shake machine. I had this theory that the longer it whizzed, the better the drink, and as the girl engaged the beaker in the whizzer I would call her over and ask, "I say, miss, is it true that you have five brothers, all of whom smoke pipes?" Anything to distract.

Scholastically I had no great problems. I liked and was good at English, and spoke French, mostly picked up from holidays in Brittany. My maths were adequate, and my mother, the classics scholar, did my Latin homework. As for music and art, I was crap but then I played games and that made it all right.

I did not know about cricket until I went to the Hall; had some coaching from Mr Rotherham the games master, who told me how to hold the bat and to which balls to play forward, which back. Having a good eye, I mastered the technique.

In my first game I hit balls all over the place and was picked to play for my house. In that game I hit balls all over the place, and at one point there was applause and Mr Rotherham stared at me and I said, "What is it, sir?" and he said, "Nice boys declare when they have scored 50" and bade me return to the pavilion.

I was twelve, picked for the First XI (my parents had bought the blazer), and the school was abuzz with the advent of our needle game against the Abbey at Beckenham: best prep school cricket team around. The Hall was in north-west London, Beckenham in the south-east. Early lunch for us cricketers and then a long journey by coach. The Hall had not beaten the Abbey for six years; we sat in our dressing room like men going into battle against fearful odds, and Mr Rotherham said, "Just don't do anything foolish."

They won the toss, batted, scored 130 runs and we had tea. I was batting No 5. Our first three wickets fell for half a dozen runs and I went in. "Don't do anything foolish," said Mr Rotherham as I passed him standing as umpire at square leg. "No, sir," said I, and the balls came and I hit them and after about half an hour there was applause. I looked at the scoreboard. The Hall total was 89 for 7. I had scored 50. I remembered what I had been taught and shouted, "I declare" and there was pandemonium. Rotherham raced to the Abbey's master umpiring at the other end and said, "Ignore him, he is a German boy and doesn't understand cricket." And their umpire said, "Like hell he doesn't — he has declared."

In my last year at the Hall I was house captain, played first-team soccer, rugby, cricket and squash and wrote regularly for the school magazine. I also played at the Oval for South Under-14s against North, had my hat signed by Ponsford and McCabe, one of whom, in his speech, looked forward to welcoming us to Oz when we represented our country. This was the highlight of my life to date.

As a consequence of being boisterous, shouting in corridors and running where you were meant to walk I had done more detentions than most boys, and as detentions meant learning chunks of poetry I left the Hall knowing "Morte d'Arthur", "The Pied Piper of Hamelin", "The Ancient Mariner" and most of Keats and Shelley by heart, also had "Albert and the Lion" as a party piece.

Why these educational establishments are called preparatory schools is a puzzle. They build you up so that you can go to your next school and get knocked down. I went from there to a public school where I was not picked for a single sports team, was taught to box, because I weighed under 6 stone and could beat other dwarves, got bullied and beaten. At Dartington religion, like so many other subjects, had failed to show on the curriculum. At the Hall, by contrast, everyone attended prayers every morning. When I went to St Paul's I found that anti-semitism was rife, as was anti-any minority. I remember going to a scout camp in Collingbourne Ducis where there was a big tent for most of the boys and two small separate ones: the first for a boy who snored loudly, the other for me because I was a Jew.

At St Paul's the masters did not beat the boys; you were sent for punishment to the porter's lodge where you were given a piggy-back, by the junior porter, buttocks hanging down. The senior porter rubbed your bum, picked a cane, swished it around a bit and hit you as many times as had been decreed. In the course of this, all three participants could be seen to have erections.

CHAPTER
TWO

In which I recall some notable bearers of my
name and my introduction to East Anglia.

At a Hunt Ball in the early 1950s a lissom English Rose
of a fair-haired, blue-eyed girl came up to me.

"I say, are you really Sigmund Freud's grandson?"

"Yes, I am."

"I say, congratulations! May I dance with you?"

I explained Sigmund Freud was not into dancing,
though strong on sex. She blushed and ran off.

In the 1950s Sigmund Freud was not as famous as
he became, but ever and anon people came up and
asked me what it was like being the great man's
grandson . . . I would admit that it must be better than
to be called Freud and be unrelated to Sigmund.

I was seven years old when it was my turn to
accompany my father to Vienna and stay with his
parents in their apartment in the Berggasse, now a
museum.

Lucian, who had already been, told me that the
waiting room was full of lunatics frothing at the mouth
who had come for treatment. Lucian was an
imaginative child. The home of Professor Dr Freud was
large and comfortable, and my grandmother spoilt me
with Viennese cakes. My grandfather, who suffered

from cancer of the mouth for his last many years, was benign and cigar-smoking and showed me his antiques and I went upstairs to my bedroom and had pillow fights with their maid, Paula, who devoted her life to the Freuds, came to London with them in 1938, stayed to look after my Aunt Anna after my grandparents had died.

While my grandmother was small and warm and busy and organised, her sister Minna was tall and blind and steadily disapproving. Great-aunt Minna had been engaged to a man who died in the Franco-Prussian War and she never got over it; she lived with my grandparents and is rumoured to have shared their bed. I did not learn of this until the 1970s when a Freud biography claimed this relationship and I appeared on a Johnny Carson show in New York: Carson asked, "Hey, do you remember your Great-aunt Minna?"

Surprised by the question, I replied, "She was six foot four and blind, smelt of embalming fluid and tried to spike me with her white stick."

"Apparently she was some dame in the sack!" said Carson, pointing to the book on Sigmund's private life.

I was too shocked to take umbrage.

In 1930s' Vienna my grandfather took his dog and me for a walk one morning. He held my hand and we chatted, and after a while came across a crowd that had gathered around a man seized by a fit who lay on the pavement twitching. His hat had fallen from his head and some of the crowd, to express their sympathy at the man's affliction, put coins into the hat. Had I been with my nanny, she would have put her hand over my eyes and hurried me away. My grandfather stood and watched for a while, then we resumed our walk.

"Why did you not put money in the man's hat?" I asked.

"He did not do it well enough."

The old Freuds were into dogs. I remember in Berlin we had a greyhound called Billy; in Vienna they had an Alsatian who was reputed to be extremely bright, as befits a Freud dog. The story goes that this dog got lost in the city, went to a cab-rank and shook his collar at a driver who examined it, recognised the owner's name and drove the dog home. At the corner of the Berggasse the Alsatian, "because he knew that there took place at the end of the taxi-ride some transaction which he would be unable to carry out", claimed the great man, jumped out of the cab window and ran home.

When the Nazis marched into Vienna in 1938 both American Ambassador Bullitt and Princess Marie Bonaparte (a patient and friend) moved into the Berggasse to ensure no harm would come to the old man. The SS arrived at the house, smashed their way in — my grandmother requested them to wipe their boots but they ignored her — broke a few things on their way to the study and, following instructions with which they were clearly unhappy, told the eighty-two-year-old Professor that he could leave the house provided he signed a statement.

He put on his glasses to read: "I Professor S. Freud am leaving my house of my own free will at the request of the SS", signed it and then asked the senior man whether he might add something to that statement.

And he wrote a post-script, "I would like to recommend the SS to everyone", after which he was driven to the station and subsequently arrived in London via Paris. I got a day off from school to greet him — I and the British Freuds and a very large number of journalists from around the world.

For the last eighteen months of his life I saw him on Sundays and got birthday presents from him, memorably an Egyptian artifact, taken from a grave, that looked very much like Queen Victoria. He asked whether I saw the likeness.

I said, "Queen Victoria 1837–1901." I knew the dates but not what she looked like.

He died soon after the outbreak of the Second World War. I was a schoolboy filling sandbags in Crowthorne at the time, and the headmaster, who had heard the news on the wireless, told me of his demise. Sigmund Freud left his estate to be divided among his six children; his six grandchildren received his royalties.

My Aunt Anna, the youngest Freud daughter, remained with her father all his life, studied psychoanalysis, was a renowned child analyst and an outstandingly brilliant lecturer. During the war she opened a centre for war-damaged children, where I used to cook on my day off. I was both fond of her as an aunt and in awe of her as an intellectual and upholder of the family profession.

The *New Statesman*, which was then widely read by people like us, held weekly competitions: on one occasion contestants were to write, in not more than 350 words, the conversation between an analyst and patient after three years of treatment. One of the prizewinning entries had the patient saying, "Goodbye, I made it all up." I showed this to my aunt, who had by this time bought a house in Walberswick, the Suffolk village where we spent our summers, thinking it would amuse her. As she read it the lines on her forehead grew deeper and she said, "The patient was not cured."

She celebrated her eightieth birthday in her house in Skibbereen in County Cork. She had been made a CBE, had honorary doctorates from universities around the world, and telegrams came flooding in. Every couple of hours the postmistress would cycle to my aunt's house with a new bunch and on one of those visits Anna said she would like the postwoman to check a message delivered last time.

"Would it be the one from Philadelphia?" asked the woman.

My aunt said, "Yes, there must be some mistake."

The woman replied that she herself had thought that but checked the text and it was right: "THE RAPISTS OF PHILADELPHIA SEND THEIR CONGRATULATIONS AND GOOD WISHES." My aunt was unworldly and the postmistress did not know the word "therapist".

Sadly, we had fallen out by this time. In 1944 I came home on leave, stayed in our Suffolk house and went that first evening to the pub where there was one other customer.

"Have a drink," I said.

He declined.

"Have one. We're the only two people here. I hate drinking on my own. I'm on leave for three days, will probably get shot by the end of the week. Have a drink."

He said, "Really not."

I said, "Really yes. Count it as part of your war effort," and I bought him a whisky, asked him to buy me one, bought him another, after which it became easier.

There are two pubs in our village: the Bell, where we were, and the Anchor, some 300 yards up the street. As no one else came into the Bell, I suggested we move to the Anchor. On the way there he made a pass at me and I told him to fuck off.

It was some years before I learnt the cause of Anna's froideur towards me: the man in the Bell had been a patient of hers, close to being cured of inebriation and homosexuality.

Let me explain Walberswick; it lies on the Suffolk coast. Between Yarmouth and Felixstowe, you tell people who have hardly any geography; between Lowestoft and Aldeburgh if they are a little more knowledgeable. The exact location is on the south bank of the River Blyth where it flows into the sea. Southwold is a mile to the north, as the crow flies; Dunwich, which once returned two Members to Parliament but has mostly fallen into the sea, is a couple of miles down the beach on the way to Sizewell, which has brought great prosperity to the region. Six years of public inquiries into the desirability of the nuclear power station meant that there was not a hotel, boarding house, B and B or camp site that did not flourish from the patronage of lawyers, journalists, civil servants, expert witnesses and protesters.

East Anglia rather prides itself on confusing strangers. Happisburgh on the Norfolk coast is pronounced Haysborough, Cossey is found on the map as Costessey, go to Hunstanton and they call it Hunston. Walberswick is known around our parts as Walsberwick. My father bought our holiday house there when I was ten. You drive up the A12, turn off to the right as you approach the village of Blythburgh (pronounced Blyboro) and make for the sea. Walberswick is where the road ends; if you don't like it you drive the 3 miles back to the A12. Before the war we had a chain ferry that took cars and people across the river to Southwold. They blew up the ferry in 1940.

"Why did you do that?" I had asked Mr Reynolds, shopkeeper, chairman of the parish council, husband of Mrs Reynolds who had the beachwear shop, brother of Miss Reynolds who did afternoon teas and made jam.

"To win the war, boy." ("Boy" in Suffolk is pronounced "buoy".)

It worked. Took a long time, one must admit, but it worked.

After 1940 a rowing boat carried people across the river; it used to cost one penny a trip, and I remember coming home on leave from the Army in 1943, asking Mr English who rowed the boat whether business was good.

He shook his head. "Not the money about, boy."

The Lloyd George concept of a community was one based on the cornerstones of church, school, shop and pub. We were a community. St Andrew's church stands on the left as you drive into Walberswick, with genuine ruins to show that it was once larger. Churches in the Middle Ages were built to reflect the prosperity of the locality, and East Suffolk was well-heeled: all that wool from the north-west to be sorted and graded for export to Holland. There was also a Methodist chapel, though few Methodists. The school was of the one-teacher variety — for the retention of which we fought so hard, which did such educational harm: nervous child throws up on teacher's shoes on first day of school, spends eight years suffering the consequences.

Mr Reynolds' shop sold most things, and there was a greengrocer who upped and left in 1939. A baker pushed a barrowful of bread through the village each day, returned to Southwold on the ferry; and a fish and chip van parked Thursday evenings on the village green. Of our two pubs, the Anchor was rather formal, people wore ties in the saloon bar throughout the year; the Bell was less square: managed houses both, selling Adnam's ales. Adnam's is one of the constants of this part of East Suffolk.

The village green was the epicentre of Walberswick: on one side the Reynolds emporia and the post office, on the other the phone box. My mother used it a lot in those "Press button A" days. All calls were via the operator, who got your number and told you how much to put into the slot before pressing button A. My mother, who was eccentric in this respect, held a collection of small foreign coins — French cents, Portuguese and Austrian and Danish pieces of hardly any value at all — and when the operator said, "Put sevenpence in the slot for your call to London" she began shovelling the coins into the aperture before saying, "There!"

"Press button B to get your money back, and put the coins in more slowly," said the operator.

She repeated the process, shouting, "I am putting them in as slowly as I can!"

At the top end of the green stood the house of Mr Block the builder. He went to prison during the war for some minor transgression of the building regulations; with no one allowed to do any construction not vital to the war effort, our prisons held a fair sprinkling of architects, builders and artisans. Mr Block's daughter was very tall and I once kissed her during a game of Postman's Knock at the Gannon Room. (The Misses Gannnon had left a substantial sum of money for the erection of halls in East Anglian villages.) On another occasion, playing that same game, I landed old Mrs Fairs, wife of our gardener, who threw herself into the embrace with such vigour I was off women for weeks. I played football for the Under-14s alongside her son Jack, who was killed in North Africa while serving with the Eighth Army.

In those days Walberswick was a fishing village with a little holiday trade and a population of around five hundred. Fishing is no longer what it was, though some Lowestoft-registered smacks remain on the Southwold side of the river, by the Harbour Inn. The Harbour is famed for having a rare music licence, and achieved national notoriety as the place where you could find Dinks Cooper.

Dinks, son of Toe Cooper who emptied our and many other villagers' Elsans — so called because a First World War injury left him with a walk consisting of a left-foot stride and right-foot drag to catch up (most Walberswick boys could do a pretty good Toe Cooper walk) — was a character of note. An ex-fisherman, he had met a mermaid and talked of the encounter on BBC radio, a talk that was often repeated and earned him drinks from all to whom he retold the tale. Dinks at the Harbour in Walberswick was like Jeffrey Bernard at the Coach and Horses in Soho, though, unlike Jeffrey, Dinks was tall and handsome and a catch for women in search of local talent — which he was, especially within a day or two of his bath night.

Next to the British Legion hall was a garage run by Mr Rogers, who repaired cars and bikes and chauffeured people to the station: miserable old sod Rogers was, doubled as a bookmaker when the pastime was illegal. I discovered the cause of his misery.

On the first Wednesday of June 1932 the Wall's ice cream man came across on the ferry, pushed his "Stop me and buy one" tricycle up the hill towards the green, stopping at the Bell for a pint of Adnam's ale. In the bar he told the assembled company that his guvnor's horse was going to win the Derby at Epsom, took up his usual position opposite Miss Reynolds' teashop selling Snofrutes (1d) and choc ices (2d) for half an hour. He then revived himself with another glass of ale at the Anchor where he repeated his Derby advice before pushing off to Blythburgh.

Mr Rogers had struck it lucky that Wednesday: a man with more money than sense had booked him to catch the London train at Ipswich — there was a perfectly good station at Darsham, only 7 miles away — and when he returned Mrs Rogers greeted him with the happy news: thirty-seven envelopes containing Derby bets had been handed in at the back door of where they lived. Each bet was for Mr Tom Walls' April the Fifth, which won at 18–1. If he had ever smiled before, I never saw him smile again.

During my school holidays I made friends with Walberswick boys of my age. At school in London I was called Freud; they had names like Jinx and Tiddler and Heron and Hairy. I tried to emulate their speech and their actions . . . especially the way they greeted people in the street: make eye contact, mention the person's name and tilt the chin towards the left shoulder and back, never breaking step. The first time I tried it out — on Mr Palmer the ferryman — he regarded my antics with amazement, turned and watched me go; I had to pretend I had this contortion and walked away snapping my chin into my left shoulder every ten seconds.

Three times a year, then, during the holidays, I became a Walberswickian. I sat on the bench outside the Gannon Room where real villagers sat and tried to remember which of my friends supported which football team — Ipswich Town and Norwich City were equidistant — keeping very quiet about my own

35

passion for Plymouth Argyle, whom I had supported when at Dartington and who kept nearly winning the Third Division South.

Though I always retained my connection with Walberswick, and we later bought a house there myself, I did not keep up with my childhood friends; exchanging Suffolk nods as we passed in the street was about it. Then, some years ago, Hairy came to my back door, looked a bit embarrassed, explained that he was taking his first trip abroad, holiday in Spain, and had this passport form and pictures which had to be signed by a doctor or lawyer or MP and I was one of those, wasn't I? I signed the form, picked up the photograph and wrote: "I certify that this is a true likeness of . . .", apologised and asked how Hairy spelt his name.

He said, "H-A-R-R-Y. What did you think? Don't they teach you anything up London?"

CHAPTER
THREE

In which I discover that life out there is neither middle-class nor necessarily celibate.

In my obituary, which David Steel, my former parliamentary colleague, now Speaker of the Scottish Parliament, has been commissioned to write for *The Independent* (hasn't yet, but rings me every few months to tell me to hang on in there until he does) it will state that C. Freud left school at sixteen to become a cook. True, but doesn't tell it all.

The war had been on for nine months; Stephen was at Cambridge and Lucian, who was always going to be a great artist if he did not get hanged for some heinous crime, was at the Slade ... though I have met contemporaries of his who swear he hardly ever turned up. My father had no work and no money to send a third son into tertiary education. He was of the generation that felt capital did not count; income was what mattered, and there was no income. I don't think my career was given a great deal of thought. What transpired was that a relative was placed as a guest at the Dorchester Hotel and instructed to persuade the manager to take me on as a trainee; I was engaged at 10s a week less 1s 4d for my national insurance stamp. Why one needed influence to get a job that paid marginally over 2d an hour is something I have yet to understand, but I went along with it.

To manifest poverty, or perhaps because he was poor . . . Freuds don't discuss money — not that generation of Freuds . . . my father let our house in St John's Wood and moved into a flat in Hampstead, a floor above Stephen and Natasha Spender who were friends. Stephen was brave enough to be a conscientious objector and worked in the Fire Service — probably one of the least efficient firemen in the metropolis. Natasha was a concert pianist.

At the Spenders' I met W. H. Auden, whose poetry I hugely admired and could recite in great wodges; Auden urinated in the kitchen sink, in full view of us all, and had the most disgusting table manners I have encountered . . . but had written *The Ascent of F6* (with Christopher Isherwood) and *The Ballad of Edith Gee*, which made it all right.

I wanted to be a poet. I wanted to go to Oxford. I wanted to do what my schoolfriends were doing, which was not going to a hotel kitchen to work forty-eight-hour weeks for 8s 8d.

By this time I had lost my Cherman accent, though Lucian kept his and my father's seemed to get more pronounced over the years. "I am Austrian, why should I pretend to be Breetish?" was his battle-cry; he had sought and been granted naturalisation in early 1939. Certificate BZ1216, I seem to recall. I worked hard on being a normal British schoolboy and could do my party piece, "Albert and the Lion", with a reasonable

Lancashire accent, though I had trouble pronouncing "horse's head handle".

To go back to 1940: I had sat my School Certificate, later learnt that I got five credits and three distinctions; my father told me that I was not exactly academic but known for being practical. (Apparently, when I was three years old my maternal grandmother came to visit us at our island holiday house in the Baltic Sea and had been accommodated in a flat over the local baker's shop. I had suggested that, when she came to us for breakfast each morning, she might bring some fresh doughnuts from the shop below. Who's a clever boy, then?)

When I went for my interview at the Dorchester the manager looked at me, told me I could start work in the kitchen next Monday and advised me to go and sit in Hyde Park between lunch and dinner and breathe nice fresh air for the good of my health. I was still puny, had boxed for my school at 7 stone 7 lbs, and managers, having done a spell in the kitchen, knew that fresh air in basements was at a premium.

So I, who could recite the whole of Chaucer's Prologue to the *Canterbury Tales* and *Julius Caesar* and *Trial by Jury* (and "Albert and the Lion"), and had set my heart on reading English at Exeter College where Neville Coghill, the great Chaucerian scholar, was a professor, went to Denny's catering outfitters in Old Compton Street and purchased the sartorial and professional requisites for an apprentice chef: blue and white check trousers, double-breasted white jacket, two tall hats . . . which are soft until they have been sent to the laundry and come back starched and a set of knives. Thus for the first fortnight in the profession that had been chosen for me I was not only useless but looked a prat, a tall hat flopping on my shoulder while I peeled carrots, the lowliest occupation on offer. The Veg commis (commis is the next rank up) asked whether my father could not have lent me one of his hats.

I explained that my father was an architect.

"Grandfather, then."

I shook my head.

"You have come up in the world," was his verdict.

The Dorchester kitchen was a hell-hole of a huge dank dark dungeon built regardless of inconvenience to staff. Like most first-class establishments it used the Carême brigade system: five departments, called parties, each with a range of stoves and a long work-surface opposite. Soup was the low man on the totem pole; after that Veg, then Fish and slightly above that Roast, then finally Sauce. Sauce was the most senior party, produced the most complicated dishes, had the most skilful chef: sauce-chefs are only one pay-rise behind sous-chefs, two away from head-chef, which is as grand as you can get.

Elsewhere in the basement was the larder with its butcher, fishmonger and oysterer, the cold rooms, patisserie, hors d'oeuvrier, bakehouse, Still-room for tea and coffee, dry-goods store, silver room for cleaning cutlery and serving dishes, plate room, plunge for washing saucepans, staff changing rooms, staff dining rooms, and a small office where the man employed to kill cockroaches slept until it was time to put on knee pads and hunt his foe at night.

The main kitchen in such establishments is hot and loud and feudal. Apprentices can talk only to commis, never speak to — but often get shouted at by — chefs. There is an indoctrination procedure in which someone tells you to get something from the cold room and locks the door on you. An hour later, frozen, you hear the outside padlock being opened and a furious chef shouts at you, "Fucking skiver! Thought it was cushier sitting here than working?" and throws a damp cloth at you.

Outside, in 1940, the war was on: the kitchen, indeed the hotel, was staffed by those too young or too old to fight, too halt, too lame or too foreign for military service. By way of provisions there were few eggs — we used powdered eggs for mayonnaise — little butter, hardly any fish that nice people would call fish, and meat was heavily rationed. We pretended it was all as it should be, and cooked as Maître Escoffier decreed in his *Repertoire de la Cuisine*, which is the chef's bible.

Kitchens work in French, whatever the language of the practitioners. A waiter comes down from the restaurant with an order, gives it to the *aboyeur* (barker), who calls out, "*Ça marche deux couverts: deux Potage à la Reine*" . . . and the listener on the soup party calls out, "*Oui*." On to "*Une Sole Florentine*" ("*Oui*" from Fish), "*Une assiette anglaise*" shouted down the speaking tube to the larder and acknowledged, then the veg order. On my second day I was deputed to listen for and reply to orders for Pommes au Four (baked potatoes) and, though I had gone into the loo and

41

rehearsed shouting *"Oui"* at the top of my voice — which might have been misunderstood by casual passers-by — no one ordered baked potatoes.

In my first week I did as the manager had suggested: walked across the road, sat in Hyde Park and breathed deeply. It was there that Fish chef, resplendent in an Anthony Eden hat and dark suit, saw me. Fish chef had taken something of a shine to me and my floppy hat; he was probably in his late twenties, unfit for the services because his nose had been severed and carelessly sewn on again. (He said it had happened while driving a racing car; rumour had it that he had fallen off his potty and cut it.)

"Boy, I've been watching you and you'll be all right. If anyone tries to make you shit, tell me and I'll sort them out."

"Yes, chef," I replied, standing up from my park bench, having not the faintest idea of what he meant but carefully locking the lavatory door until I discovered, some weeks later, that "making you shit" is kitchen-speak for giving you a hard time. I had feared worse.

Like a frog who hovers around waiting to be kissed and returned to being a prince, I waited to be discovered by my workmates. I dreamt of the Grill Room manager coming down and asking if anyone could help translate the final stanza of *Beowolf*, and being identified and rescued. It wasn't a bit like that. Veg cook was an old French drunk who had been recalled from bibulous retirement when war broke out. He smelt of garlic, which he chewed as others chew

42

gum, and his favourite trick was to garnish restaurant-bound silver veg dishes by filling his mouth with chopped parsley and shooting the now garlic-scented herbs on to his vegetables through the gaps between his teeth. This was particularly effective with new potatoes, where the evenness of his aim made the dish look impressive.

And he sang, continuously, tunelessly, and if you should be unfortunate enough to get close it was always the same "Oh Susannah, won't you marry me?" tune, to which his words were:

Down in Alabama where the darkies shovel coal
A darkie shoved his shovel up another darkie's
    hole
The foreman came along and said, "You're here to
    shovel coal
And not to shove your shovel up another darkie's
    hole."

He also stole my shandy ration. In the extreme heat of service, Arthur, the senior kitchen porter and assistant in the head-chef's office, would come round with a huge jug of shandy and pour each of us a silver sauce-boat full. Glass was not allowed in kitchens lest there were breakages and splinters.

Arthur was Indian.

"Allight, chef?" he would ask after pouring the drink for the four of us. "Allight, Arthur," said chef, draining the shandy of his two boys.

43

Being an apprentice on the veg was a rotten job, widely considered to be a rotten job, but I was a creep and did it to the very best of my ability and simply by being there I learnt about veg cooking. Being an orderly boy with a retentive memory I mastered Escoffier's 131 potato dishes from *Le Repertoire*. Chips went from Pommes Pont Neuf, which are very large fried potatoes, to Frites, Allumettes and Paille, which are so fine you must cut the raw potatoes on a mandoline . . . as you do game crisps and Pommes Gaufrettes, which are like crisps but thicker and with holes in them. Then there were Pommes Soufflé, which were magic.

You peel a medium-sized King Edward potato with your veg knife into a smooth barrel shape, cut off the ends and mandoline the tubes into half-centimetre slices. These you wash before drying each slice in a cloth. You use two deep pans, the first containing fat that is just hot enough for the insertion of the potato slices to cause ripples rather than bubbles, and you leave them at that temperature, agitating the deep fat constantly. After a few minutes you notice that blisters appear on the slices. When all are nicely blistered you remove the potatoes (with a big pan you can do about twenty at a time) on to a cloth to drain the surplus fat from them. Then you plunge them into smoking hot fat in the second pan and the blisters cause the entire potato slice to puff up like a pillow. Cook until they are a light mahogany colour on each side. Put them back on the cloth to remove the fat, and serve. A soufflé potato amazes people; for me it was as close to proving that one plus one makes three, made me proud to be a chef . . . Then I went back to washing spinach, making crosses in the stalks of brussels sprouts and stringing French beans. Some months later I was promoted to apprentice tournant, working on a different party each day, covering for apprentices on their days off.

Meanwhile there was my life to think about. I was sixteen, still a virgin but now constantly aware of sex. On the bus to work I would habitually get so large an erection that in order to hide the bulge I got off and sloped down Park Lane looking like the Hunchback of Notre Dame with a hernia.

Kitchen boys stopped work at 9 p.m. when I would go to Soho to find Lucian and slowly sip a drink at the Coffee Ann, which was frequented by artists: these were altogether more interesting human beings than I encountered in the hotel. I never met any desirable girls in the Quality Inns — sort of trendier cafés than Lyons, where young cooks bought each other teas between shifts and propositioned the waitresses — whereas the Coffee Ann was replete with beauteous and available talent. I was in love with love . . . desperate to find something on two or at a pinch four legs on which to focus.

In the autumn of 1940 the hotel, unable to attract suitable restaurant staff, employed girls to take the places of young male waiters called up for military service; I thought one called Avis was particularly fetching. I told my senior commis chef, a tired Italian plucked out of an old people's home.

"That Avis," I said, "she is so beautiful."

"Boy," said the chef, "if she hadda as many pricks sticking outtaher as have beena stuck into her she'd be a porcupine."

At night in bed I closed my eyes to visions of Avis with all those penises, and at the earliest opportunity invited her out to dinner on her day off. She said her mother wouldn't let her, she'd never been out with a boy, but thanks for asking.

So it was back to the Coffee Ann, where there was a really available girl whom I invited to supper on my next day off.

She said, "How about half past ten day after tomorrow?"

I said, "Fine". Bought her a small box of chocolates, got to the Coffee Ann at ten o'clock after work, saw her sitting with some other people and after about half an hour she came and joined me.

"Shall we go out?"

I said, "Yes indeed", having booked a table in what was supposed to be an artistic restaurant that stayed open late.

She said, "I haven't got long. Let's go to the park", and we went to Russell Square and she sat on the grass and said, "Come and sit next to me." I took off my mackintosh so that she could sit comfortably, sat next to her, and she grabbed my prick and I noticed she was wearing no knickers. In hardly any time (less than hardly any time) I was inside her but, as I was about to come, realised that this would give her a baby and I would have to marry her and, while attractive, girls who wear no knickers are not wife material. I withdrew. So

46

much for going to a "progressive" co-educational school. She pouted, lay there for a short while, got up and said, "See you". I set off to walk home to St John's Wood.

Passing Lords Cricket Ground, I realised that I had left my mackintosh on the grass in Russell Square and walked back. Clothes were on coupons during the war; losing a coat would have been a blow. It was October; there was hardly any moon as I walked up and down looking for it. An air raid warden came and joined me, asked what I was doing, and when I told him I had carelessly left my mac somewhere round here in the grass he kindly lit his torch — air raid wardens were allowed to use torches so long as there was no raid on — and we found it . . . with a nasty dark stain on the fawn material. That experience put me off sex for several days.

Bombs fell throughout the nights and on my way to work in the mornings, I found Park Lane littered with large pieces of shrapnel from our anti-aircraft guns. Being a civilian became an embarrassment. "Young man, why aren't you in the forces?" women would snap at anyone over the edge of puberty. Lucian had his stock reply: "Madam, why aren't you having a war baby?" I took up knitting . . . a cotton reel with four nails and you lifted the wool with a hook and a useless woollen pigtail emerged from the bottom of the reel. It looked a patriotic thing for a civilian to be doing.

As my seventeenth birthday approached, I volunteered for the Air Force. Not long after that I was called for an interview at RAF Uxbridge, took a test and was passed

PNA — the letters stand for pilot/navigator/air-bomber, the highest category — took an oath, was given a number and told to consider myself an airman.

My next communication from the Air Ministry informed me that pilots etc. were not getting killed at the expected rate and there would be a slight delay in my joining up. A few days after that I received a personal letter asking me to attend the Ministry the following Tuesday at 4p.m. I realised that they had done a bit of homework and come to the conclusion that I was a man of quality who should be left in civilian clothes for not a day longer.

I arrived punctually, was shown into a large waiting room, then ushered into an office where a senior officer with many medals on his uniform sat behind a desk. I saluted (creep) and he said, "Frood, sit down."

I sat down.

"Frood," he said, shuffling papers that I recognised as those I had filled in at Uxbridge, "it says here that you were born in Berlin. Tell me, Frood — Berlin, Germany?"

I was surprised that two years into the war there were people who did not know the whereabouts of Berlin, and said, "Actually, sir, Berlin, Sussex."

"That's more like it, Frood," said the wing commander "Berlin, Sussex, eh?"

"No, sir," I said, "Berlin, Germany."

I was asked to go back to the waiting room, then summoned to another office where an altogether brighter wing commander explained that people born in enemy countries are not, other than in exceptional circumstances, recruited as PNAs.

I could think of no exceptional circumstances and volunteered for the Navy — it took a year before I was called up into the Army. A good year for me, with the handicap of virginity out of the way; my high culinary ambitions dampened by the inevitability of joining up and getting killed on some battlefield, I enrolled at Pitman's College to learn shorthand (and meet girls); joined a dog-racing fraternity; briefly became a waiter (the manager remembered that I was a "trainee"), then worked in the Control Office where you ensure that every docket received in the kitchen is charged against someone's account. I was now earning £3 a week and had left home, moving in with acquaintances who became friends in a wooden house in Charles Street, 200 yards from the Dorchester's staff entrance. With incendiaries falling nightly on the metropolis, the market for rented wooden buildings was depressed. My share of the rent was two roast chickens a week (about par for a thieving apprentice cook).

I read Norman Douglas' book about aphrodisiac food and was much taken by it, especially a recipe for a love potion made of hock and seltzer poured into an iced glass coated with angostura bitters, topped with apricot brandy. Miss Hill worked in the Bill Office and I invited her to dine in Charles Street, told her I would cook. We ate some coley, which was the only fish available, and I, with my unique position in the hotel enabling me to assemble the ingredients for the potion, prepared this and persuaded her to drink it. It worked.

A few days later, as one of my hotel friends was boasting of his sexual conquests, I was able to tell him about the glamorous Miss Hill and detailed the drink that did it, stressing the icing of the glass, the bitters . . . and that final flourish of apricot brandy. I thought he would be impressed. I was wrong. He said he had fucked Miss Hill after half a pint of mild ale.

Three afternoons a week, after service, a taxi waited outside the staff entrance to take those of us who liked that sort of thing to Stamford Bridge greyhound races. I went often; just how I managed on 8s 8d a week I no longer remember, but I had a Post Office savings book and medium-generous relatives and won almost as often as I lost. I gambled instinctively, watching the shifting of the odds rather than assessing the form, the draw, the going and the trainer. Bovril was my afternoon drink.

There was an occasion when I had won a forecast and got something like 7s 6d for my half of a 2s ticket. After I had collected my winnings, a man I did not know bowed to me, looked at me again and walked off. Following the next race he approached me, asked whether I had noticed him coming up to me earlier, explained that he used to work at Buckingham Palace and that I bore a striking resemblance to His Royal Highness the Duke of Kent, that it was only when he got close that he perceived I was younger. He apologised for intruding — he expected many people had made the same mistake. He was not an habitué at The Bridge but had been sent by a nobleman, whose

50

name shall remain undisclosed, to have a substantial bet on a dog in the next race.

It was he who proposed, as compensation for accosting me, that he might put a few pounds on for me, to show he was really sorry.

I said I did not bet in pounds.

"Ten shillings then."

He was such a decent-looking man — and the unlikelihood of the King's youngest brother spending an afternoon in the cheap enclosure at Stamford Bridge did not occur to me till later — that I gave him 5s and agreed to meet him in the Bovril bar after the race. "Which dog are we on?"

If I wouldn't mind, he'd really rather not say in case it affected the odds — "but the dog will win".

The 6 dog won, at 20–1. A fiver was a very substantial sum and I went to the Bovril bar with a big happy smile on my face.

The man, he who had worked at the Palace did not show, though I waited a long time.

For other afternoon diversions there were the waitresses at the Quality Inns. I don't recall what we ate, but with eggs, butter and sugar rationed, dried fruit in short supply and lemons and oranges non-existent, it was basic stuff. Going out was what mattered, getting away from the heat and the shouting and the bullying.

Another destination was the Astoria Ballroom in Tottenham Court Road, where there was afternoon dancing. This was the time of the rumba. Carmen Miranda, a South American sexpot with a huge mouth and full figure, was the "in" movie star — her "Aye,

Aye, Aye, I like you veery much" would have been top of the hit parade, had there been a war-time hit parade. It was there that I met a dark-haired girl of about my age called Josie who was a waitress somewhere and taught me a variation to the quickstep called — I am not sure whether I got the name or even the step right — the "fishnet". From guiding your partner along the floor doing slow-slow-quick-quick-slow, you suddenly appeared at her side and did a shuffle. We looked forward to that a lot. I asked her out one evening and she said she couldn't, but she did know some people who ran a pub on the river near Windsor and they had rooms upstairs, and if I liked, she and I could go there one Saturday night, only it cost 3s 6d for a room and breakfast. We agreed a date and a meeting place on Saturday afternoon. She didn't turn up. There is a lot of that when you are young.

My best friend in the Dorchester kitchen was a Hungarian aristocrat called Count Anton von Diersztay, some six years older than me but probably the only other person who did not feel that the world began and ended in a hotel basement. He worked in the stores awaiting the call to be a receptionist on the way to becoming a manager. For the months before he donned a morning coat and learnt *Debrett's* by heart we went skating at the Queen's Club in Bayswater. I learned to skate on the frozen Baltic Sea when I was two and was fairly good. He had learnt on a lake on his father's estates and was better.

What he did brilliantly was finding us women — well, girls.

I would be skating and he would go up to some girls standing by the bar and say, "See that boy with the black and white jersey, the one over there? You'd never believe that he is the heir to the Cadbury fortune, may be the only person in London who could find you a bar of chocolate." When there was a break in the skating, so that the rink could be swept, I was extremely popular with girls who would be far too grand to accord a second look at a puny seventeen-year-old apprentice cook.

The reason why kitchen apprenticeships take such a long time is that you start on, say, the Fish department and after a couple of months you have the hang of it and want to move — only Fish chef finds you useful and won't let you go. As apprentice tournant, I did a day a week on Soup, Veg, Fish, Roast and Sauce, with an occasional stint in Hors d'Oeuvres and Patisserie, and in a year and a few months I was ready to move — upwards as a cook or sideways as a hotel trainee. I became a waiter.

Let me try and sum up what I had learnt: to chop and slice and carve and "turn" potatoes (with a sharp veg knife you cut off the top and bottom of a new potato and turn it with seven sweeps into a barrel-shaped Pomme Château). The fact that new potatoes are much better scrubbed and poached is irrelevant. Haute cuisine, which is what we were at, is not about being good, it is about being right . . . and new potatoes got "turned". Escoffier had so decreed. Nor was peeling potatoes the job of a chef; it was done by a man who spent the livelong day taking potatoes out of a sack, peeling them and throwing them into a bucket of water. He was called "Sailor". The spuds from his barrel were collected by the boy on Veg and used for boiling, steaming, roasting and frying. Sailor was not a chef, did not wear white, had no future.

Universities have departments of pure and applied sciences. Nothing "pure" about kitchens then. Research and innovation was the road to professional excommunication. A Sauce Hollandaise was egg-bound butter seasoned with lemon juice. Béarnaise was egg-bound butter spiked with herbs, Dijon mustard and a reduction of wine vinegar. Put cream into a Hollandaise sauce and it becomes Sauce Mousseline. Put in too much cream and it is wrong, throw it away, start again. Put some minced anchovy into the Hollandaise (which is delicious) and you get the sack. Not just for doing it wrong — "wilfully wasting anchovy" they would call that.

Rather as prayers are deemed to be more effective if you are kneeling on a stone floor, so was food considered to be more authentic if it was really bothersome to produce. Machines, though some existed even then, were out. Fish for quenelles was passed raw through a hair sieve. Rotary whisks had no place in patisserie, where boys spent forever whisking egg whites with a fork; commis were allowed balloon whisks. The argument is that the more air you get into the albumen, the better is the meringue mixture; and while this may be marginally true, the difference in taste is absolutely minimal, that in labour tremendous. Soups and sauces were not sieved to achieve smoothness — that would have been far too simple. A sieve was placed over an empty pan, a tightly woven tammy draped over the sieve and the soup or sauce poured into the tammy cloth which was gripped by two men, one each end, and turned in opposite directions until the liquor spurted out of the heavy cloth, through the sieve, into the pan. "There's smooth", as they say in Wales. Whether it tasted good was no criterion: go in for culinary competitions like Hotel Olympia (the catering Olympics) and texture is what wins the medals.

Hors d'Oeuvres, which are now often based on reinvention — like yesterday's boiled chicken emerges as part of celeriac remoulade garnished with chervil — were then absolutely prescribed. The HdO trolley in the restaurant had room for twelve dishes and they had to be the same twelve dishes. Surprise never figured in the seduction of customers — you gave them what they expected to get in a first-class hotel: sardines, anchovy fillets prettily criss-crossed to look appetising, potato salad, tomato salad, lentil salad, Russian salad, Italian salad with slivers of meat, celeriac salad, baked beans, hard-boiled eggs on a bed of chopped lettuce in mayonnaise with a pinch of cayenne pepper, leeks in vinaigrette, mushrooms à la Grècque.

There was a wet afternoon when I had insufficient money to go greyhound racing and sat instead in the larder where a tired old Belgian called Edgar, recently reclaimed from an old people's home, made sandwiches for afternoon tea. I watched him take a sandwich loaf, 18 inches long by 5 inches high and 5 inches across.

Using a carving knife, he removed the entire top crust, then the crusts on the other four sides of the loaf, putting them into a box from which breadcrumbs were made. Next he made beurre maître d'hôtel — softened butter into which are blended chopped parsley and lemon juice — and spread the top of the loaf generously therewith before cutting a horizontal slice a third of an inch thick. He continued buttering and slicing until there was only the bottom crust left and his worktable was filled with large buttered slices. He took these two by two, garnished one with slivers of cucumber gently salted and pressed, arranged in cunning patterns to lie two deep all over the bottom slice, given a modest sprinkling of chopped chive. The top slice, butter side down, was then put in place, the sandwich aligned and cut into 1½-inch fingers, arranged on a dish bearing a doiley, garnished with mustard and cress.

"Edgar," I said with youthful enthusiasm, "that is a great sandwich."

"No, boy," said Edgar, looking at me through his wire-framed glasses, "that is a sandwich."

What was different then was our constant awareness of "class". There have always been "them" and "us", but here this was accentuated in that we were downstairs, they upstairs, also "we" had never met "them" — we who spent all our time doing things to give them pleasure. So they were the natural enemy and anything we could do to hurt them was a blow for us. I saw in my first week, while I was still noticing these things, a commis pissing into the stockpot.

"Why are you doing that, chef?"

"That'll teach them — bastards!"

When your weekly salary was what they spent on a portion of grilled lamb cutlets with Broad Beans à la Crème and allumette potatoes, the feeling that we were part of the same human race flew out of the window. When there was an air raid warning — and they came and went all the time in that period of 1940–1 — we hoped the bombs would kill our customers, especially that sod who ordered Pommes Anna . . . a potato dish that is complicated and time-consuming (though delicious).

You peel the potatoes, shaping them into cylinders, and cut them into thin slices. We used small round copper oven dishes with lids, brushed the bases with butter and covered this with overlapping circles of potato, starting the first layer with slices overlapping one way, and on the next layer (having applied more melted butter, and salt and pepper) overlapping the slices the opposite way. After some eight layers, each anointed with butter and salt and pepper, you put on a tight-fitting lid and bake in a medium to hot oven for forty-five minutes, when the middle of the "cake" will be soft and buttery and the outside crisp and brown. Preparing this for someone you love would be rewarding; doing it in response to a barker shouting, "*Un Pommes Anna*" is truly joyless.

For my new role as a waiter I went back to Denny's (outfitters to the catering trade) in Old Compton Street and this time bought two pairs of dinner jacket trousers, a modified tail coat, black shoes, black socks, a white bow tie and a packet of a dozen cardboard dickies with collars. Commis, the lowest order of the species, wore no shirts. There was no one in my family, the way there were in all the other waiters' families, to tell me to wear the best shoes and change socks at least after every service. The kitchen was three stone flights of stairs beneath the restaurant and I got blisters on day one and kept them for the three months that I stood around answering shouts of "Hey, you!" and going up and down the stairs to fetch food.

The restaurant head waiter was an elderly, elegant Alsatian called Monsieur Smid, who had a penchant for drinking bottled Worthington before service. It was the job of the most junior waiter to open this bottle and pour it for the overlord of our profession. Worthington is volatile; open the bottle and you lose half of it in fizz, pour it any way but with extreme care, a few drops at a time, and it will billow out of the glass and froth over the side. I brought what was left to Smid, who swore and aimed a blow at my head which I learnt to side-step.

Smid wore well-cut dark suits on his way to work, impeccable morning coat and cravat for luncheon, stunning white tie and tails for dinner. He organised the seating plan. About 70 per cent of our customers were regulars or resident; if he did not know a name, the person would be seated in a crap part of the restaurant; Smid walked about his empire speaking only to the most desirable clients.

Next in seniority were two reception head waiters, who had long forefingers and guided customers to their tables. The room was divided into stations, each with six or seven tables, a head waiter to take the order, a chef waiter to serve the food, a commis waiter to fetch and carry and keep the sideboard equipped with cutlery and crockery; occasionally to serve water to the bad customers (water was then tap water, ordered, we felt, by people too mean to buy wine). I was lucky in the station I was given. While still a cook I had gone upstairs to help prepare a buffet, lost my way, walked into a store room and come upon an Italian head waiter being given a blow-job by one of the new waitresses (we all knew that having female servicing staff at the Dorchester would lead to trouble).

He said, "If you tell anyone I kill you."

I said, "I won't tell."

The participants of this interesting act I had disturbed had a whispered conversation and he said, "If you don't tell, she'll give you one."

She was large, about twice my size, and had red hair. I said, "No thank you, sir" and he said, "All right, I owe you."

When I got to the restaurant it was he who claimed me as his station commis.

Being a head waiter was reasonably skilled, like you had to know how to fillet a Dover sole tidily in front of a customer, carve chickens, ducks, saddles of lamb and contrefilet of beef, make bespoke salad dressings. Chef waiters had to be able to use a spoon and fork for silver service and commis waiters needed to be fleet of foot, tireless, neat and try very hard, when tasting the food they were bringing up to the restaurant, to spill as little as possible on their dickies and make sure to wipe them clean if spillage occurred. We always had teaspoons tucked into the outside breast-pocket of our jackets and mounting the stairs would sample the sauce, taste a piece of stewed venison, eat a chip or two . . . generally get the flavour of the food we were serving.

Those were the days when the chefs' names were obscure but everyone knew the head waiters. Indeed, the serving staff did a realistic job of fucking up what the chef had prepared. We had lamps on our sideboards and would rewarm the food that came from below and with a flourish turn the peppermill at it, add Worcestershire sauce, mix things around, turn things over. What motivated waiters was the need for customers to appreciate that the good meal they got was down to them, and tip accordingly.

Instead of leaving a bottle on the table, wine waiters would pour minimal amounts into the customers' glasses and place the bottle in some distant ice bucket . . . so that if someone wanted a refill, the watching wine waiter would hurry along, ask if he might replenish the glass, go off, come back with the bottle, pour hardly any into the glass and replace it afar. The idea was that a parting customer would say, "But for that wine waiter I wouldn't have had nearly so good a time."

Each station wrapped the tip in the bill and the Tronc-Head-Waiter assessed the average percentage gratuity received by each station. The tronc, which is the box in which all tips were put, was then distributed. Commis waiters were paid steady amounts, like £3 a week; everyone else got "points". Smid had two, the senior head waiters one and a half, and head waiters between one and one and a quarter depending on performance. My head waiter, Mr Van, was steadily at the top of the head waiters' league table. Chef waiters got upwards of half a point.

When the statutory payments — to commis, bus boys and cleaners — had been made, all the other points were added together, the total tronc divided by that number and a point declared at somewhere between £20 and £30; waiters were paid accordingly. With the average salary in 1941 under £5 a week, this was good money.

You can learn all there is to learn about being a good waiter, as far as the customer is concerned, in a couple of days at the most. That is not the point. Let me explain. We had, on our station, a regular luncheon guest called Captain Frazer-Nash. The Dorchester restaurant had chairs with arms and chairs without, and Frazer-Nash was particular that he wanted an armless chair. Every day, when laying up, it was essential that the captain's place had a chair with arms, so that as he approached I could be sent hurrying along to replace the chair that was there with the one he wanted. The mistake would have been to have left his chair *in situ*, which might not have let him realise that we did it specially; this could have affected the tip.

The highlight of my time as a waiter was New Year's Eve 1941. We were two years and a bit into the war; new shortages were announced all the time and that winter there was a paper shortage. Newspapers were confined to four pages and the hotel, wanting to be seen to be patriotic, decided that the New Year's Eve dinner menu should be printed on a piece of card the size of a large postage stamp. Turtle Soup. Beluga Caviar. Fillets of Sole Bonne Femme. Tournedos de Boeuf. Poires Belle Hélène. Stilton.

For this event there were no stations; each waiter had ten customers to care for, my ten all at one table. Lew Stone's band played . . . with Carl Bariteau on the clarinet; the lights were low, the mood as festive as the war allowed, and it occurred to me that the print on the mini-menu was so absurdly small that no one could read it. At my table, the guests went straight from their turtle soup to the Dover sole.

At midnight, while they sang "Auld Lang Syne", I went to the bake-house and got a freshly baked flute to go with my ten portions of Beluga; obtained a quarter of a pound of butter from the larder; asked Mr Van which table would not notice if I put a bottle of Dom Pérignon on their bill, and sat in a store room having the most memorable New Year's Eve meal of my life to date.

CHAPTER
FOUR

In which I don the King's uniform, fight, mostly behind public houses at closing time, and am court-martialled for misappropriating ducks.

My call-up papers arrived when I was eighteen, working in the hotel's Control office with Alma who was plump and had a moustache and BO but such stunning handwriting and impeccable arithmetic that I loved her. From my desk I watched admiringly as she drew the straightest margins in the Business Done book. Her father was a Swiss body-builder, she told me; I was seriously considering replying to Charles Atlas advertisement: "You too can have a body like mine. Send a postal order for 12s 6d." Atlas was a fine figure of a man; I was weedy, very keen to have a body like his with all those muscles.

The Army had sent me a warrant for the night train to Glasgow, also a pass that would take me from Glasgow Central to Maryhill on a No. 13 tram. In common with other men who were summoned to leave the dangers of the metropolis and its bombs and fire-hazards for the security of distant outposts of the United Kingdom I was given farewell parties, at all of which I ended up drunk, in bed with someone, quite often Miss Hill, but also with others. Never with Alma.

On the appointed evening I went to Euston Station, found the night train was full, and stood for seven hours in the corridor idly chatting to a boy of about my age who had also been called for the Initial Training Course that all soldiers take.

In Glasgow we had a coffee, found a tram, went to the barracks where we showed our papers and some time later a sergeant came to shout at us: "When you hear your name called, come to attention, call out, 'Present, sergeant' and move off to the quartermaster store to get kitted out . . . Turnbull," he barked.

Turnbull, who had come straight from the station without stopping for a coffee and had therefore been the first to hand in his papers, sloped off to be given the King's uniform, also socks, grey, three pairs; pants, cellular, white, three pairs; housewife, one. (This, lest you should think otherwise, was a sewing kit and is pronounced "hussif".)

Then he shouted, "Frood."

I came to attention, said, "Present, sergeant" and was on my way to the store building when I heard him shout "Jung", looked around and saw that the man with whom I had travelled, had a coffee and shared a bacon butty was marching towards me. My tiredness disappeared and I said to him:

"This is the most extraordinary coincidence. You may have heard the man call me Frood; actually my name is Freud, and for a Freud and a Jung to be brought into such close contact is astonishing, don't you think?"

He said, "Don't know what you're on about. My name is Young."

Basic training was pretty straightforward. We learnt how to assemble and take apart a .303 rifle. How to march in step, turn, salute, fire, fix bayonets, remove bayonets, take orders, give orders, and at 4.30p.m. we were free to do what we liked. Some men in my platoon said I could go into Glasgow with them: at Green's Picture Playhouse there were always girls with well-paid jobs in munitions waiting to pick up soldiers. "Just one thing," warned my comrades-in-arms. "Keep your fucking mouth shut. They'd run a mile if they heard your posh accent." I held hands with a substantial assortment of Scots lassies, was taken out for drinks by them, sometimes ended up in a bed in a single-end — Glasgow accommodation at the very bottom of the luxury scale — with them and their families. I was the "quiet one"; over the weeks I learnt a few words . . . like I could say, "It's aboot a quarter past six" in a fair Glaswegian accent, which was passed by my friends as authentic; I then became known as "the cuckoo clock" because I could only speak at half-hour intervals, then didn't say much.

After the first six weeks we got a weekend leave and a rail warrant to take us where we wanted. I came back to London, walked along the platform at Euston and was grabbed and hugged and kissed and fondled by a girl, which I enjoyed a lot. After a couple of minutes of this she shoved me away, saying, "I want to see if you've changed", and her face fell.

I had changed too much; she was waiting for her fiancé.

London hadn't changed a lot. I went to the Dorchester, where they admired my uniform and Alma smiled and Miss Hill said, "Usual place at 6.40?", and I went to the Coffee Ann, where I was known as Lucian's brother (the crowd considered having a uniform pretty pathetic), and I drank "my drink" — rum, lime, ice and soda — at the first-floor bar of the Café Royal where the barman, who knew me, said, "The usual, is it?"

But said it with limited enthusiasm. A private soldier was some way from being the desirable customer West End barmen cherished . . . unless he was a fag. I was not a fag. "The usual" is what people who want to be considered "in" ask for, so that surrounding punters know that they are folk to be reckoned with. When I had my own night-club certain members came twice a year, brought guests, went to the bar and asked for "the usual"; my barman had instructions to smile and pour a gin and tonic.

I had a friend called David Chancery who worked in the City, made a lot of money but knew little about life. One day he met a girl whom he wanted to impress, asked her out to dinner, rang a restaurant of which he had heard good reports and spoke to the head waiter.

"My name is Chancery. You will recognise me by the fact that I am six foot two and have fair curly hair and will be wearing a green tie. I want to impress my companion, who is gorgeous, and would be so grateful if you could pretend to recognise me and make a fuss."

He arrived with the girl, the head waiter cocked an inquiring eyebrow, got an imperceptible nod, called out, "Look, everyone, Mr Chancery is here again", took him to a table and said, "Will it be the usual?"

The story has an unhappy ending: he was brought a bottle of Dom Pérignon and foie gras canapés.

I returned to Glasgow for further "initial training" — we were sheep, did as the others did, ate the same, worked the same, slept the same. Had one shown initiative, they would have had one on a charge for insubordination or failing to obey orders. Promotion came by default: whoever had not done anything wrong ended up with a stripe more than they started with. To succeed, you needed to dubbin boots with skill, shine badges and buttons for longer than any sane person would say was necessary, blanco webbing over and over and, when you did a left turn, end up exactly 90 degrees from where you began. It is quaint to believe that that is how you discovered the men most suited to lead others into battle.

At arms drill, we took it in turn to command the platoon. "Atten*shun*!" we shouted at our mates under the eye of the drill sergeant. "Platoon left *turn* . . . . Platoon quick *march*." One of my fellow soldiers got that far and lost it. "For God's sake," shouted the sergeant, "say something if it's only goodbye."

With a month to go before we were posted to our regiments, I was told to do a fortnight on the bike. I said, "Yes, sergeant", and though it sort of wrecked my social life, it taught me much. Such success as I had in later years owes something to those two weeks on the bike.

Every night the hospitable folk of Glasgow organised events for the poor wee soldier laddies, so far from home, paid such a pittance, also — looking at what was happening to our troops around the world — not long for this life either. The adjutant's office would get invitations for fourteen men to come to a whist drive in Milngavie, eight were invited to a fish dinner by the Women's Institute, the Darby and Joan club had dances to which a dozen of us were bussed. Being "on the bike" meant getting yourself over to these events, liaising with a chosen representative, mingling for a few minutes and then making the speech of thanks.

"Ladies and gentlemen of Glasgow," I would say nightly at four or five different venues, "we who have come to this city from afar did not realise the kindness, hospitality and generosity that are part of the Glaswegian character. We are so very grateful to you for inviting us here tonight and . . .", now I looked at the piece of paper our rep. had handed me when I arrived . . . "I feel particular thanks are due to Mrs McLeggan for the wonderful sausage rolls, Miss Fraser for organising the raffle, the Misses McGhee for playing the piano and cymbals, and all of you who helped to make this evening so very enjoyable." I hung around for two or three minutes, then slid out into the night, pedalled to the next destination, did it all over again.

The weekend before I was posted to the Royal Ulster Rifles in Omagh (no, I do not know why either)

Company Sergeant Major Alexander, Highland Light Infantry, a right bull of a bastard of a man with wiry black hair and a very loud voice, told me that if I had nothing better to do on Sunday evening I might like to look in on a party he was giving . . . and passed me a card with his address. I pressed my uniform with especial care and went.

There were about twenty men at the party, mostly non-commissioned officers and one second lieutenant whom I had seen being bullied by the CSM, and there was no food — the way there isn't at Scots parties — but large amounts of drink, mostly from the messes — you could tell by the fact that the whisky labels were upside down on the bottles. Beer was served by the pint, there was music from a gramophone ("La Mer", "We'll Meet Again", Jack Buchanan's "And Her Mother Came Too" . . . by this time "We're Going to Hang Out the Washing on the Siegfried Line" had lost its popularity) and in a corner of the room stood a three-seater settee. Suspended over the two arms were two naked soldiers, their four feet chained to the legs of the sofa, their hands cuffed together on the middle seat, their bare buttocks jutting out.

"Help yourself," said Sergeant Alexander. "They're the entertainment."

I knew one of them by sight, leaned down to ask him what on earth had happened and he said, "It was this or three weeks' jankers."

Funny how you forget all about some parties while others remain embedded in the memory. I left Glasgow a couple of days later. When I visited it again in the

1960s, as a football correspondent for the *Observer* covering an Old Firm match, Maryhill Barracks had been pulled down and a housing estate built in its place.

I spent just on five years in the Army, held ranks from rifleman to acting major, and came out at the end of 1947 a lieutenant. During my war I did not as far as I can remember kill anyone, but was drunk a lot. Jeffrey Bernard once put an ad into the personal column of the *Daily Telegraph* to announce: "I Jeffrey Bernard having been asked to write an autobiography for Lord Weidenfeld would like to hear from anyone who knows what I was doing between 1953 and 1977."

My time in khaki was marginally more memorable. After the joys of Glasgow, I settled into life as a rifleman in the mixed Irish brigade. Our commanding officer in Omagh was a miserable old shit called Major Weeks who rode into barracks every morning on his bicycle. For a month I was daily on a 7a.m. duty that occupied every crossroad on the major's journey to work in order to salute him. It was the hope of the regimental sergeant major who organised this campaign that the major, while answering the salute, would lose his balance, fall off his bike and get run over.

In the winter of 1942 I played at scrum half for the Green Gates (British Forces in Northern Ireland, so called because our insignia was a green gate), knowing that if I did not get the ball back I would be posted to Africa. I stayed.

My background made me a prime candidate for posting to unlikely assignments. There was a notice on the officers' mess board stating: "If any officer or man has an aptitude for languages, applications are invited for training at the School of Oriental Languages in Poona." I applied. Explained that I was bi-lingual in English and German, had fair French and a smattering of Danish (holiday house in Baltic), and if the best use that can be made of this is to teach me Chinese I apply under notice FRP 4316 W. I was posted to India, then I was posted back. I was transferred, became attached to a unit that was going to blow up railway installations behind the lines in Germany in 1944, I was about to be sent over there when I was recalled — the Germans were doing what we were going to do — and I went on a course to stop people blowing up railway installations.

I was stationed in Lancaster in a barracks on the Garscube Road. A girl accused a soldier of raping her outside the barracks in a sentry hut. The regiment was assembled and she walked up and down the ranks of men with the adjutant. At length she identified her assailant by touching him on the shoulder. She was asked to finish her inspection of all the men, lest she had made a mistake, did so, confirmed her original selection. The adjutant addressed the serried ranks of some four hundred men and announced: "If there is any other soldier here who has had intercourse with this woman, let him take one pace forward." The entire regiment took one pace forward; it was hard to keep a straight face.

I was put forward for a commission after nine months in the Ulster Rifles. Like other riflemen I marched at 140 paces a minute, which is fast, trailed arms, sloped arms and on occasion presented arms. Took apart and put together again a Bren gun, was neither better nor worse than any other man at firing a PIAT . . . which stands for projectile infantry anti-tank, and were you to try and fire it from the hip, the kick would break your bones. One Ulster Rifleman did this in action, knocked out a tank, and got a VC — posthumously, as far as I recall. My one distinction in that initial period could not have been responsible for any commendation, though it was an occasion on which I showed flair and initiative and kept cool. It was when my rifle and I parted company.

A rifleman and his rifle go together like a dog and his identity tag. By day you carry it around, at night you place it in a rifle rack in your hut, where, for security, a metal rod is threaded through the trigger housings and secured with a padlock at each end. I lost my rifle.

I had it at lunch, I obviously had it on parade in the afternoon and at weapon training, before we did arms drill at 5p.m.; then I went to the NAAFI, which is the cafeteria. Later, when it was time to lock away the weapons, mine was not there. I looked everywhere, could not ask anyone whether they had seen it because rifle-losing, even rifle-mislaying, was a heinous crime, a cardinal sin, punishable by a week in the glass-house.

That night I could not sleep — riflemen without rifles don't sleep. And at about 2a.m. it occurred to me that what made me different from the other men in my platoon who were sleeping all around me was that they had rifles; if they didn't we'd all be in the same boat and safe.

The Army is actually all about being in the same boat as the others.

I knew where the key to the padlock was, crept towards the rifle rack, unlocked the pad and withdrew the rod gently, silently. I stuck three rifles under my nightshirt (my grandmother had given me Grandfather's nightshirts when he died in 1939 and I wore them — should have kept them and sold them for a fortune in the USA) and over the next hour and a half I disposed of all thirty rifles, throwing them into hedges, into a stream, or hiding them under the boundary fence. Finally I crept back into bed and slept.

Reveille was at 6.15a.m. By 6.30 someone had noticed that the rifle rack was empty and by 6.45 the platoon hut was full of military policemen, officers and warrant officers. At 7.15 Major Weeks, having survived another bike ride, arrived. It was the IRA who had done it, no doubt about that. Thirty-one rifles taken soundlessly at night; one really rather had to admire them. As the day wore on and we were excused arms drill the rifles started to appear, one after another, until all but two were found. Mine had been one of the first to turn up, and the two men whose weapons were still lost were under considerable suspicion. I mean, they might have lost theirs and committed this dastardly act.

I was less fortunate attempting an act of chivalry during my first day in Omagh. When I joined the Army they had asked what was my religion. I said, "None." They wrote, "Religion: o.d", which meant "other denominations", and on Sundays it was Protestants here, Catholics over there, o.d.s. piss off and clean the shit-house. So, for convenience sake (my convenience), when I was posted to Ireland I went along with the flow and left the latrines to be cleaned by people who had real faith. We had church parades when, with our boots shone, our webbing blanco'd, our cap badges polished and our uniform pressed by placing it meticulously under our palliasses and sleeping on it, we marched behind the band of the Irish Fusiliers into the centre of Omagh and filed into church. The service was long and, by the time we had been marched back to barracks, the morning, the first part of which had been spent bull-shitting, was gone.

There was an alternative. You could go to 9a.m. communion wearing civilian shoes and be out for elevenses of bacon butties. So that day I had gone to early communion and was on my way back when a soldier came up to me and asked if I could help him. I did not know him but had seen him around; he was, like many of my colleagues at the barracks, an ex-IRA soldier who had come across the border to see some action. There was then no agreement between the two armies, and when he went home on his first leave he was arrested for desertion, got three months in the glass-house, returned to the British Army — who posted him as a deserter and sentenced him to three months in our glass-house.

"Look it but," he said, falling into step beside me, "my wife is at home in Donegal, one of my bairns is ill with the whooping cough and they need to see me."

"If there is any way I can help . . ."

"What you must do," said the Donegal man, "is go to the barracks, give your name and number to the guard room and then, before 10.30, slip out under the boundary fence, come back through the guard room and give my name. I'll sneak back under the fence tonight so I can answer my name at roll-call tomorrow."

I considered the man's plight, the lonely wife, the coughing bairn and said, "Of course I can do that. Tell me your name and number."

"McGeoghan 629," he said.

"McGeoghan 629?"

"You've got it perfect. I'm really grateful."

I hurried to catch up with some colleagues on the way through the guard room, said, "Freud 533", stood by while my name was crossed off and went for a stroll along the boundary fence . . . Within half an hour I was back outside the guard room, tagged along behind an incoming Enniskillen Fusilier and said, "McGeoghan 629."

The military policeman opened the book to find the name, looked at me and asked whether I was one of the Sligo McGeoghans.

I told him that some of my family certainly came from Sligo and he said, "Do they now." Then he said, "Come look at this" and I followed him into the guard house and suddenly the cell door closed on me. "You fuckin' liar," said the MP. "What's your real name?"

"McGeoghan 629," I replied.

They called an officer who knew who I was, read me the riot act, told me that if I wanted not to be confined for life with not much bread or water, I must tell him the whereabouts of the man I was impersonating. They picked him up on the Donegal bus before it had crossed the border, but the Army was not pleased with me. Nevertheless I was eventually sent to one of the selection boards where they assess whether you would make a good officer.

At the beginning of the war, according to Evelyn Waugh's novels, people telephoned their army friends and asked if they might have a vacancy as an officer in this or that regiment. By the time it was my turn to join up and the war was going badly for us, WOSBs were in place. If your commanding officer put you forward for a commission you went on one of these War Office Selection Boards where they watched and tested you over three days and decided whether or not you should do four months at OCTU, the Officers' Course Training Unit. My CO nominated me for a WOSB not because I was the best marksman, the best marcher, the most able tactician, the brightest, smartest, or fittest man under his command. I was nominated because I had been to a public school. There were men around me who would have made better officers, but as their parents had sent them into the state sector of education, they remained "other ranks".

WOSBs were located in grand country houses requisitioned by the Army for that purpose. There was a major in charge, a second-in-command captain and three or four officers or non-commissioned officers to supervise the action. There was also a psychiatrist: the one at my WOSB told me he had had a wet dream when he learnt that Sigmund Freud's grandson was in the next intake.

They gave us a four-course dinner and watched what cutlery we used. When we went to bed, they had someone prowl around at midnight to examine where and how we had hung up, folded and put away our clothes. There was a day when the twenty-four of us did the sort of exams you do to join MENSA, and a day and a half of tests to assess our qualities of leadership, courage, dexterity and fitness. A fifteen-minute session with the psychiatrist was also scheduled on day two; mine lasted an hour and a half, in the course of which the shrink boasted of his secretary's big boobs and her willingness to share her assets with him. I took her out that first night . . . and on day three, rather than wait for my regiment to hear whether or not I had passed the selection board, the CO told me that in view of my "outing" with the psychiatrist's secretary, I would be sent back to Ireland with a commendation that I wait three months to become more mature.

I think I did pretty well in the tests. The written exams caused me no problems, and in the one in which they assessed who was the natural leader of our group of four I alone acted while the three other potential officers shouted: "All right, you men, go there and do that." In the courage/fitness test we had to jump from a river bank on to a 2-foot-wide diving board in midstream about 7 feet away. We did this in full uniform, carrying arms, and, anxious not to land on the side of the board, slip down and castrate myself, I took a leap and missed the target by 4 feet. The officer in charge said, "Bad luck, Freud, but that was a really gutsy jump. What we are after is effort, and you showed plenty of that."

Perhaps the most pointless "test" was the obstacle tunnel. Each team was given a long, heavy log of wood which they had to manhandle through the obstacles of a 200-metre tunnel, one team east to west, the other west to east. Points were awarded not only for overall speed but for the team that came out first.

So I went back to my regiment and my place behind the scrum in the rugby team, and found a café in Killiclogher where they served eggs and bacon and sausages, and the woman who ran it had a daughter who told me she was lonely and asked whether I was homesick. I became a lance corporal, which meant more pay . . . like 1s 6d a day instead of the shilling awarded riflemen. And I became fitter and stronger, excelled at "battle inoculation" when we ran, keeping low, along a valley while warrant officers fired live bullets over our heads. People were being killed all around the globe; I felt it would be both comfortable and convenient to get shot in County Tyrone but I escaped.

Three months later I was at another WOSB, this one at Monk Fryston outside Leeds, home of the Duke of Rutland whom I had served when a waiter in the restaurant at the Dorchester. It all went swimmingly — the psychiatrist was a Jungian, uninterested in Freud. The written exams were the same, therefore even easier the second time, and the tests went well until we got to the obstacle course.

The two teams were briefed about the tunnel, told how our performances would be assessed, shown a diagram of the obstacles we would encounter: a wall, a net under which we would have to push the log, a water hazard . . . and then given five minutes to plan before we started. I went to the other team, explained that I had done this same test recently and suggested, in order to save ourselves much strain and heartache, that we each drop our logs 40 yards into the tunnel, amble through and pick up the other's log on the way out. All concurred. We met in the middle and some of us had a smoke; the other team agreed to let us get out first, but would themselves come out very shortly afterwards so that they too would receive praise. So we did as planned, dropped our log, picked up the other team's log at the end of the tunnel and started to run to the finish, where a sergeant sat with a stopwatch. He used a field telephone to summon the adjutant. It emerged that this test had been going on for eighteen months and we had not only beaten the record, we had shattered it.

A photographer was called and a fuss was made of us until one of the officers-to-be couldn't take the adulation and confessed. It was all my fault and the CO of the unit, far from acknowledging initiative, told me I should be ashamed and not to bother waiting for his report to my regiment re their verdict.

So I returned to Omagh, saluted everything that moved, painted what didn't, was posted overseas and, by the time the whistle-blower had gone to OCTU and come out a second lieutenant I had been commissioned. Just like that. I was sent back to London to buy my officer's uniform and walked past Buckingham Palace in order to be saluted by the sentries outside. I liked being saluted.

Later, when I came out of the Army, I joined the Automobile Association because in those days their men saluted members who had the AA insignia on their car bonnets.

During the First World War, officers got rapid promotion because of the multitudinous deaths of their colleagues. After the Second World War, promotion was fast because people got demobilised on a first-in-first-outbasis: now men who had joined two years into the war, because they were previously too young, rose to dizzy heights . . . temporarily. How did one reach such an exalted rank? One was there; the man who held that rank was back in civilian life.

After the peace I was in charge of an employment exchange for Germans who worked in our messes in Bad Oeynhausen, was briefly attached to Field Marshal Montgomery's staff as a sort of catering adviser. My job was to ensure that Montgomery was never given anything messed about or "frenchified" to eat; he was especially suspicious of salad dressing.

He was guest of honour at a party in Minden, Westphalia: cocktails from 6.15p.m. to 8p.m. Officers from all around were invited, turned up in their best dress uniforms. Monty arrived at 7.30, was saluted in by two sergeants at the door and, recognising one of the men's African campaign medal, spent twenty minutes chatting to him. Bastard.

A story went the rounds about the field marshal . . . which may well have been apocryphal. On an inspection of an Army cook-house Montgomery saw a pastrycook roll out some dough, remove the false teeth from his mouth, then use these to cut out nice circular shapes.

"What the hell are you doing?"

"Making jam tarts, sir," said the cook.

"Haven't you got a tool for that?"

"Yes, sir, but I use it to make holes in the doughnuts."

Being bi-lingual has both pros and cons. A Major Bacon of the Wiltshire Regiment was officer i/c provisions and asked me, as a fellow member of the mess, to come with him one early evening to a duck farm which he intended to requisition. I was to act as his interpreter.

We went through the rigmarole of telling the poor sod that as from this day all his ducks were the property of the Control Commission for Germany and giving him requisite papers so that he could claim compensation in Deutschmarks (which were wholly valueless, like we could get 160 for a packet of cigarettes). Bacon decreed the sale price of a duck to be 10 marks, and as we had won the war there wasn't a lot the duck farmer could do. A password was agreed without which ducks would not be released.

Soon after that I was posted to a War Crimes Investigation Unit elsewhere in Westphalia, where the food was very average though the bar, for some strange reason, had been assigned a ten-case crate of Cordial Médoc, a little-in-demand liqueur which is a blend of port and brandy; we had that for breakfast, lunch, tea and dinner; also late at night. One evening it occurred to me that our mess fare would benefit greatly from ducks. I telephoned the farm first thing in the morning, gave the password, and requested thirty-six ducks to be plucked and prepared for collection. When the man asked who would collect, I told him, "That nice officer who was with me when I requisitioned the farm — the one who spoke such good German."

Our mess got something of a reputation for food. Fellow officers invited guests, who said, "This is much better food than you get at our mess. Duck, is it?" And we said, "Our chef is so talented he can make anything taste like duck. Have some more."

My day job was to locate minor war criminals living in the British Zone of Germany — people whose names had come up at the International Military Tribunal in Nuremberg. I had a batman/driver and an interpreter/police-heavy who carried handcuffs, and if you should wonder why I, who drove perfectly well and spoke fluent German — though my vocabulary was limited to words I had learnt in the nursery, amongst which "I therefore charge you with being an accessory to repeated assaults on concentration camp victims in Magdeburg" did not feature — needed these men, that was the regulation War Crimes Investigation Unit team; also I was then drinking more than drivers should.

82

The court martial came as a consequence of an early morning expedition to the duck farm, my tenth visit to the establishment. I arrived, made small talk with the farmer, told him how pleased Herr Major Bacon continued to be with his produce ... when Bacon appeared from one of the stalls with a military policeman.

I forget the actual charge at the Court Martial but pleaded guilty on the advice of my "prisoner's friend", a King's Counsel who worked for War Crimes and decently agreed to represent me. The court decided to sentence me to "loss of seniority". It was an inconvenience rather than a blow and meant that I was unlikely to rise to major general.

Throughout history, after a war the winners would kill the men and rape the women of the losers, whereafter life started over again. Not this time. To show the world that we lived in civilised times, we prosecuted the men with laws which we conveniently made up, and bought the women ... for cigarettes or coffee. Women worked out at two cigarettes, a cup of *Bohnenkaffee* (which was our coffee made of coffee beans as opposed to the mainly acorn-and-gravy browning liquor they had perforce come to drink). Fraternisation was prohibited for the first many months after the end of the war, so if men caught venereal disease, which they did a lot (women with syphilis felt they were doing their bit for the defeated Fatherland if they could infect enemy soldiers), they had to ask for compassionate leave on some excuse, depart from Germany, come back and register sick.

In Bielefeld in the winter of 1945 the entire Sergeants' Mess got clap from the same attractive, enthusiastic, patriotic barmaid. I was briefly VD officer, was instructed how to give penicillin injections, slap the man on the bum, stick in the needle where you slapped and he is slightly anaethetised, pump in the penicillin and give the puncture point a wipe with cotton wool dipped in Dettol.

"Won't it hurt them?"

"Serve them right," said the doctor.

I received one complaint during my short tenure of office. A soldier came to me confidentially, to complain that he had gonorrhea and for his daily visits to the hospital had to share transportation with men who had syphilis. I called him a snob and told him to sod off.

Let us move on to weightier matters. There were serious war criminals who, after any war, would have been shot or lynched. We tried those at Nuremburg, paid for them to have defending counsel, kept them in food and drink while all around their countrymen were starving. Begging children stood in the streets, and when they saw an occupying soldier or car or truck they would wave with one hand and hold out the other for food or sweets.

After the first big trial, the International Military Tribunal, Nuremberg was running smoothly and prosecutions went on and on. Each time a German was appointed editor of a newspaper, head of a film unit, teacher in charge of a college, or to civic office under the guidance of the Control Commission, the letters of accusation would come in from jealous citizens.

Depositions, for instance, that on this date of that year, the man about to be appointed/promoted/selected was in a crowd that had watched an Allied airman bale out of a bomber which had demolished their community; and that when the man had parachuted down and landed in a field the crowd had pitchforked him to death, "the prospective appointee being particularly active in this killing".

Our job was to investigate, find evidence and hand the matter to our prosecution department. In the case above, the man's defending counsel had found evidence of a German airman being shot down in 1940 over Louth in Lincolnshire, where he was castrated by the outraged locals. The judge ruled that to be inadmissible evidence — nothing to do with the case he was trying.

If any case gave me satisfaction it was that of Sergeant Whitehead, ex-Intelligence Corps but demobbed under schedule B, a category involving businessmen whose release from the forces was crucial to their work. Schedule B demobs were conditional and could be revoked. A woman guard in a camp in Hamburg-Wandsbek had had a reputation for cruelty and I received details of some of the rotten things she had done, along with her picture and her most recent address. She had since moved several times but, accompanied by a Hamburg CID officer, we found her, arrested her and left her in prison for a couple of days before interrogation. I faced her across a table in an interview room.

She was belligerent. "What is it this time?"

I explained that we had evidence that, while a guard at Wandsbek, she had drunkenly assaulted women under her care, broken the nose of one, fractured the skull of another.

"That has been dealt with. I was accused of that charge by Sergeant Whitehead in July, pleaded guilty and told I could do three years in prison or accept two weeks' corporal punishment."

Most accused gave reasons why prosecutions should not be carried out; they usually claimed they had obeyed orders (which is not a crime) or accused the informant of making trouble because of this or that. "My case has been dealt with" was new. I asked to be left alone with her, got her a cup of coffee and sat back.

She had been at Wandsbek two years ago, hated it, drank a lot, hit and kicked women when she felt like it — everyone else did — and in July 1945 a unit investigating the camp arrested her. When Sergeant Whitehead, who was in charge, gave her the alternatives of jail or punishment she chose the latter, and for a fortnight Whitehead raped her, whipped her, set an Alsatian on her and called in friends to help themselves to her body.

"Do you have any witnesses?"

She said there was a witness. She was having an (illicit) affair with a British soldier who tended her wounds when she came home after the ordeal.

I asked if she had his name.

She said he was called Jock, was Scottish, and added that if she could go home she could find his address. I escorted her home and when she produced a full name and address I received permission from my commanding officer to pursue the case while she remained in prison.

I had not been to Glasgow since my twelve weeks' initial training there and it seemed even more dirty, run-down and hopeless than I recalled. "Jock" lived in Gorbals Cross. I gave a boy 6d to call on him and say, "An army friend is in the pub across the road — come and join him for a drink", and when he arrived, I explained who I was and showed him a photograph of the accused.

"Ilse," he said. "Fucking Ilse from Hamburg. Better not let my wife see that."

I asked him about the "corporal punishment" she had received.

"That bastard," said Jock, "should be horse-whipped. I should have killed him but my mate was caught fraternising with a German and got put away. I couldn't do anything."

I asked if he would mind coming back into the Army for a few weeks, to give evidence. He was without a job and willing.

The scene moves to a downstairs office in a building in London's Edgware Road — it is an import-export business. The Provost Marshal (the senior military policeman in London), an MP corporal and I come into reception. A girl looks up.

"We've come to see Sergeant Whitehead," said the Provost Marshal, a major who was well over 6 feet tall with a moustache under a Cold-stream Guards hat pulled down over his forehead.

"Do you have an appointment?"

"No. We'll wait."

We waited for a good ten minutes before being ushered into the office. Whitehead was small, balding, nervous.

"Sergeant Whitehead?"

"Mr Whitehead; I was demobilised under Section B."

"Demobilisation revoked," snapped the Provost Marshal. "Stand to attention, left turn. Handcuff him, corporal," followed by a quick march to the car parked outside.

Whitehead got his come-uppance — a couple of years, I seem to recall — and I stopped being an investigating officer and was posted to Nuremberg as liaison officer.

Nuremberg is where War Crimes were at. For an investigating officer to be posted to Nuremberg was like a priest being sent to the Vatican, a footballer to Manchester United. Amazing talent had gathered to attend the trials: men of law and letters and the arts; politicians and psychologists, doctors and surgeons and pathologists. At night, there being no entertainment, we drank. Apart from drinking, I collected witnesses from the British Zone and brought them to the Tribunal, did a little interpreting, received daily complaints from the German police about the damage done by the British soldiers to bars and clubs and cafés in the town. Our soldiers were paid a fraction of what US personnel received, which was the main reason our men fought; theirs just passed out. It was my job to find appropriate punishment for transgressors . . . like confining them to barracks for forty-eight hours; with no one to supervise detention it was a useless exercise.

I was also in charge of looking after visiting VIPs. On one occasion the wife of Mr Justice Lawrence — he who later became Lord Oaksey, father of the race rider and journalist — had listened to the proceedings and wanted to go back to her hotel; I was to accompany her. As we walked down the road a US military police vehicle with a loudspeaker saw this Allied officer and a dowdy civilian woman old enough to be his mother, thought they knew what was going on and followed us with speaker blaring: "Beware, VD walks the streets!"

In the 1950s people went around saying so-and-so had had a good war; I am not sure that applies to any of the three Freud boys. My brother Stephen, who had written home from Dartington aged thirteen claiming to be wasting his precious youth, joined the Royal Horse Artillery after two years at Cambridge. When asked whether he wanted a commission he replied, "I hate all the men and they all hate me, but I can't go on sleeping in blankets" (other ranks did not get bedlinen) and went to officers' training in Catterick. He was commissioned with seven hundred other cadets and celebrated by going to Catterick races. On his return he found that he had been posted duty officer for the day but had not looked at the noticeboard, and got into severe trouble. Odds of 700–1 against this happening.

He was posted to Italy to join his regiment and went to the transit camp at Dover . . . where they lost his papers. Most people spend thirty-six hours at transit camp. Stephen was there for months and for some of that time worked for my father, who ran an equipment hire firm for an interned friend.

I happened to meet up with him in Westphalia in 1946 where he was a captain at a sort of WOSB for Germans about to take important jobs under the umbrella of the Control Commission. He told me that one of the tests was to sit them down, tell them they had been appointed mayor of a town where there was a food shortage, an infected water supply, the electricity was cut and the police on strike. "What would you do first?" was his question. It appeared that the majority, anxious to give the answer they thought the selection board wanted to hear, said, "Immediate de-Nazification, Herr Captain." I think Stephen had the best brains of the three of us — just the worst luck.

Lucian disappeared in about 1941, came back, said he had joined the Merchant Navy and sailed to Nova Scotia where the locals, for recreation, drank beer and head-butted each other into the long nights. I think he may have been invalided out — he was never a natural taker of orders — a fact I had discovered way back: in the nursery, at Dartington and when we shared a bedroom in our parents' house to which he brought girlfriends, explaining that I was (a) a very sound sleeper, also (b) deaf. It would be less than honest to claim that, but for the participation of us three Freud boys, the result of the war would have been different . . . I have heard the same said about Field Marshal Montgomery.

CHAPTER
FIVE

In which I gain further experience of the hotel trade, alcohol and the roulette wheel in an altogether sunnier climate.

I was demobilised in late October 1947; the first twenty-three and a half years of my life had been spent doing what others had ordered me to do . . . though not perhaps always as they would have had me do it. Now it was to be up to me.

I was given a brown and white herringbone demob suit, pants and shirts and ties, shoes and socks, an overcoat and a trilby hat. Also quite a lot of money: my gratuity. No advice. Oxford was where I had always wanted to go but I considered myself to be too world-weary for further education. A career on the stage? My rendition of "Albert and the Lion" was only average, and I was too full of myself to be an actor and play other characters.

In a moment of cowardice I had written to the War Office asking to become a regular soldier; the response had been unenthusiastic: "A vacancy as Second Lieutenant in the Ordnance Corps" was their best offer . . . which is Army-speak for piss off. The trouble was that, having done little but wait to be called up before my war, I was unequipped for harsh civilian life. I had barely ever made a decision of my own, or worn clothes I was not told to wear. When it comes to fending for yourself, two years of a batman and a driver obeying your orders and superior officers telling you what to do is poor preparation for striding out on your own.

I spent a little of my gratuity taking a taxi from Chester, where the Army bade me farewell, to Plymouth — which is where the Argyle, the football team I had watched when at Dartington, played their modest version of League football. Train to London. Found a room for rent in a friend's flat.

London was awash with returned servicemen. My last War Crimes Investigation Unit CO had been a Polish colonel and I went to him for advice. Should I try banking, journalism, go into medicine after my success with the VD hypodermic?

He said, "You ran the officers' mess so well, I'll try to get you the management of the Polish Club in Green Street. But you'll have to learn Polish."

I had lunch with my father, asked him why he had never tried to persuade me to become an architect.

He said, "I looked at the talents of all three of you. None were suited to architecture." My father told me about the last six months of the war: he had a map of Europe on his study wall and every time a country was liberated from the Germans he would book a table in that country's best London eating house and help them celebrate. He loved food and had drunk victory toasts in Belgian, Dutch, Danish, Polish, Romanian and French restaurants.

I had known Diana Ashton when I was in charge of the labour exchange in Bad Oeynhausen. She was a subaltern in the ATS, chestnut hair, soft, eager to help. I asked her if she spoke German. She said, "No, I took geography." We had been lovers. Now I sought her out and took her to dine in a Soho restaurant called the Venezia, owned by Rienzo, Italian ex-chef at the pre-war German Embassy; until recently interned on the Isle of Man, he was sponsored by his friends and family to open shop and cook something that they could eat . . . like pasta made with eggs, and real sauces made with olive oil and tomatoes and garlic and herbs, also pizzas. He was elegant and capable, with no business acumen. His brother-in-law, Gibby, had been a mechanic and was the waiter. Two Irish girls called Kitty and Eenagh did the dishes and cleaned, sleeping upstairs on the second floor of the building in Great Chapel Street, Soho. Chef's wife, Gibby's eldest sister, came to help out when they were busy, which was actually never.

I loved the Venezia and its emptiness, took all my girlfriends there during my first month as a civilian and then, like the man who so admired the electric razor that he bought the company, I took it over. After one evening on which my friend and I were again the sole diners I said, "You never get any customers. I've spent most of my money here — why don't I buy the Venezia for last month's take, and you can buy it back from me for my last month's takings whenever you want."

They had to ask a few people, but the next day it was agreed. Damn it, no one could have done worse than them. Chef was good but reclusive. Gibby was small, pale, nervous, sullen, uncommunicative, bit his nails to the quick and had only come into the trade because (a) his sister had told him to and (b) there were no jobs around.

Let me describe the place. Great Chapel Street runs south off Oxford Street, between Berwick Street and Wardour Street and is a culde-sac. On the ground floor was the restaurant, seating thirty people if they sat in twos and fours as we laid up for them, which, of course, they did not. A few steps down, at the back, was the kitchen, which would today pass neither Planning nor Environmental Health scrutiny.

On the first floor were Rooms One and Two. One had a table for six and a sideboard, was available for private parties. Two had a table for two and a sofa; could be, and was, booked for assignations. In accordance with London County Council bye-laws there was no lock on the door. Mr Berkeley came for Fish Tea every Tuesday at 5p.m. with a woman who, when they first started to go out together, may have been young and fetching, was now blousy and dowdy. They arrived separately. Always ordered, but seldom ate, baked haddock. When this was served, he said, "Leave us now" and moved towards the sofa . . . which creaked. You could hear it down below. They paid £1 12s 6d, had done for years.

The Venezia opened for lunch and dinner, six days a week, and on Sundays Rienzo's family and friends came and ate the poor man out of house and home.

This, then, was my inheritance.

I promoted Gibby to a managerial position, mostly behind the cash desk, and took Kitty, the prettier of the two Irish sisters, as a waitress employing an Indian kitchen porter in her place. There was then a 5s limit on restaurant meals, though places like the Dorchester were allowed an extra 3s 6d because of their grandeur. Meat was rationed and hard to come by — restaurants got meat based on the number of meals they had served the previous year, so expansion was no easy thing. I expanded.

I found a man who sold horse-meat for human consumption and delivered it in laundry baskets for security — his security. We marinated the rumps to eliminate the sweetness of horse, rubbed it with mustard, called it "steak" and won customer appreciation. Only the splashing when it was fried (horse contains more water than beef) remained to give it away, but the customers were out of earshot of the kitchen. "Is it venison?" asked someone (venison was not rationed, just hard to obtain) and I put my fingers to my lips and said, "I am not allowed to tell." One ex-Army friend of mine said, "Tell me honestly, what is this?" and I said, "Horse" and he explained to his guests that I had always been a very funny man.

Kitty with her light blue eyes, dark brown hair and soft Mayo brogue took to waitressing and was loved by the clientele . . . all my Army and family friends and their friends. Some nights we were full. Rienzo's family came on Sunday evenings as before and I charged them and they paid with grace. I upped Mr Berkeley's fish teas to a fiver and he said, "Time your prices went up."

On one occasion, after he had left, I found his wallet in a crack of the sofa. His name was Sanderson. I looked him up in the phone book, rang him, told his wife, who answered, that I was Lost Property, Baker Street, and when he came to the phone told him we had his wallet. Perhaps I should have gone for the Diplomatic Corps.

In February 1948 *Time* magazine had a small paragraph headed "London". "Sigmund Freud's youngest grandson runs the trendiest restaurant in the metropolis. For 35 shillings (seven dollars) he serves . . ." and outlined my menu. I got out before the police came in. Gibby and chef told the Fuzz, "*Time* got it wrong. Here is our 5s menu — they must have kept one for old times' sake," and I left England to further my career.

The odd Venezia incident remains in the memory. A customer came in one Monday night, did himself and his guest very well and paid by cheque, leaving a sizeable tip; he came back the next day and spent even more. On day three he came on his own and gestured to me to come to him in the street outside, where he admitted that both his cheques would bounce and the law was after him. As he realised that I was a one-man band he wanted to (a) apologise profoundly and (b) try to make up. All he had was a room at the Mount Royal Hotel in which he had left two Danish girls who would make me very welcome and gave the key to me. I went to the Mount Royal after dinner service that night and let myself in with some apprehension, but they greeted me with much enthusiasm.

I am not sure the 5s limit on meals really worked. If you were determined to spend more, you had to have a 5s portion of smoked salmon in one place, a 5s lamb cutlet somewhere else and so on. But it was not only our British Ministry of Food that imposed restrictions on spending. A friend called Tony Wheeler, a Don Quixote of a bizarre, enterprising, louche leader of men, bought a guest house in Majorca and charged huge sums to guests who came for holidays. The Spanish tourist office sent an inspector, who classified him as a Class IV establishment at which bed and breakfast cost 250 pesetas — which is hardly any money at all. Wheeler framed the notice, hung it outside the front door and added an amendment: "Cooper's Oxford English marmalade is served compulsorily with all breakfasts at an additional charge of 2000 pesetas."

I was still uncertain whether catering in some form would be my profession, but the Venezia experience persuaded me that I had some talent as a host. A friend who worked at the Hotels and Restaurants Association told me that France might be a good place to go. Foreign travel, albeit with restrictions as to how much money you could take out of the country, was starting up and the French Government had taken into ownership all property owned by "proven collaborators with the Nazis". As hoteliers have never minded too much with whom they collaborate the Government ran hundreds of hotels and had decided that, to encourage visits from foreigners, their hotels would be jointly managed by one Frenchman and one national of the country that had supplied the majority of their pre-war trade.

The French hotel industry, rather than going on strike, sensibly amended the legislation. Absolutely OK about joint management, but the French manager indisputably is senior; as for the representative of the country that had provided pre-war tourism, he must be kitchen-trained, speak fluent French and have held officer rank during the war. There cannot have been many takers, for I was shown a list of hundreds of grand French hotels and was told to choose.

I chose the Martinez Hotel in Cannes. Sounded a nice name and a good location. Telegrams were exchanged between our Association and the Martinez' management, and in February 1948 I bought a single sleeper ticket on the Blue Train, arriving at Cannes Station in the early afternoon. I had sent a letter giving the time of my arrival and was met on the platform by a porter, who took me and my luggage to the hotel bus waiting on the forecourt. My suitcases, which I had requisitioned from a German luggage factory (as Major Bacon had done with the ducks), were chrome leather and rather smart. At the hotel I was met by a delegation comprising the manager and senior staff — which was impressive in view of the assurances that I would be a *very* junior partner in running the place — given a glass of wine and taken up to a third-floor suite which had three windows overlooking the Croisette.

"Does it please?" asked the manager.

"It overwhelms," I said. "Far grander accommodation than junior management would be given in my country."

"*Merde alors*," said the manager and disappeared.

At length a porter arrived, said, "Follow me" and led me to a broom cupboard which, when my luggage had been put in, afforded insufficient room for me to join it. We compromised with a smallish room with a wide bed, bath en suite. Not a good beginning to my stay, but, as I learnt later, when my letter on handmade paper had arrived, (I had requisitioned a handmade paper business near Hanover) asking to be met, no one thought that was something a member of staff would do; then me and that luggage, and the rarity of a customer in February.

Cannes in winter is a village. There is no industry but tourism: for six months they prepare for six months of fleecing. A casino stands at each end of the promenade and there are grand hotels from the Majestic at the Napoule side of the town to the Martinez at the eastern end. The Carlton, then owned by Jimmy Goldsmith's father, stands proudly in the middle.

The railway described a loop of the town, rejoining it just where the Martinez had been built, so that we had rooms that had a sea-view and rooms into which you took customers — ensuring that this was between train times — threw open the windows and pointed to the hills beyond: "*Voilà, messieurs, dames, les Collines Californie. Quelle vue, hein?*" Had they looked down they would have seen the railway track. One ensured that the *vue sur le chemin de fer* clients were entirely satisfied with their rooms before the slow train to Toulon came past and a furious procession of recently arrived clients would besiege the reception desk.

In the end they got used to it — didn't have much choice — and we had to put up with endless jokes from people who were leaving, asking whether instead of a car to the station they might not just jump out of the window with their luggage.

"*Très drôle, monsieur*," one said.

Once my status had been sorted out, the managing director, a Government employee, who was very busy and spoke French very quickly, told me he hoped I would be content and that, as a gesture to international cooperation between our countries, I should drink a litre of wine per week with my meals, with his compliments, and good luck. I did not see him again for a month.

As I explained, he spoke quickly. I missed the "per week" bit, had not at that time gone metric, and was surprised, when I ordered a litre of wine with my first lunch, at the size of the bottle. My colleagues looked on admiringly as I did my best for the old entente and finished it within the half-hour lunch break. That night I had another litre, and again at the next lunch and the next evening.

In those first weeks in Cannes I became captain of the hotel football team though I played rugby; bought a second-hand motorbike with sidecar which I had no licence to drive; proposed marriage to several customers and the housekeeper, who was fifty-eight; and on my twenty-fourth birthday won a substantial sum of money playing No.24 in the casino. Throughout that time I moved in the oysterlight of an alcoholic haze, mistook customers for each other, gave people the wrong room keys, the wrong messages, the wrong bills, and quite often fell asleep behind the reception desk — but I never let down the generous managing director. That litre of wine was drunk twice a day, and on my day off I had lunch or dinner out and then returned to the hotel to claim my tipple.

At the end of the month I saw the managing director for the second time. He said, and he now spoke more slowly (or I understood him better), that the reports he had received about me were less than totally satisfactory.

"It appears," he said, "that you drink."

"Only," I answered, "what you so kindly asked me to drink for the sake of national amity."

Indeed, I assured him, there was little opportunity after that to consume other liquor and I promised I had not done so.

"But you drink two litres a day," he said, looking at his notes.

"With your compliments," I said, belching gently and trying to get him into focus.

"I offered you one litre a week."

There was not a lot I could say. My casino winnings went to pay my wine bills and Cannes took on an entirely new appearance — not just because it was spring. Customers emerged from their cocoons of anonymity; keys achieved an identity. The Croisette outside remained static when it had previously refused to settle down and my eyes returned to the colour specified on page two of my passport signed by Ernest Bevin.

There was one customer called George Dawson who was about five foot six tall, solidly built and rich; he had well-cut suits, a red-headed wife and lots of money. I got to know him a bit and asked him how one becomes affluent, a state I wished to attain. He said he had been on the look-out for ways to turn a few quid and chanced on scrap metal. Sold a hundred tonnes of steel here, bought similar quantities of tin, had a go at copper, arbitraged silver . . . you know how it is? I nodded as if I did and he ordered me another glass of Alpes Maritimes rosé.

Some evenings I drove my motorbike up into the mountains above Nice, found an agreeable bar in a village square and drank. One night I was sitting drinking in the village of Castellane, next to a table at which locals were playing cards, smashing them down with ever-increasing force as Frenchmen do. When there was a break in the game I took the pack, shuffled it, glanced at the bottom card, arranged them on the table face-down and asked one of the players to touch one . . . having deliberately made all but one card equally easy to touch. The player touched the partly obscured card. I told him it was the nine of clubs. It was; he was hugely impressed and by something of a fluke I did the trick again with another player, thereby becoming the best thing that had happened in Castellane since the baker's wife had triplets.

I went back to that mountain village every now and then, always declining to do my "trick" again, drinking, chatting, noticing that the hardware shop in the square sold firewood at 2000 francs a bundle while the Cannes price was 9000.

One evening I said to George, "If I were rich it would be so easy to become richer. I've found a place that sells firewood for less than a quarter of the price it costs here. If I had a van or two and drivers to go with them, I could clean up, find myself a red-headed wife and buy my suits from a proper tailor."

George asked me when I would do this . . . or would I resign from the hotel and set up shop?

I told him that for starters I would do it in the early mornings, like get up at dawn and be done when my shift started at 9a.m.

He said, "Thursday OK for you?"

I said, "Fine."

The following Wednesday evening I went to the casino, as I did most nights, ate a lot of the foie gras canapés which were served to players, drank champagne with people who had won, danced with a pretty and willing girl and got to bed at 3a.m.

At 5.45 the *concierge de nuit* telephoned my room to announce, "The lorries have arrived, four of them. How long will you be? Because I don't want them parked at the front of the hotel."

I told him to let them go and slept out my hangover. Perhaps I was not meant to be a trader and make money. I kept out of George's way from embarrassment and when we met up some days later he had the good manners not to mention the lorries. For my part, I ceased to talk about the injustice of his being rich, me not.

Tony Mostyn, a painter from our village in Suffolk, had emigrated to Antibes where he lived in a small house near the beach with his beautiful wife and elderly parents. I liked him and we both liked drink; neither of us had enough money. Some evenings I would drive over with a 5 litre flagon of *vin ordinaire* and we would reminisce about Walberswick and single malt whisky — and about his wife's brother Alfred, who had always welcomed me to his Walberswick house and sometimes took me greyhound racing. We visited remote East Anglian flapping tracks while I was in my early teens, stopping at pubs on the drive back, Alfred never forgetting, however drunk he was, to bring me out a glass of cider. In 1946 a Newmarket friend had told him that Langton Abbott would win the Lincoln Handicap and, being a gambler, he had £10 doubles: Langton Abbott with four horses in the Grand National. The winning double gave Alfred more money than he had ever had before.

When I was thirteen Stephen had warned me about Alfred: "Don't you know he is a well-known homosexual? You are to stop seeing him."

"He's never homosexualled me," I replied. "Anyway, it's my life — fuck off." We were never that close, Stephen and I.

Alfred was tall, languid and Catholic, with fair curly hair and wore good clothes. Thirteen years my senior, he gave me a first edition of Hilaire Belloc's *Cautionary Verses*.

Tony, his brother-in-law, had a small pension which, he said, allowed him to have a better life in France than he could have in England, "and then there is the weather". He called me at the hotel one evening, having walked into the village where there was a phone box. "Great news," he announced. "We've been asked to a party at Auguste's in Antibes. There's to be real drink. Come and meet at my house at 5.30 and we'll be in good time for the kick-off at six." On arrival he took me to his studio in the garden, where two glasses and a bottle of olive oil graced the table. He filled the glasses. "Drink this, it'll allow the alcohol to slip down more easily and we can drink more."

I drank the oil. It was pretty disgusting and, with mouths sorely in need of hard liquor, we hurried to Auguste's — to be told that the party had been the night before.

My best friends in France were Michael and Caty Coates, who lived in a small house in Cagnes, up the hill from Cagnes-sur-Mer. Michael was Arthur Rank's nephew and had some family money. He had been a subaltern in the infantry, like me; and missed it, as did I. Late at night, after the local hotel, Le Cagnard, closed its doors on us, we would drill each other around the village. "Atten*shun*!" we would shout. "Queek march. Left-right-left-right-left-right. Pick up those steps, you miserable bunch of morons. *Halt*. Left turn." Neither of us could understand why Caty told us the neighbours had complained again. We had won

105

them the war; they just provided women to be laid by Germans.

Popette John and her friend Barbara Skelton came to live at Le Cagnard while the Tour de France came by. They bought glossy cycling magazines with pictures of the contestants and circled the men they fancied. I liked Popette the better of the two; she was Augustus John's daughter, large, dark and extrovert. I invited her to have lunch with me at a local restaurant and on the way told her she was beautiful and I fancied her a lot. A few minutes later, passing a small inn with a table for drinkers outside, she said, "Let's go in", negotiated the rent of a room for half an hour and took her clothes off. I was unprepared for this and could not rise to the task until she went over to a piano under the window and played lots of very loud chords to turn me on. She was older than me, more honest too. I was a pissy young man, an opinion shared by my employers.

Then I got jaundice. I was standing behind the reception desk one afternoon when the Blue Train passengers decanted and an English doctor looked at me and diagnosed jaundice. I went to the hotel doctor, who told me to go away and get better, drink no alcohol nor eat fat but boil up globe artichokes and take a cupful of the stock every two hours. Going away and not drinking was a problem, for all my friends were drinking friends. I remembered Princess Marie Bonaparte, she who had helped to rescue my grandfather from Vienna, who had a house in St Tropez.

"May I come and stay and not drink and sip artichoke broth?"

She said she would be in Paris but I could go, so long as I tipped the staff.

I spent a month at her house, some of it wondering whether I had chosen the right career. In an attempt to make money, I went to the local bookshop and asked if they knew of any vacancies for an English teacher. The bookshop manager said the village was rotten with Englishmen trying to teach people their language, but if I could write a pornographic book — quite short, as long as it was explicit — there was a good market and an up-front payment.

He loaned me the sort of book that sold well and I read it with interest. The author knew so much more about sex than I did, had nine different names for a penis, a dozen for a vagina. He set his story during the Spanish Civil War where a sex-maniac had been put in charge of a prison for the daughters of noblemen, whom he chastised several times on each page with the help of three lesbian nuns and a German Shepherd.

I declined the commission but did compose a short story and sent it to the *New Yorker* with a letter:

Dear Editor
I am thinking of engaging on a career as a writer and would like to start my collection of rejection slips with one from you, as I am a great admirer of your magazine.

Money continued to be a problem, but my share of Grandfather's royalties was now worth over £100 a year and that helped.

I recovered from my illness, went back to work and spent the mornings of my days off motor-biking to Ventimiglia just across the border, loading up my side-car with Arborio rice, eating a drunken lunch, driving back and selling the rice in France at about twice the price I had paid in Italy. Not a George Dawson road to riches but worth about as much again as my salary and there was always No. 24 on the roulette wheel. "*Vingt-quatre noir, pair et passe*" was the music my ears sought. I was born on 24 April 1924 and 24 was my number, although 5 and 16, neighbours to 24 on the wheel, were used to hedge. In that twenty-fourth year of my life I agonised about when would be the right time, the right place — which table at which casino — for my coup.

Between now and infinity every number on a properly balanced roulette wheel will come up an equal number of times; the trouble is that infinity is a long way off. Using statistics gleaned from the tables of Monte Carlo's Salle Privée it is known that if you draw a graph of each of the thirty-seven numbers, once one of them is fifty hits lower than the average top six numbers, wait for it to hit a couple of times and then back it to catch up. Casinos who know this now regularly change the wheels at the expensive tables, just in case. I was looking for quicker results.

In the summer of that year, on the 24th of a month, accompanied by a girl who looked as if she would bring me luck and a diminutive mouth-organ player who was down on his luck and sleeping under my bed at the hotel, I put the minimum stake on 24 over and over and, when it finally came up, left it there. It came up again. One thousand two hundred and ninety-six times my stake. I shoved 460 francs to the croupiers to shouts of, "*Merci, monsieur, pour le personnel*"; blew some on celebrating my win at the bar, as people do; rented a small house in Cagnes for the rest of the year; bought Tony Mostyn a bottle of single malt; organised that the housekeeper spend a few hours with a gigolo she much admired but could not afford and drove to St Tropez and re-tipped the Princess' staff, for they had not done well out of me.

The big win made me bet less, though when someone at the black-jack table got an ace and a picture I would still slip some money in behind the gambler's stake for the next deal, and, more often than not I won. I loved casinos: the atmosphere, the opulence, the different ways different people gambled, the old women at the inexpensive tables who tried to claim other players' winnings with appeals to the croupier: "You saw me put it on — 29 has always been my number." When you play a lot, as they did and as I did for those months, you begin with a number and play that and its neighbours; sit next to someone who wins consistently on another number and emulate the play; meet a girl who says, "Final 7s are best", have a spell on the zero sector 0, 3, 15, 26, 32 until, in not that long a time, every number on the board has, at some time, been your number. Nineteen comes up —

dix-neuf rouge, impair et passe — and it is as if you've caught your wife in bed with your friend. "Nineteen!" you say with incredulity. "My number and I did not back it."

When guests came to the hotel and asked the *concierge* about going to the casino, he would occasionally recommend me as a guide; it was one of these men who caused me to be banned from the Summer Palace. The man was tall, fat, from Shaker Heights in Cleveland, Ohio.

"Call me Chuck."

I called him Chuck.

He asked whether a bank of a thousand dollars US would be about right for an evening's play and I opined that it depended on his wealth and he said, "Damn it, then. Five thousand dollars." I introduced him to the casino manager, we had foie gras and champagne and he exchanged a bundle of notes for a huge pile of chips and played roulette without any rhyme or reason, other than always waiting until the ball had been thrown into the wheel before placing his bets. Suspicious gamblers do that in the belief that a croupier can hit numbers at will and avoid those that are heavily backed.

He lost some, we had another drink and he returned to the table, increasing his bets until the pile of chips in front of him had almost disappeared. Quite a decent-sized crowd had gathered to watch, as crowds do when high rollers are at work.

The croupier shouted, "*Faîtes vos jeux*", spun the ball and Chuck, now nicely drunk, tore a button off his jacket, placed it on No. 16 and said, "Gentlemen, this button represents one thousand dollars US." He sat back; the croupier tried to rake in the button with his croupe and was shouting, *"Le bouton ne compte pas"* when the ball landed on 16. There was pandemonium and I was requested not to return. Chuck neither.

Around this time we realised that my job was genuinely futile; since my arrival at the hotel I had dealt with English bookings, replied to clients reserving summer accommodation and answered their queries about golf, pasteurised milk for children and were there in-house hair-dressing facilities. Now they started to arrive, and the scene went like this. The bus brought the guests from Cannes Station and they were ushered to me at reception.

"Good afternoon, Mr Wilkinson. Welcome to the Martinez Hotel."

"Je suis Monsieur Wilkinson de Huddersfield."

"You are very welcome. You may recall that we corresponded."

"Voilà Madame Wilkinson et les petits Wilkinsons."

It was the first year of foreign holiday travel after the war. People had looked forward to it and were determined to make the most of it, which meant speaking French.

After filling in the forms, he said,

"Maintenant nous voulons monter aux chambres."

I glanced at the timetable, realised that the stopping train to Marseilles was about to pass, inquired about their journey, offered them a cup of tea.

"Nous voulons monter."

I explained about the children's bathing pool, heard the rumble of the train in the background, asked the client whether he would like to go up and see his rooms, threw open the window and pointed up to the Californie hills, dreading the scene when the express to Milan came by half an hour later.

I particularly remember Mr Wilkinson because after he had been with us for three or four days he came up to me at the reception desk and said: "*Est-ce qu'il y a des autres ici de Huddersfield?*" His wife was at the beach, his children in the pool; he was lonely.

At a weekly management meeting my situation was discussed. English customers had complained about me. I spoke English. If they had wanted to speak English to staff they could have gone to Bognor Regis. The senior manager suggested that, as it was classy to have English staff, I might take over the welcoming of the French guests . . . though as my accent was now a bit too French, could I speak so that guests would know I was English.

I got a letter from the editor of the *New Yorker*.

Dear Mr Freud
We like very much your story about the professor and the prisoner of war and would like to publish it . . ."

The summer was drawing to a close, guests were leaving. I had a short article about me in *Nice Matin* headed "*Petit-fils de Freud et le Yorkshire pouding*" and got invited to lunch with Somerset Maugham, who had the worst halitosis I have encountered. Picasso asked me to visit him at Vallauris where a friend of mine was on a journalistic assignment. When I arrived and was introduced he asked whether I was from England.

I said, "Yes."

"*Comment vont les eezes?*"

I had to explain that "eezes" was not a word I knew. It turned out he wanted to know how ICI shares were doing.

By October Cannes was a village once more; guests had gone, temporary staff were laid off and I went to restaurants to which I had sent customers during the high season, claiming my free meals. Felix of the Blue Bar on the Croisette, the loudest and funniest of the personality barmen in town, stopped beavering away behind the counter and again stood outside his premises offering drinks, spreading gossip, telling people that if they wanted to have for lunch what other people had for dinner, swim in the Mediterranean. The sewerage system kicked out into the sea about 40 metres from the beach.

I spent afternoons on the beach, witnessing a very tragic accident in which two boys of about fourteen on a pedalo were capsized by a wave and by the time a boat got to them a quarter of an hour later one of the boys was stiff and green and swollen with water and dead. The other, seeing his friend's corpse, had loud and uncontrollable hysterics, screaming with anguish and shivering. A woman who ran the seafood bar on the beach came and put her arms around the grieving boy, sat him down, opened her blouse and let him suckle her breast. I was very moved and considered this as a theme for my next *New Yorker* story. The seafood bar woman became a friend. She told me that mayonnaise always curdled if made by one having her period; I believed her.

My private life became more settled: I worked in the mornings and evenings; read books on the beach in the afternoons; and spent weekends in Cagnes, seeing a lot of the Coates and having a regular Saturday afternoon rendezvous at the Abbaye de la Colle, a hostelry bought by an ex-head porter of Ruhl's Hotel in Nice and his blind ex-Ruhl housekeeper wife. They had two pretty twin daughters who lisped and I loved them both, never quite sure which was which. I took an upstairs room there and they came to visit, one of them staying in the bar where her blind mother knitted. The gramophone played songs from *Oklahoma* like "The Surrey with the Fringe on Top", which meant that both parents were in view. When the music stopped and did not instantly restart, the twin who was with me would lisp, "*Attenthion, monthieur! Papa vient*" and disappeared.

When my year's work permit expired and the hotel gave me a farewell party, the housekeeper finally accorded me a chaste kiss. I travelled back to London an adequate if seldom sober hotel man, a published writer aged nearly twenty-five with a suntan and more holiday friends than anyone. My Martinez customers who on departure gave me their cards and bade me visit them ranged from Maurice Chevalier and Jack Benny down to fifteen-minute-fame-and-fortune post-war pop stars.

114

I took out to dinner (at the Venezia, where they were pleased to see me again) the woman from the Hotels and Restaurants Association, told her that I was grateful for her guidance in getting me to Cannes, but now felt like packing in catering to work at something more cerebral. I showed her the copy of the *New Yorker*.

"What a pity," she said. "I have been holding a job as manager of a seasonal hotel in North Devon pending your return."

I started work as manager of the Saunton Sands Hotel near Braunton, not that far from Barnstaple, at Easter 1949.

CHAPTER
SIX

In which I perform a seasonal job, whereafter
I fall in love and marry.

From afar the Saunton Sands Hotel looked like a huge
public lavatory; on closer inspection it did indeed turn
out to be designed by the *toilettiste* school of
architecture: rectangular is a good shape; white cement
a good finish; who could want for anything more?
Saunton had been built on the sand-dunes above a
stunning stretch of beach, so endless that it was picked
as the location for filming *Here Comes Mr Jordan* to
depict the balmy featurelessness of heaven. Three sides
of the hotel had sea-views; the front overlooked the
Braunton to Croyde road and the gorse and heather
beyond.

Despite my position of "junior manager" at the
Martinez, I had never managed anything, knew nothing
about hiring and firing, purchasing, food cost,
stocktaking or holiday entitlements. In the weeks before
I was to take up my position I found out a bit; saw Mr
Williams, the staff manager at the Dorchester (Alma
had gone to draw tidy lines in her father's new
gymnasium's account books; Miss Hill had aged), and
he was friendly and forthcoming. After he outlined the
rudiments of the job, I asked . . . now that we were

116

almost equals . . . whether he could tell me about a few things that had gone on while I worked at the hotel which had puzzled me.

"Why did you sack someone from the silver room nearly every week?"

"It kept people on their toes and any cunt can work the silver room."

"Why was Roast chef paid less than Fish chef when everyone knows Roast is the senior of those two parties?"

Williams looked at me, smiled, said, "You ought to know why. Roast chef used to nick more food from the kitchen than Fish — you must have been sent out to put stuff into his bicycle bag when you were the apprentice."

That impressed me. He also advised me not to employ friends — "If you bawl one out, the other sulks" — nor couples and "never more than one Portuguese, else they take over"; most importantly, "most people can do any job in our trade if they have the right attitude." We went out for a drink and he told me he had finally sacked Monsieur Smid, hoped the old bastard now got Worthington froth down his own trousers. I had not realised how much management knew about what we believed to be our private hell.

Mr A. H. Brown was the resident managing director of the seaside hotel: a tall, plump, slobby man in his sixties. I had met him at the interview in London and he met me at Braunton Station, driving me to Saunton at a steady 29 miles per hour. A law-abiding man. He called the shots. I ran the place. His office dealt with bookings; I was told the number of customers and given an allocation of staff. There was an absolute minimum skeleton staff: one each cook, kitchen porter, waiter, housekeeper, maid, porter and cleaner, and only as guests arrived was I allowed more employees.

All West Country hotels advertised for seasonal staff in spring; the *Caterer and Hotel Keeper*, our trade paper, was full of job ads. On the advice of the waiter *in situ* I put advertisements into the *Liverpool Echo*; and on the advice of Mr Williams, after describing the vacant situation, be it waiter, cook, maid, porter, whatever, added: "Previous experience disqualifies."

The afternoon arrival of guests who were staying for Whitsun remains in the memory. The A. H. Brown rule about not engaging staff until there were customers meant that I stood at the door as the coaches arrived from the station, saying, "Good afternoon, sir, welcome to Saunton Sands Hotel" to a Liverpudlian kitchen porter-to-be, adding "Piss off round the back", when he identified himself. "Good afternoon, sir, welcome to Saunton . . ."

I invited Alfred Holland from Walberswick, deeply down on his luck at the time, to come to Devon and take over the bar; a waiter called Griff, who had been commis at the next station when I worked for Mr Van, joined the restaurant staff; and a girl called Victoria whom I had met on the train (she was going to Exeter University for her interview and was looking for a summer job) came to work in reception. This was a mistake. Victoria was competent but possessive and

118

jealous, and ensured that no women under forty were given bedrooms anywhere near mine.

When we were a quarter full, everyone had a dining room table facing the sea. As more guests arrived, my main income came from the pay-table: this was a table for four placed between the in and out doors to the kitchen, as far from the sea-view as a table could be. I would greet guests warmly, look up their names on my chart and lead them there proudly, ensuring that as they sat down a door would smack against one of them and a waiter would push closely past another.

"Could you not find a better table?"

I searched my chart, looked doubtful, said I would try to do better, perhaps next week . . . "You are staying a fortnight . . ." and as I walked slowly away would be pursued by the paterfamilias pushing fivers at me.

On one occasion that summer the pay-table did not work. "Nice table," said the man. "Like it here — close to where it all happens" — this as Griff banged a door into the back of his chair. A whole week without income from that source.

Food was rationed, though not as tightly as it had been. Meat was still on a percentage-of-what-the-place-sold-last-year allocation and, as Mr Brown had decreed that being a three-star hotel there must be a choice at every course, I juggled meat with chicken or fish or braised ox-hearts (a great meat-rationing standby), steadily trying not to make the one in short supply sound more desirable than the alternatives.

I had trouble here in first courses: for a full house of 140 guests we had smoked salmon or melon and the first 90 guests ordered smoked salmon. Come early to avoid disappointment.

A late-comer ordered salmon; the waiter said, "I'm afraid we're right out of salmon, but I can recommend the melon."

Man said, "Call the manager."

I arrived.

"Freud," said the man. "See here, I ordered smoked salmon like it says on your menu and this dunderhead says he's run out and tries to sell me melon. See to it."

I went to the kitchen, found that there was no smoked salmon, left and reported this to the complaining guest.

"Do you mean to tell me, Freud, that in a bloody big building like this you cannot find a single small slice of salmon?"

I wanted to explain that there was no connection between the size of a construction and the availability therein of selected foodstuff, remembered that I was the manager rather than the proprietor and said, "No, sir."

He said he was disgusted, had thought better of me.

I apologised.

As the summer progressed, work actually got easier. Every disaster that occurred was recognised and dealt with: flooded bathrooms, bed-linen on fire, man snoring in the room next door, wrong breakfast served to the wrong room at the wrong time, a mouse . . . it had happened before and we had learnt the answers. Our clientele was upper middleclass: husband, wife, two children, one nanny. At night husband got drunk, wife read a book, nanny got laid by a waiter — the more superior the nanny, the more senior the waiter.

On my day off Alfred, not a great success as a barman although he had spent such a substantial part of his life in bars, and I went into Barnstaple where we found an unlicensed bookmaker and had a few bets after a bibulous lunch in a hotel in the High Street. The hotel had a bow window giving on to the road; Alfred decided that when he won the pools he would come here to lean out of that window — perhaps employ someone to hold his feet to prevent him from falling — and give pints of ale to people walking by. We both thought that an admirable ambition. Sadly, Alfred was killed in Kenya in the 1950s during the Mau Mau uprising.

A. H. Brown was not much in evidence as the hotel filled up though he came to the kitchen one morning and told me that the way to make tea is to heat the teapot with boiling water, pour this away, put in the tealeaves, add half a pint of boiling water, let the leaves stew for *two* whole minutes and then add the rest of the water. "You get stronger tea for fewer tea-leaves — remember that, Freud."

In June we had a genuinely desirable customer: a Lloyd's insurance broker, member of Boodles, connoisseur of fine wines, there with his wife, children, nanny, under-nanny (who had it off with kitchen porters) and chauffeur, who was popular with the waitresses. He came to me on the morning of Ascot's Ladies' Day and said, "Mornin', Freud, d'ye have a bookmaker?" I told him I did. He opened his wallet, pulled out twenty crinkly white £5 notes and said, "Put these on Benny Lynch in the Gold Cup at 100–1, there's a good fellow."

I took the money and went to the residents' lounge to confirm that Alycidon was going to win the Gold Cup. Benny Lynch, also owned by Lord Derby, was Alycidon's pacemaker, had never won over a Gold Cup distance and was 100–1, rightly so. I stuck the bet; put the money in my cash hiding-place, which was in the lining of one of the two chrome leather suitcases in the cupboard in my room.

This was pre-television, but the BBC Light Programme broadcast from Royal Ascot and I listened to the race, Raymond Glendenning commentating. He mentioned that Alycidon was favourite — the BBC did not give odds, ever, not even when they announced racing results after the evening news. Benny Lynch took the lead, as pacemakers do, and after half a mile was ten lengths ahead of the field; at the mile post he had, if anything, increased that lead. Coming to six furlongs from home Glendenning opined that the pacemaker had got away and looked like winning.

One hundred pounds at 100–1 was £10,000. Fifteen years of my wages, the cost of 250 acres of land, twenty times as much as caused the average suicide to jump off Beachy Head. I felt a trickle of ice-cold sweat run down the back of my neck — actually felt it, had previously read that this happened but had not believed it. I saw a life of disgrace and penury ahead.

Alycidon won the Gold Cup — Benny Lynch was not able to stay the distance, just as I had worked out, but that was the last time I acted as a bookmaker.

Among other guests Michael Redgrave came to Saunton with his wife and three children. He had been a friend of Stephen and Natasha Spender and I looked after him well, ensuring that if he was late for dinner there *would* be smoked salmon and on his arrival took him straight to a window table rather than make him buy his way to it. Before they left I gave the Redgraves a small farewell dinner, made the Béarnaise sauce myself, promised that when I returned to London I would go and see Michael in *A Month in the Country* at the Comedy and come backstage for a drink.

Up the road from Saunton was the village of Croyde, and at Croyde Bay NALGO, the National Association of Local Government Officers, had their holiday camp . . . a big, bustling, Butlinesque place where policemen and postmen and council office clerks took their families for an all-in charge of very little. "All-in" included accommodation, breakfast, lunch, tea and dinner, also a creche for children, dancing and cabaret at night; and every camper was given a nickname which was printed on a plastic disc and worn on the lapel.

Sitting on the terrace of the hotel bar, which had access to the Croyde road, we would see figures come towards us from afar and take bets on what would be their nickname. I got to win most of the time for I knew how it worked: everyone under five foot four was called Lofty, bald men were Curly, anorexics Fatso. A regular caller at the bar was the local landowner, Sir William

Williams Bart. who missed being in the Army but unlike the rest of us had not become used to it. "Freud," he would greet me from 50 yards. "Atten*shun* quick march left-right-left-right *halt*. I'll have a Gordon's and tonic since you asked."

Our staff got nicked by nearby hotels at Lynton and Lynmouth, and Mr Brown had to be despatched down to Torquay and Paignton to steal waiters from there.

Insurance brokers came to stay, always tried to sell me policies; stockbrokers came and, instead of leaving tips, whispered, "Buy Metal Box shares, you can't go wrong."

In September Michael Redgrave telephoned and asked me to come and have dinner at the Woollacombe Hotel 6 miles away.

"What are you doing there?"

"Staying a week.

"Did we do anything to upset you? I thought you had enjoyed Saunton."

He said, "Come to dinner tomorrow night."

I drove over to Woollacombe. He was staying there with his boyfriend, Tony Hyndman, whom I knew because he had been Stephen Spender's boyfriend when we shared a house during the war.

Some years later I had dinner with the Redgraves in Chiswick. After the meal Michael went across the road to his workroom, where there was a boy in residence. I said to Rachel, "I didn't know this went on so openly. Do you not find it humiliating?"

"It's humiliating for Mike."

The Saunton Sands Hotel closed at the end of the summer. I got a bonus from Mr Brown and went to Braunton to call on the butcher who had offered me twopence in the pound for any hotel purchases from his shop. He gave me a drink, asked me whether I was coming back next year, and I said, "I feel one season in a summer holiday hotel is enough. What's my commission?"

He said, "What commision? Piss off." One is always learning.

On my return from Devon I called on Beecher Moore, a man I had known since I was sixteen in the early days of the war. A friend at the Coffee Ann had taken me to the Players' Theatre, in Albemarle Street, a Victorian music hall with a chairman who used long words and a dozen acts, all of which I learnt by heart. On that first night there was an air raid alarm and we stayed at the Players' until the all clear six hours later, by which time I was in the kitchen making sandwiches with only part of Edgar's skill and had got to know most people there.

Beecher was American, a kinsman of the author Harriet Beecher Stowe. He had sailed for the USA in the 1936 Olympics, inherited from his father a company called Moore's Modern Methods which printed account books and wages sheets and by virtue of being a fire-watcher had been allocated a fifth-floor flat in Inner Temple Lane by the Law Courts. He lived there with an actress called Joan Gates, who worked at the Players' and sang:

There was I waiting at the church, waiting at the
   church, waiting at the church,
When I found he'd left me in the lurch, Lord how
   it did upset me, blimey,
All at once he sent me round a note, here's the
   very note, this is what he wrote,
"Can't get away to marry you today, my wife
   won't let me."

I went to the Players' a lot: to listen, make sandwiches, chat and drink and one night asked Joan whether I might walk her home. She said, "Yes, fine", and when we got to where she lived she said, "You can come in. Beecher said it would be all right." That is how I found out they were living together; I excused myself from coming in. "Important appointment, didn't realise it was so late. Goodnight, see you."

My friendship with Beecher blossomed over the years, through his many girlfriends and both his marriages. He was best man at my wedding and died in that flat in the Temple while I sat at his bedside; died quietly, decorously, of old age.

In the 1950s he was one of four partners who owned the Arts Theatre Club in Great Newport Street, off Leicester Square. When Beecher asked what I was going to do next and I said I just might try something new — become a teacher, get into medical school — he said he might be able to offer me a job. A few weeks later I was catering manager of the Arts, wages £10 a week and my food. A proper London job. I took a large room in a friend's house in Drayton Gardens for £2

10s a week. An economist told me that if your living expenses are less than one third of your salary you will be all right. I was all right.

My first job was to enhance the Arts Theatre snack bar, which was open to all-comers during the day and did a fair pre-, post- and interval trade when plays were on in the afternoons and evenings. If you take over an existing establishment, it needs courage to bring about radical changes. People go to this or that place because they like what it does. Replace the lunchtime moussaka and mushroom risotto with boiled gammon in parsley sauce and Scotch eggs and, while you may well succeed in the long run, the core clientele will go elsewhere. Changing the snack bar was a bit like playing Grandma's Footsteps. I introduced new coffee, but kept some of the old in case anyone really complained. Went to a new baker for my bread; reorganised the sandwiches so that they bulged a bit more and were fresher by virtue of being made in smaller batches, more often. I bought mugs with names on them for a dozen or so of the most regular customers and told the staff that bussing — cleaning up after a person has finished — is actually more important than serving.

By November the snack bar was going smoothly, taking more money than it had previously done. I turned my attention to the lounge bar and restaurant, and appointed Mr Matta as supplier of wines and spirits to the Arts Theatre Club. Mr Matta deserves a chapter to himself. I first encountered him on a Sunday evening at the Venezia. He was a friend of a friend of the chef: small, slight, very Italian and spoke of himself in the third person — "Matta will see to it." When he sent bottles of his wines to people sitting in restaurants, the waiter was always to say, "With the compliments of Matta."

Matta was a wine merchant, though after the war you would have been right in calling him The Wine Merchant. He was steadily good to me and I learnt about his rise to fame and fortune over the years.

Ferdinando Secundo Matta was the second son of a family from Cuneo in northern Italy. Like other Italian boys he became a waiter and after the First World War, came to England. Worked at the Trocadero, got his own station, thrived. Twice a year he went home to see his parents, brought back with him a barrel of Chianti and between lunch and dinner service he collected Chianti bottles — which were then handsome and elliptical with the bottom half covered with straw — on which his wife stuck labels declaring "Chianti Casa Matta" followed by a year, not necessarily the year it was bottled.

He sold this wine to hotels and restaurants and after a while applied to become a member of the Wines and Spirits Retailers' Association. They looked him up, found that he had neither applied for an import licence nor paid duty on his wines and declined membership.

Uniquely among London eating houses, the Trocadero had a system to ensure against staff larceny, which was rife. The Trocadero method entailed having a menu on each table and a cashier in the kitchen; as waiters emerged from below to take food into the restaurant they paid for what was on their trays and reclaimed this from the customers they served. Matta had a commis with whom he got on well and one day took him to a tailor to have him fitted for a bespoke waiter's jacket. It was loose-fitting and had oiled silk pockets and he said to the boy, "Now when you go to the kitchen and getta the food, you putta the meat in this pocket and the fish in that pocket and you pay for the veg, *capito*?" He prospered.

Proprietary whisky at that time was wholesaling at 60s a case, got sold on to restaurants at 66s. Matta, on learning of his rejection as a licensed victualler, undersold the other merchants by advertising whisky at 63s a case, just about cornered the London whisky market: first Soho, then most other places that felt three shillings a case was worth saving.

The three shillingses mounted up, and Matta left the Troc and concentrated on whisky when war broke out. In 1939, having never bothered to become a naturalised British citizen, he was interned on the Isle of Man as an "enemy alien" for Mussolini had joined the Axis; famously, when Churchill was informed of this, he said, "Serve them right; we had them last time."

Matta was not held very long on the Isle of Man — a few months, I think — but when he came back to London he found his wife gone and his office in Westminster Bridge Road closed, his manager having been called up. Among the piles of unopened mail he came across a letter from the Proprietary Whisky Wholesalers' Association, informing him that whisky was now strictly on allocation, "such allocation being based on a fraction of the previous year's purchases

129

which in your case is . . ." and they had filled in 2496 cases a month. If you wanted to buy whisky during the war, there was nowhere else to go. Matta, to his infinite credit, never overcharged customers for whisky, but did rather expect anyone who bought a case of whisky from him to purchase six cases of his wine. And his wine was not very terrific and cost a bit.

Matta was delighted to get my business at the Arts. It was a prestigious account — there were no Italians there, so landing it was a feather in his cap. He not only quoted me decent prices but gave me a personal allocation of a case of whisky a month, which was worth £36. "Compliments of Matta," he said as his driver delivered the bounty to my gofer, whose name was Ted and whom I trusted above all people. Ted had been a Covent Garden market porter; at the Arts he ran the goods inward, cellar, laundry, empty bottles, employment of minor staff and did all the dirty jobs others did not want to do. His motto was "Quicker to do it yourself than argue the toss."

We were pathetically uninspired in the kitchens of Britain at that time. After a decade of rationing, price control on meals and no history of innovative English cooking (France, by virtue of having poor raw materials, invented stunning sauces and garnishes) we failed when produce reappeared in the shops. Our sausages had contained so little meat for so long that no one remembered how delicious an 80 per cent meat banger was. There were angry young men in literature, politics, architecture and drama, not in the field of culinary art: fish cakes went on being made with more breadcrumbs and mashed potato than fish. Symington's pretty ordinary powdered soups ruled the starter section of menus in all but the most select eating houses, bread remained awful and when cream returned to the shelves people had quite forgotten what to do with it.

Indian and Chinese restaurants flourished — not necessarily because they were good, but it stopped the little woman saying to her man: "What are we doing spending our money on roast lamb at 3s 6d a portion when I can do it better at home for half the price?" She could not say that about lamb biryani with okra, let alone a portion of No.36 with pilaf rice at the Cantonese.

In Paris, home-going revellers could go to a café in Les Halles and obtain a bowl of *Soupe a l'Ivrogne*, drunkard's soup: finely sliced onions, simmered in best Normandy butter until soft, the volume provided by champagne, the oniony buttery vinous liquor decanted into a *marmite* pot, covered with a scraped Camembert cheese, topped with breadcrumbs and baked until the golden crumbs set on the melted cheese lid above the broth.

In London you left the Bag of Nails in Beak Street and, if you were lucky, found an all-night caff selling Bovril.

The Arts Theatre Club, with its membership of arty-farty women of a certain age, was not the place to stage a culinary breakthrough . . . or perhaps I was just lazy. Under my management things went on pretty well the way they had, nor was there anywhere that seemed to do much better. Our wine list was goodish; I worked on it, partly because I was learning about wine and went to auctions and tastings at Beaver Hall in the City, partly because I was not oversure of my job and someone had told me that no manager is ever sacked while constructing a new wine list.

I did introduce some innovations in the restaurant; cold soups, dried fruit salads, vegetables served on a skewer. The members were deeply conservative and suspicious of new dishes, had become really fond of Escalope de Jour which was always, every jour, made of boned thighs of rabbit floured, egged and breadcrumbed. Rabbit was never mentioned. Had one appeared in Great Newport Street, London WC2, my punters would have thought it was an escalope.

What did succeed was the establishment of a gastro-connection with the production in the theatre. During a Noël Coward play we served 1930s' cocktails in the interval. Eugene O'Neill's *The Iceman Cometh* was cause to home in on Irish stew, colcannon and Guinness. There was a half-page picture of me and the top table in the *Evening Standard* when I organised an ambigu to boost public awareness of a not very successful rendering of Vanbrugh's Restoration comedy *The Provok'd Wife*; I had gone to the British Museum Library and read up a bit on the subject. Ambigus consisted of a dozen or more dishes served simultaneously — peas, raspberries, potatoes, oysters — and the great boon was the drink: warm beer and cheap gin — helpful when it came to profit and v. authentic.

What was special about the Arts was the quality of the people I met. Actors, writers, artists; up-market hookers; Bernard Shaw, for whom we gave a Club Supper, who came and did not eat anything we served him, but beamed at Florence Desmond for whom he had written a play. The Club Suppers were monthly events, if we could find a speaker. A hundred members and their guests bought tickets, got a decent meal and listened to a speech by a man or woman of the moment. They included Peter Ustinov, Christopher Fry, Margaret Rawlings and Alec Clunes — a formidable actor of his time, now best known for fathering Martin — who was one of the four owners, though in my first month there he came close to severing all connections.

It was 1950 and a great year for poker. Casinos had not yet been licensed, the backgammon vogue was still to come and as good a poker school as any was that run by Johnny Stais, owner of the White Tower restaurant in Percy Street. The White Tower had the most literate menu, wonderfully well-prepared Greek Cypriot food and the charismatic Johnny, who disappeared nightly around 10p.m. to run his poker game upstairs. Alec was a keen player. I heard this story from my friend Beecher Moore, who was there.

Late one night, with not too many contestants left, Clunes held a full house, kings high. There was £50 in the pool ... which was a lot. Stais raised Clunes, Clunes raised Stais, backwards and forwards until there was a massive four-figure pot and it was Alec's turn to call or raise.

Alec said, "The Arts Theatre."

Stais replied, "The White Tower."

Beecher knocked over the table and said, "That's enough", and no one ever found out what cards were in Johnny's hand.

I had nearly made a similar error of judgement myself. On Christmas Eve 1949 there was a matinee of the Arts pantomime. Then we closed and everyone wished everyone else a Happy Christmas and I took Ted out for a drink, and then another, and Ted said, "I've got to put the bar-take into the night-safe"; I said, "Give it to me, I'll do it." And he did and we had a few more drinks.

An actor called Michael Aldridge, who was keen on racing, had told me who was likely to win a chase at Towcester on Boxing Day and we decided to go. The weather was horrible and it snowed for the big race, the one we had come to bet on specially. Michael met the owner and trainer, came back and said, "The thing's a certainty, can't lose" and as I still had the Arts bar takings in my pocket, about £100, I thought it prudent to lend this to a bookmaker for the duration of the race and pick it up threefold when it was over. Towcester is probably the stiffest course of any in the land and with a couple of days of heavy rain and now a covering of snow they should have called it off. Today's stewards would have abandoned.

Not then. Seven runners went down to the post for the two and a bit circuits and passing the stands for the second time there were but three left standing, ours among them. Towcester is a right-handed circuit with an uphill finish and one of the three that were left was down to a walk. At the last fence, to our right, through the snow, we saw our horse and its opponent stop, having insufficient impetus to jump. The walking horse still staggered on a couple of fences behind. I ran down to the fence, shouting to the jockey that I would give him £100 in cash if he just got over the fence. The wind howled, the snow blew and I am not sure he heard me, but it was no use — their race was run. The jocks got off.

When I reached the stand, promising myself that I would never bet again, not with other people's money, not in large amounts, not for some time . . . there was an announcement that as no horse had completed the course the race was declared void: bookmakers and Totalisator would return all bets.

Back on firmer ground, on 2 April 1950, in the Arts members' lounge on the first floor, I was introduced to an actress called Jill Raymond who had played Michael Redgrave's daughter in *The Father* and was appearing at the Embassy in a new play called *Home Before Seven* (hailed by critics as *Asleep Before Eight*). I proposed to her four days later and then concentrated on marrying her, which meant sessions with her Catholic priest and finding a church where an unconfirmed unbaptised Jewish atheist (or were we agnostics?) could marry a religious God-fearing convent-educated girl. I met her parents, who were a delight, introducing her to mine — which required a drink in the pub down the road to stop her shaking. "How many languages do you speak?" was my mother's opening remark.

As June Flewett Jill had won a medal at RADA and then gone into films, starring with Jean Simmons in *Woman in the Hall*, for which the J. Arthur Rank Corporation held a competition to rename her. Thus she became Jill Raymond, until the 1980s when she opened her own theatres on the Suffolk coast under the name of Jill Freud.

At around the time of my twenty-sixth birthday we announced our engagement in the *Times*: "Clement Raphael third son of Ernst and Lucie Freud of St Johns Wood London to June Beatrice second daughter of H. W. Flewett M. A. and Mrs Flewett of Gipsy Lane London SW15" . . . though Jill still insists that I never proposed to her properly.

I was by now five foot ten, weighed 12½ stone and promised to try to hit 12 stone for the wedding. I had nearly £100 saved in the Cox and King's branch of Barclay's Bank in Piccadilly, where the Army had directed my monthly pay cheques (Pricks and Queens, it was more commonly called); had an income of £10 a week from work, the same again from Mr Matta's whisky and indeterminate sums now and then from Grandfather's royalties, which were on the up. My father and the publishers had engaged James Strachey to re-translate the complete works, which had originally been done, apparently with only limited understanding, by A. A. Brill. This meant that everyone . . . well, everyone who wanted to or needed to read Freud . . . bought another load of books. By way of worldly goods I had lots of books, a monogrammed dressing gown bought from Simpson's of Piccadilly with my demob money and two chrome leather suitcases.

Jill spent that summer playing juvenile leads at Salisbury Rep. We would meet late on Saturday evenings after her show, at some station usually in the New Forest, and spend our weekends together. Monday to Saturday I worked at the Arts, played cricket for *The Stage* and squash with a friend called Tony Dawson, went greyhound racing, had bets on horses, called on Jill's parish priest ("He's giving me a terrible time," he is reported to have told my mother-in-law-to-be). For the rest of the time I organised the wedding invitations and guest list.

St James's church in Spanish Place had agreed to marry us, the director of the Arts had consented to our holding the reception there at cost price plus 20 per cent, and the neighbours to the theatre had been wondrously helpful. Victor Gross, a Czech refugee who had a jewellery shop nearby in what is now Chinatown, gave me a huge discount on a filigree gold and garnet engagement ring. The Arts florist fell over herself to give flowers. The car-hire firm we used to bring guest speakers to Club Suppers offered a limousine on the house. Beecher agreed to be my best man and gave me a bachelor's party. And my father, who had good relations with estate agents, especially St John's Wood estate agents, said he would try hard to find us somewhere to live. As for Matta, he said, "Leave the wine to Matta. Compliments of Matta."

Invitations were tricky. The standard ones read: "Henry and Freda Flewett invite you to attend the wedding of their daughter June to Clement Freud at 2p.m. on Monday Sept 4th at the church of St James Spanish Place and afterwards at the Arts Theatre Club Gt Newport St WC2."

The ones for my parents and their friends, because we were Jewish atheists . . . or was it Jewish agnostics, they were never quite sure . . . requested the pleasure of people's company at the Arts Theatre Club on the occasion of their son's wedding. The old Flewetts were not told of this. Jill was upset; I was upset; Father Mangan of Farm Street, a kindly Jesuit who had agreed to marry us, was upset; and on the wedding day we arrived at the reception to find my father and mother and an aunt waiting for us: they said they had not wanted to be late, had been there half an hour.

People got married on Saturdays; I felt Monday would be good, showed that your Friday pay-packet was not instantly spent . . . also Jill had said that she might be in a play that had a Saturday matinee. Acting for Jill had been, was, still is the absolute priority. As I write she is in the next room learning her lines for a play at her Summer Theatre in Southwold.

The month before, Jill had opened in the West End in a play called *They Got What They Wanted*; it was an Irish play, with the great Irish actors of the day, and was not only bad but played to very small houses at the Phoenix, which is a very large theatre. Jill played a bride. She opened the show, perched on the sofa in a typical Irish farmhouse sitting room, with the words, "It says here that the residue of the Gilscire fortune could be worth onythin' up to half a million." And it did not

138

get much better after that. We thought it would come off in time for our wedding; the management, because she played a bride and was going to get married and was quite well known as an actress, believed that our wedding would generate enough publicity to keep the play on for another week or so.

My father had found us a house to rent: a really excellent mews cottage off Sussex Place in Regents Park, where the London Business School stands today. Downstairs there was a sitting/dining room and a spacious cupboard, also a door leading to a garage; upstairs a double bedroom, single bedroom, bathroom, kitchen. The rent was £6 a week. Our landlord was a bill-broker who went to work in a black silk top hat and had married the daughter of *Times* editor Geoffrey Dawson, he who had been held responsible for the abdication of King Edward VIII.

The wedding went wonderfully well. Our picture leaving the church was on the front page of the London *Evening Standard, Star* and *Evening News,* and there were further pictures of our page, looking angelic in green velvet and gold braid, being eyed by half a dozen raggedly dressed boys. Presents had arrived in quantity: bedlinen and towels, furniture, carpets, pictures, vases, a gross of green-and-white striped napkins from Ted ("S'nothing really — picked them up as a job lot"), a twelve-sector hors d'oeuvres dish from my secretary Shelagh who had wanted to marry me and cried throughout the ceremony, and a cheque from Beecher. Good friends are allowed to give each other money. I walked my wife to the Phoenix Theatre after the reception, glowing with pride and happiness. "Your wedding," said the company manager, waving the evening papers at us, "was a complete flop. Not a mention of the play in any of them." The notices for *They Got What They Wanted* went up that night, the play came off at the end of the week and the happy couple went away on honeymoon, hiring a car and driving west.

We went to the races at Bath and won enough to buy a twenty-four-piece nineteenth-century tea-set in an antique shop in Frome. Drove to Bristol and saw a play at the Old Vic there. Made for Dartington so that I could show her the whereabouts of my mis-spent youth, but the car blew up on Exmoor. An AA man came by to examine the situation, picked up pieces of metal and said, "That'll have been part of the sump . . . that's the front of the back axle . . . don't know what this is."

We stayed the night in an inn where they sang about Tom Pearse's grey mare, feeling like actors in a B-movie, going to sleep to the sounds of Bill Brewer, Jan Stewer, Peter Gurney, Peter Davey, Dan'l Whiddon, Harry Hawk, old uncle Tom Cobbleigh and all. We made plans. Jill decided that we would wait six years and then have lots of children.

"Ten?"

"Ten or thereabouts."

I had determined that by my twenty-eighth birthday I would have a wife, a child, a house, a car and £1000 in the bank; I was 20 per cent there already, with eighteen months to go.

140

That year, 1950, had been the best yet. I had a decent job, had met Jill, got married and made a lot of new friends, mostly actors and directors, through the Arts, also neighbours like Louis McNeice and Robert Kee and BBC producers like Reggie Smith (who was married to Olivia Manning), with whom I played cricket, and Ken Tynan and Ludo Kennedy and David Gascoigne and Dylan Thomas, with whom I drank. Dylan slept a night at our mews cottage and threw up on our carpet, and I left a note for Jill saying: "Do not go gentle into that sitting room."

In the country outside "Don't you know there's a war on?" was still said when you asked for a spoonful of sugar in your tea, but "a second lamb cutlet" and "a bar of chocolate" were gradually reappearing in the everyday vocabulary of ordinary folk.

Jill was cast as Beauty in *Beauty and the Beast* that autumn. A splendidly difficult actor called Alan Badel played the Beast. His opening line was "Good morning" and at the first read-through he had stopped and said to the director, Charles Hickman, "What exactly am I thinking when I say, 'Good morning'?"

I bought my first car. Stanley Baker's uncle was a taxi driver whose London cab had done its statutory sixteen years; he told me the man was selling and I negotiated a price of £55. Its registration number was AXP 628. We called it Taxpi. If it had one fault it was the starter mechanism, but our mews was on a slope and a push in second gear and then letting out the clutch tended to do it. Jill and I pushed, then I jumped in. I promised she would get driving lessons so that I could do all the pushing. I had brought back a wooden wine crate from work and Jill covered it with some material, so we had a passenger seat up front. We drove around happily, occasionally having to argue with strangers who got in at traffic lights and wouldn't accept that we were not for hire. If they were nice, I quite often took them where they wanted to go. If they insisted on staying in the cab, I drove them where I was going.

A fortnight after we returned from our honeymoon, I lost my job. My fault really; I went to my first board meeting as a married man, said cheerfully, "Did you miss me a lot while I was on my honeymoon?" And they looked at each other, realised they had not noticed I had been away and felt they might save money and not suffer substantially from my permanent absence.

I told Matta to stop sending my whisky to the Arts because I was leaving, and he said, "Come and work for Matta. Have dinner with Matta tomorrow at 8p.m. at the Caprice and we speak. Bring Mrs Freud, I bring Mrs Matta."

Matta was thriving, had bought agencies of decent clarets like Château Pape Clément, kept Taittinger champagne, which James Bond drank, was negotiating British rights of Campari and also Strega a sweet, sticky, yellow liqueur the like of which I had not drunk since my Army days when suppliers were as likely to send Amaretto when we had ordered Amontillado. Dinner with Matta was always an experience and with his new young buxom Italian wife, who I think had been his secretary and was thirty years his junior, he was unstoppable. Each time he recognised a face at another table, he would summon the sommelier and order him to send across some bottle of a wine he shipped, "Compliments of Matta." After the meal he turned to me and said, "You know Campari?"

I denied this.

"Is a populare Italian aperitivo made of oranges of Seville best served with ice and soda and a slice of orange."

"Sounds good," I said.

"You sell it," he replied. "Same pay, same whisky. You worka for Matta."

So I worked for Matta.

A Mrs Gaskin, big cheese at Batchelor's Peas in Wadsley Bridge, Sheffield, had been appointed chairman of British Railways catering. Matta had met her, persuaded her that every decent bar in the land stocked Campari and that, if her railway bars did so, the stuff would sell itself. As an earnest of his prediction, he would give her a case; it would be there in the morning. I was to be the person who made Campari sell itself.

"You goa find it and buya it," Matta told me, "and there bea a bonus when it is all gonna. Is a simple. Goa to the bar and when you see the bottle say, 'Ah, I see you sell Campari, the populare Italian aperitivo made of oranges of Seville best served with ice and soda and a slice of orange. I buya a glass.' And if you see someone else at the bar, offer him one."

I worked from eleven in the morning till eight at night. Located Campari at Liverpool Street, Fenchurch

Street, Waterloo, Victoria, Charing Cross and Marylebone. There would be a dozen people waiting for service so the foreplay was useless.

"A Campari," I would say.

"You what?"

"Campari . . . the bottle on the top shelf, second one in."

The barman got a ladder. The natives around got restless.

He poured a measure. I suggested he used a larger glass, added ice and soda and a slice of orange, asked the next man in the queue if he would perhaps join me. Next man in queue said he'd have a pint; I had to tell him that pints were not on offer, not part of my brief.

Campari is Vermouth-like in consistency, pervasively bitter, orangey, alcoholic. I went to each station each day, changing the order and the times of day of my visits. I smelt of oranges, tasted of bitter oranges, staggered around in an orange haze. At night I dreamt Campari, dreamt that I went to a station and found that someone had ordered a nip and the bottle, instead of being nine-sixteenths full, was down to half full . . . and one day my dream came true. I looked at the bottle in Fenchurch Street with delight. Before I could say anything, the barman said, "Your dad was in earlier, Mr Campari. Asked me to give you his regards."

It took a month. Marylebone ran out of Campari first because Marylebone was closest to where we lived, then Victoria. "Make a scene," advised Matta. "Aska whatta happened to Campari, the populare Italian aperitivo made of oranges of Seville best served with ice and soda and a slice of orange." And a few days later his manager telephoned to say that I could lay off the drink. British Railways had ordered some more; I told Matta he had been right, Campari did sell itself.

I continued going to restaurants, ordering Matta drinks, until early 1951: after I had my third crash in Taxpi following a lunch of Campari, Taittinger, Pape Clément and Strega, I decided it was time to move on. The *Caterer and Hotel Keeper*, our trade paper, carried an advertisement for assistant manager at a club associated with the shortly-to-be-opened Festival of Britain 1951, and I got the job.

The Festival Club of Great Britain was built on a roundabout just south of Westminster Bridge. Hope and Anchor Breweries of Sheffield were the instigators and there were eight bars each with tables for two dozen people, also cloakroom and toilet facilities, so that firms inviting guests to the Festival could feed and water them and keep their coats and bags while they explored the exhibits.

It was a brilliant idea. Hope and Anchor, who were a power in the Yorkshire brewing world, kept one suite for themselves and let three others on a permanent basis to Time Life of America; Aims of Industry — a political lobbying outfit with politics to the right of Genghis Khan; and the Association of Travel Agents. The other four were let on a weekly or daily basis, or not let at all.

Brigadier Ryves Hopkins was appointed managing director, while a five-foot-five man in pinstriped trousers, black jacket and pebble lenses called Arthur Figg managed. I was his assistant, and employed friends of Jill's and mine to act as barmaids and kitchen helps. Food was pretty basic: egg sandwiches, sausage rolls and pieces of roast chicken, with Heinz tomato soup as starter and Fuller's walnut cake as dessert. We employed a telephonist, bookings and accounts clerk, cleaner and night-watchman, for Asprey's had show-cases in the corridors.

The Festival had its problems, particularly in relation to the amount of stuff stolen each day; nor was this confined to after it had opened. As the site was being built, Sir Gerald Berry, ex-editor of the *News Chronicle*, who was overlord, one day called in the Metropolitan Police, so alarmed was he at the losses. Every incomer and outgoer was to be searched.

At 7a.m. on the day the Fuzz began investigations a man tried to leave the site with a heavily laden wheelbarrow.

"No you don't," said the law. "Empty every item in the barrow on that table." And the man filled the table with straw and rubbish, bits of wooden cases and empty cartons. They let him go.

Half an hour later he wheeled out another load.

"Empty it," said the law. He emptied it; it was similarly legitimate rubbish, as it was every other time he passed through the gates.

A day or two later one of the searching policemen was in a pub, saw the wheelbarrow wielder and said, "We're off the case, but I'm damn sure you were up to no good. Tell me what you were doing and it'll go no further. Promise . . . what *were* you up to?

"I was nicking wheelbarrows."

146

Our clientele was impressive: authors and publishers, through *Time*; politicians, via Aims of Industry; stars of stage, screen and dogtrack all appeared, drank, asked us to look after their wives, coats, briefcases, dogs. And we had television, which no one had, not in 1951. I saw Turpin beat Sugar Ray Robinson.

A month into the Festival I was appointed manager. The brigadier had come in one evening, found the club reception deserted and walked into the telephone operator's cubicle to find her on the floor accommodating an untrousered Mr Figg. To her credit she still had on her headset and speaker, though whether, as I told Jill, she actually said, "Have you finished? I am putting you through now" may not have been absolutely true.

Like the Dome, the 1951 Festival promised more than it achieved. Jill was expecting our first child in the autumn and Sir Gerald said there would be a big celebration if she would have it in the Festival. We chose the Elizabeth Garrett Anderson maternity hospital and Nicola was born there on 24th October, my half birthday.

One of the few notable events of my tenure at the Festival Club was when the police telephoned me at 3a.m. to ask whether I employed a Patrick O'Flaherty as night-watchman. I said I did. They said, "Come here straightaway." Paddy, a six-foot-five ex-Irish Guardsman recruited by the brigadier, had been apprehended selling Asprey's watches in the local pub for 5s each; Asprey's had identified the time-pieces as those in the Club's show-cases and Paddy was for the high jump.

Stupid bugger, charging 5s for a 100-guinea gold and diamond watch.

When his case came up after a number of remands for character references, the brigadier asked me to go to court and do what I could to help. Paddy, looking even taller and thinner and yellow with fright, was marched in and confirmed his name.

"O'Flaherty," said the magistrate, "how do you plead?

"guilty but insane, sorr," said Paddy.

He got bail and used to hang around cleaning cars. Did mine for free.

When the Festival ended it was back to looking at Situations Vacant in the *Caterer and Hotel Keeper*, and as we needed money sooner rather than later I went to Victor Gross's antique shop on Mondays, to receive from him a £20 job lot of assorted items bought at auction houses under the heading "sundries": vases, belt buckles, ornaments, miniatures, paperweights, dessert forks . . . whatever. We sorted them and cleaned them and on Friday loaded them into one of my chrome leather cases and lugged it out to Taxpi. Our well-to-do neighbours thought I was off to Switzerland for a weekend's skiing and called out, "Have a good time." I rented a table in Portobello Road market, at the northern end where the antique stalls were, and flogged what I could.

I did not know enough about antiques and, as the other traders sensed this, I would see something I had sold for 3s 6d marked at 12s down the line of stalls. So does one learn. Jill brought my lunch and our daughter in a wicker basket; we could have sold her over and over, but we hung on. Sometimes Jill minded the table while I went for a walkaround, once sold an early Irish solid silver teaspoon for a shilling and, when I told her, felt so badly about it that I had to buy a Fuller's walnut cake to make it better. If she hadn't polished it up so nicely, no one would have known its origin — Victor certainly hadn't. She still feels badly about it.

In November the *Caterer* advertised a vacancy for manager of a London night club. A Jewish greengrocer's accountant had heard that the Knightsbridge Studio Club was for sale, did not realise that it was used as a money-laundering device, that its figures were plucked out of the sky, that the previous owners were charging illicit sums for most things (price controls were still in force). Having been extremely successful selling vegetables and fruit in Covent Garden and three shops, he thought (a) he could do anything and (b) it would be rather impressive, especially to his wife's people who were in the smoked salmon business, if he emerged as a successful night-club owner. He had a Rolls. He treated me as a son. He wouldn't keep his hands off me. During the day I went to his office and he patted me on the shoulder, shook my hand when he heard his shops had sold more spinach than last week. On an average night at the club he would ring up every forty-five minutes to find out how we were doing. He was loud and brash and when he came in to dine, like three nights a week, it did nothing for the quality trade that I was trying to attract to "my new venture."

As I was coming to terms with working until 2.30a.m. every night and auditioning a new band, for the one *in situ* was duff, my father heard about a house. An estate agent told him that No. 7 Boundary Road was going to be for sale: it was a British Railways-owned corner house on three floors, front and back garden, indefinite lease as a sitting tenant: £1000, plus £2 10s a week rent. The purchase price included a lot of furniture and curtains and carpets.

We hurried round to the house, bringing Nicola in her basket; sadly the vendors, a Dr and Mrs Ashton, had agreed to sell to someone else the previous day. Mrs A. admired our baby; we admired her house. She showed us her garden, admitted that they were leaving because the London County Council were going to build a school in Marlborough Hill across the street and she and her husband would not like the noise.

Jill said the carpet in the dining room was one of the most attractive she had seen. Mrs Ashton said it would not fit into their new house and she was leaving it. We said how really sorry we were not to have come yesterday.

She asked whether we had a dog because the man who was buying hadn't got one.

I said we had left it behind because you never knew with vendors of houses, but perhaps she would see it, if anything happened to the purchaser, like if he changed his mind . . . an unlikely occurrence, because the house really was a terrific bargain. We left sadly.

The next day Mrs Ashton, to whom we had given our phone number at the mews just in case, telephoned to say that she had been thinking about us. "That man who is going to move in — I sense weakness there. If you want the house, you can have it."

I raced out to borrow a friend's dog, we got to the Ashtons' in ten minutes, agreed to buy, and went down the road to a shop where we bought a dustpan and brush and asked whether we might leave them there as a mark of ownership. My dear father, the bank and what was left in our Post Office accounts helped raise the money and shortly before Christmas 1952 we moved, Taxpi making some ten journeys to transport our worldly goods.

Boundary Road is the boundary between St John's Wood and Hampstead; the house had three bedrooms and a bathroom upstairs, two large rooms on the raised ground floor that went from front to back, a kitchen and two further rooms downstairs where there was also a coal cellar. The property was 40 feet wide, the front garden 20 feet long, the back 120 feet, just beyond which was a vent for the railway line from Euston to South Hampstead which is why BR held the freehold.

So entering 1952, aged twenty-seven, I had a house and a car and a wife and a child. Pity about the £1000.

The Knightsbridge Studio Club taught me a lot. There was a bar, a downstairs restaurant with dance floor and band, a kitchen on the mezzanine. I employed a doorman, a hat-check girl who also dealt with membership, a barmaid, three waiters' a chef with an assistant and a kitchen porter. A cleaner did three hours each morning.

Dinner was fixed at 5s with a 3s 6d permitted surcharge because we had live music. The existing clientele was recently enriched black market Golders Green veg merchants and people who couldn't get into the Wellington Club next door which was classier than the Studio. I gave free meals to the porter of the Normandy Hotel opposite and the Hyde Park Hotel up the road if they sent clients ... whom we quickly claimed as members, joining them up on the spot, or not if they did not want to pay a subscription. It was a place to which men brought their mistresses ... though Sir Hugh Wontner, chairman of the Savoy Hotel Group and erstwhile Lord Mayor of London, did in one week bring his mistress and two days later his wife.

"Sir Hugh, it is such a long time since you were here! Welcome back," I greeted them, wondering again whether I should not have gone for the Diplomatic Corps.

Business built; the band had something of a following; our chef, a Japanese, was not bad though he had this nasty habit of eating food that customers had sent back because it was off. "Is allight," he would insist, munching a Dover sole that had been in the fridge so long we knew it by name. As a consequence he was unable to come to work quite often, when I would cook, which I did well. I made desirable salad dressings, gooey Crêpes Suzette, was pretty good on food you can read by, which is called "flambé." Flaming brandy poured into lobster soup stops anyone examining the taste of the bisque and allows you to charge extra for cognac. My relations with the greengrocer deteriorated, and after New Year's Eve, when we were fully booked but I had not taken deposits for the bookings and hardly anyone arrived, they broke down completely.

I went back to Portobello Road with Victor's cast-off antiques having made a whole host of new friends, found suppliers of quality, learnt that "The customer is always right" is a lie coined by some customer who was wrong, and realised that customers do not change. If they behave badly one evening, however much they apologise and insist it will never happen again, it does. God was wrong; to forgive is a mistake.

I also yearned to be my own boss. If a guest comes to a restaurant and starts moaning about the soup tasting like dishwater and not being hot enough, a manager has to apologise. As an owner you can say, "Sod off. Never mind about your bill, just don't ever come back." As an owner you can give food and drink to people you like, overcharge those you don't, sell booze after hours, change the décor, wear a lounge suit. Not as a manager you can't.

CHAPTER
SEVEN

In which I become my own boss and do an awful lot of other people's work, as good bosses do.

I spent January 1952 looking for somewhere to start up my own business. With the Dorchester, the Venezia, Martinez and Saunton Sands, the Arts Theatre and Studio Clubs behind me, I had a reasonably clear idea of what I wanted: a place where I could sell honest food, to theatre-related people, ideally into the early hours of the morning.

Seven years into the peace was an excellent time to start up a catering establishment: meat rationing was about to end, fish was no longer coley — you could get Dover sole and turbot and skate and mussels (where did mussels go during the war?) and the incoming Conservative Government had abolished fixed-price meals. We were approaching the "you never had it so good" era.

The new gastro-climate did two things: (a) it persuaded more people to go out to dinner in the evenings and (b) it caused caterers who had depended on restriction and cheating to move into other trades, like extortion and the black market. Sophistication was an "in" word. Sophistication meant exuding elegance, using long words like "marmalade" and "wheelbarrow", never "damn" or "bum", avoiding the common, pursuing the exclusive, drinking cocktails, wearing off-the-shoulder dresses (women) and white carnation buttonholes (men). Jack and Daphne Barker had been a sophisticated couple who sang contemporary ditties at the piano — I think Jack played and Daphne sang, but I might have got that wrong. They were like Noël Coward without the bite or the wit.

The Royal Court Theatre in Sloane Square had been bombed and was then rebuilt under the aegis of one Nevil Blond, who had been our Lease-Lend ambassador in Washington during the war and must have done something unspeakable not to have got a knighthood. Now he and his friends and family — his wife was the elder sister of Lord Marks of Marks and Spencers — were going for glory the artistic way. They furnished the theatre and constructed a sort of salon for the Barkers upstairs where the circle and gallery had been. Apparently no one had patronised this since the Barkers, except the bailiffs, who had waited a while, then taken away what was easy to carry. Now the theatre was looking for a tenant. A friend of a friend told Jill, who told me, and I went and had a look at it then made an appointment to meet Oscar Lewenstein, the theatre manager.

I was early, so I wandered down the Kings Road to chat to the butcher whose meat I had bought at the Studio Club, negotiated two pigeons for 1s 6d, tucked them into my alligator skin briefcase (I am not sure whether I mentioned requisitioning an alligator skin briefcase factory in Ulm after the war) and was given a tour of the theatre by Oscar. There were problems, like no separate entrance unless I wanted to use an emergency door at the side of the theatre that was four long stone flights of stairs before achieving the carpeted bar area. The derelict restaurant on the top floor would seat a hundred and the kitchen was small — but adequate; the bailiffs had left the ovens and refrigerators.

I was keen, possibly over-keen. Oscar said the rent was £20 a week, payable quarterly in advance, saw me gulp and remarked that he had heard I was not exactly rolling in money.

I repudiated this, pointed to the bulging briefcase and asked whether that looked to him like the briefcase of a man with cash problems.

The premises had been shown to a number of people, none of whom felt they could make a go of it despite the splendid location. Those stairs were the problem, combined with the fact that, while the Club had a 2.30a.m. licence, the theatre shut up and locked its doors at 10.15 and the guests and the band and the deliverers of goods and the staff would all have to use the emergency exit at the side of the building that led to the said stairs. I decided to take it.

"Sure?"

"Sure."

The agreement was signed in accordance with the Landlord and Tenant (Business Premises) Act whereby I stayed while I paid and behaved responsibly and did not contravene the small print of the Refreshment

156

House legislation, like getting caught making chicken curry using Kennomeat. I sat down and made a list — I spend much of my life making lists, also lists of the lists that I am going to make — to distil from what I had learnt those things that would be useful.

In 1940 I had spent four days making Pommes Parisienne, cutting marble-sized pieces of potato with a scoop that blistered my palms; a week later, for a 300-guest banquet, I made Pommes Olivette, olive-shaped potato pieces, using a different scoop that also gave me blisters. By 1952 I had decided that the shape of the potato was less important than its taste.

I had learnt to pass sauces through a tammy cloth. Now I bought a sieve, also an electric whisk. At the Dorchester we spent our time looking after the stockpot, adding to it, removing the scum, clarifying the liquor with eggshells and egg whites. Having insufficient space or time for this, I would in future put onions, leeks, carrots and parsley into a roasting pan with a little olive oil, brown it in a medium oven, decant it into a pot and add water; this would go to make soups and sauces.

They teach you, as a waiter, to serve from the left, clear away from the right; I decided to perform these acts from whichever side least distracted the guests. I had learnt to hold five plates of smoked salmon in one hand; gave that up for being over-intrusive. People do not go to restauraunts to be impressed by the waiter's prestidigitation. (When we first got married and had a dinner party, I tried to teach Jill how to hold three

157

plates in one hand. She said, "And make people think you married a waitress?")

I determined not to employ waiters who smoked and breathed tobacco fumes over guests, and avoided complicated French on my menus. Filet de Sole Walewska, for instance, became Dover sole fillets garnished with prawns and lobster.

If someone was unhappy about their food, my staff would look at the complaint sympathetically, not start grovelling apologetically as soon as the guest started to moan. As for the wine, I had a really satisfactory way of dealing with customers who ordered and tasted and sniffed and twirled the wine in their glass, held it to the light and took another sniff and a taste, looking into the middle distance as experts are believed to do. I would come bouncing along, explain that the customer clearly knew a great deal about wine, was almost certainly correct in suspecting the quality of this one; please will he allow me to replace it with something he will find impeccable ... and brought him the bottle the last customer had made a fuss about. No one has the bottle to complain twice about wine; it also meant that we never stocked more than one "ullaged" bottle.

When it came to receptionists, I wanted to employ women who looked pleased to see customers rather than try to catch them out for getting in on friends' membership cards. (When I found people who did that I would add a fiver to their bill, telling them that this was for the liqueurs that they had had last time — "The ones you asked me to put on your account next time you came.")

The logistics of staffing were going to be a problem. With a hundred-seater restaurant you needed a head waiter, a wine butler and four stations, with maybe two boys to buss and tidy and clear tables and a cashier; also a chef and an assistant and a kitchen porter, a downstairs carriage attendant to greet the guests and call taxis, a receptionist to check membership and take coats, an orderer of food and drink and a good inward clerk, cellarman, cleaner and secretary.

What I definitely needed were pots and pans, cutlery, crockery, napery, tables and chairs, and sideboards. Fortunately the bailiffs had left the piano; I had £300 which my father had loaned me, found a catering wholesale shop opposite Kings Cross Station and I went there to have a look round. When I told the assistant what I wanted and my price range he said, "Come back on Saturday," out of the corner of his mouth.

I heard a story about a man who went into a tobacconist's and asked for a packet of Passing Cloud cigarettes.

The man behind the counter said, "That'll be threepence."

The customer, surprised, asked the price of "that box of Havana cigars". The shop man said, "Ten shillings."

"And the gold Ronson cigarette lighter in that leather box?"

"One pound."

"Excuse me," said the customer, "do you own this shop?"

"No. I'm doing to this shop what the man who owns it is doing to my wife."

The man at the Kings Cross catering suppliers seemed to be on a similar mission. I bought everything I needed for hardly any money at all; he delivered on Saturday evening, helped me put things away and asked me to take my business nowhere else. "Just remember: Saturdays." As if I would forget.

I started to call in favours. London Linen Hire Service gave me four months' credit. Mr Batten, the butcher in the Kings Road, allowed me three months. Matta said, "I trust you. Paya when you've gotta the money."

In the end I compromised on staff. I had a secretary called Mrs Carrington . . . and I went on calling her Mrs Carrington for ten years. She was not very good, but by the time I found that out she had worked for me for two years, after which time you cannot sack anyone for incompetence. My cleaner was called Elsie; she also stayed with me for ten years. I negotiated with the theatre's commissionaire that after the show he would move across to my canopied side entrance and work for a small hourly rate and big tips; I would give him dinner.

I did a fair number of jobs myself. I bought the food and wine, cellared the latter, cooked most of the former during the day and employed an Italian who worked in a lunchtime City restaurant to come and put together my food for the evening's service. I was also head waiter, cashier, wine butler — and bouncer when one was needed.

Kitchen porters were friends, like D.R.W. Silk who got Blues at Cambridge for rugby and cricket and went on to be Warden of Radley and President of the MCC. We didn't just employ anyone. I had four waiters, one each French, Greek, Italian and Spanish. My band played from 6 to 9p.m. in a cocktail bar in Piccadilly, then came on to work for me for cash — not very much cash, and free food. Jill's sister did reception, a friend of hers was barmaid. That was the staff.

The Royal Court Theatre Club, proprietor C. Freud, opened its doors the night Laurier Lister's *Airs on a Shoestring* opened the theatre downstairs. That was one of the worst nights of my life. We were plum empty until 8.45 when there was a theatre interval. Two hundred people stormed upstairs, about eight of them got served.

I had made a table plan for when the show was over; we were fully booked, mostly with friends and family. Then in came the owner of the building and the producer and the director of the revue, plus all the actors and most of the audience, everyone expecting dinner. Very few of my customers with reservations got in, let alone obtained food or drink, and many never came back. I had prepared twenty-five portions each of duck in orange sauce, chicken roasted with tarragon, poached Norwegian salmon, and moussaka. The waiters went around taking orders; chef ended up with seventy-six orders for duck and got drunk and my landlord said, loudly, that he knew it had been a mistake leasing the place to someone of my youth and inexperience.

We had opened on a Tuesday so that I would have enough cash to pay staff on Friday. After that first night Jill — we now employed a mother's help called Pauline so that Miss Raymond could work in plays and films and come on to Sloane Square — said, "It can only get better", which was true. It did. Slowly.

For a year and a half I worked six days a week, spent Sunday with Jill and Nicola and the mother's help of the day, having lunch which I had brought back from Sloane Square. (One Sunday lunchtime Jill, eating a fillet of turbot, said, "That would have lasted". When I asked what she meant, she said that every other Sunday meal I had brought back would have been dicey had I tried to serve it for Monday dinner.) In the afternoon, we went to the club and tidied up.

Jill got a job in a film, playing a handmaiden in a TV drama called *Moses*. Nicola played Moses, dressed in swaddling clothes, put into a basket among the bulrushes.

The director said, "This baby is too big for the basket".

Jill told him that in the bible it was exactly when Moses became too big to hide that he was floated off ... and the director said, "Not in this film he isn't". The director also distinguished himself with the casting of Ruth, a part given to actress Ruth Gorb.

"Is she Jewish?" he asked the casting department.

"We aren't sure," they said.

"If there's one thing I don't want in this film, it's anything Jewish."

162

In St John's Wood we had an Irish cleaner who brought her baby to work, and Nicola bit her. The woman came to me and said in an outraged voice, "Your baby has bitten my baby. One of them will have to go."

We said goodbye to the Irish cleaner and her daughter. I sometimes think we made a mistake there.

In those days I would get up at 9a.m., drive to the Royal Court, do the empties, order food and wine, deal with membership problems and answer letters. Then I made Tartare sauce: best mayonnaise with chopped capers, gherkins, chives, onions and lemon zest; also Cumberland sauce — redcurrant jelly melted over a slow heat with one third its volume of English mustard and whisked smooth, finished with ruby port and garnished with a julienne of orange and lemon zest marinated in angostura bitters. I made velvety parsley sauce for boiled ham, using some of the ham broth and lots of cream; orange sauce for duck; mornay sauce for poached eggs on spinach; caper sauce for boiled legs of mutton. And I portioned up under-roasted duck, cursing the designer of the beasts who could so easily have caused the legs to protrude and make themselves as easy to segment as chickens.

We wanted to have more children. Boundary Road deserved more children. Jill had miscarriages, we were absolutely wretched.

The Royal Court flourished and by the end of year one we had 650 members paying £3 a year, just about covering the rent. I was doing nine people's jobs and, while at the beginning I did this for two people's pay, it gradually became more profitable. I began to make money.

Of course it had been a huge help getting ninety days' credit, being able to sell a bottle of wine sixteen times before I had to pay for it, ditto meat, but by 1953 we were free of debt and took a holiday in early August. We stayed at an hotel in the Lake District and while there saw in the newspaper that Queen Elizabeth the Queen Mother had celebrated her birthday at the Royal Court, watching *Airs on a Shoe-string*. We were sorry to have missed seeing her; very much sorrier when, on my return, I found a letter from the Palace informing me that Her Majesty was visiting the Royal Court Theatre and had expressed a desire to come upstairs for a drink and something to eat afterwards. I cursed my luck.

That autumn we introduced a floor-show, nightly at midnight. Our first performer was a buxom actress with a great voice, a frightened pianist and an agent who was her boyfriend and tried to get me to pay more than the £10 a week I could afford for an act. The average spend per head was under £2; the cabaret was going to be the profit on twenty dinners.

We sent a newsletter to our members telling them of the cabaret, urging them to book tables, reminding them of the excellence of our Reform lamb cutlets (Reform sauce is made of *Sauce Espagnol* spiked with Worcestershire sauce, garnished with slivers of boiled tongue, beetroot and hard-boiled egg-white), and on that first show night I said to my bandleader, "Announce the cabaret."

He said, "You do it."

So I asked the artiste's pianist, who declined. I tried her agent/lover, who asked what I was paying for the intro . . . so I did it. Went to the middle of the dance floor, said, "Ladies and gentlemen, in cabaret tonight we present Miss . . ."

She came on, gave me a foul look, said, "Is that all you're going to say?" and began to sing "Nature Boy".

After the show her agent/lover (artistes and their friends had a table and free food and wine for the evening) told me I should have mentioned the fact that she had sung at the Palladium, been in a Richard Tauber musical and was appearing in revue in Notting Hill. I decided against that, but later that week I did try a joke.

"Good evening, ladies and gentlemen. There was this man who went into a shop in the Kings Road and said, 'Do you castrate cats?'

"Shopkeeper said, 'Yes.'

"Man said, 'I have been going up and down the street looking for you. Why do you have an alarm clock in your window?'

"Shopkeeper: 'What would you have me put in the window?'"

No one laughed. So I said, "In cabaret tonight we have . . ."

I tried that joke over and over. Had I been employed, I would have lost my job; as I owned the place, the odd person asked when I was going to try a new joke. At length I tried a new joke.

"Two Chelsea pensioners were sitting on a bench in the Kings Road in the afternoon sun when one of them said:

'Do you remember those pills they gave us during the Boer war to take our minds off women?'

"The other said, 'Yes.'

'Well, I think mine's beginning to work.'"

Someone laughed. My career as an announcer of cabaret was launched.

I told a joke every night, sometimes two jokes. Cabaret was nominally at midnight but there were times when the kitchen was so overloaded with orders that I went on early (we did not serve food during the cabaret) so that chef could catch up. We averaged fifty dinners a night and tended to be full at weekends.

I fell out with the police. When I opened the club, the main influx came at 11p.m. when the pubs kicked out and at midnight I sent my waiters round the room for last orders. Some people asked if they might just have one more drink even though it was 12.15a.m., and the waiters said they would have to ask me, and did, and I would come over and say, "Oh, all right", and on many an evening there would be lots of punters drinking into the early hours.

If people behaved badly — became abusively drunk, as did the stammering Irish journalist and TV personality Patrick Campbell, who interrupted the cabaret or threw up more than once — they would be barred. Let me tell you a story about drunken behaviour. In the 1950s the late Gilbert Harding, who knew much about the insides of bottles, achieved great fame and fortune by being himself on television and radio. He was, for those who do not date to that era, a kind of academic Groucho Marx. During his humbler years he had drunk at the Stag in New Cavendish Street, a popular BBC pub much frequented by features producers who were easy to recognise by their dandruff. (Rumour had it that the Head of Features had a daily roll-call at which he shook dandruff over the jackets of his staff.)

There came a time when the manager of the Stag had done well enough to buy his own free house in the Home Counties. He asked Gilbert if he would come and preside at the opening ceremonies of his new establishment and the great man, who was as generous as he was intolerant, said he would be honoured to do so. Gilbert arrived in his chauffeur-driven car, smiled at the photographers from the local newspapers, pulled the first pint, made a short and witty speech and remained for a while, drinking and chatting. About half a bottle of gin later he went up to the bar, squinted at the wife of the ex-Stag landlord, said, "D'ye know, you're one of the ugliest bitches I've seen for many a long day", and flicked the contents of his glass in her face.

Pandemonium. She shouted, the crowd milled. The chauffeur plunged to the rescue. A shamed Harding was bundled into his vehicle and departed to the boos of the local populace.

Absolutely overcome with remorse, he sent the landlady a huge bouquet of flowers and a grovelling letter of apology. A year later he returned, by arrangement, to the pub to wish them well on the first anniversary of their enterprise and to pledge his friendship. He was welcomed, made much of, delivered a short speech, chatted and drank, but some time before they muscled him out of the place for the second and final time he had gone up to the landlady, flicked his drink in her face and said, "I washright, you're a bloody ugly bitch."

A drunk is consistent, and if he is objectionable in his cups he goes on being objectionable in his cups.

When you run a night-club, everyone knows where to find you. I had bought a Rolls Royce 1934 Tickford Cabriolet with a silver-plated windlass which could be engaged to wind down the back. As I had to go out from time to time, I would take taxis and leave my car, with its CF 6915 number plates, parked outside the club so that people would think I was in. This ploy occasioned my brother Lucian's last social call on me.

He had come to our St John's Wood house for Christmas dinner in 1954, or it might have been 1955; brought Francis Bacon, and we had a happy time. Some months later he came to my night-club, told the receptionist he wanted to see me urgently as he needed some money and when I arrived, admittedly ten to fifteen minutes later, he had gone, having left a message with the girl at the desk re what I might do to myself.

When my son Dominic was eight, I picked him up from prep school one day and we went to Marine Ices in Chalk Farm for afternoon tea. The place was full. The owner asked whether we would mind sharing a table, we said, "not at all", and, as father and son approached it, the occupant looked up and raced out.

"Why would that man have done that? He hasn't even finished his ice cream."

"It was your Uncle Lucian," said I.

I became food and beverage editor of the *Observer* magazine in 1964, and devoted one of my first articles to eggs.

"'On a chalk white plate you lie
With loathing in your yellow eye
Swimming in sickly fat. Ugh.'

Wrote my brother Lucian before he abandoned the writing of verse for painting," was my opening paragraph. Lucian tried to sue the *Observer* for breach of copyright, abortively.

But I digress. Out of spite, some of those members whom we barred from the club went to the police and reported me for selling drinks after hours.

"Until when?" asked the Fuzz.

"Well after midnight," they were told.

The police looked up my file, said, "The Royal Court has a 2.30 licence", but on a couple of occasions came to tell me that I was making them look foolish by pretending to serve drinks after hours.

"A bit like arresting the wrong man, is it?"

They did find out that I was serving late drinks on Saturday nights, midnight Saturday being the beginning of Sunday when you could not serve alcohol, which was ludicrous: the one night in the week when people could drink without getting to work on a hangover and it was banned. The Government promised to improve matters when they were next changing the licensing laws.

So on Saturdays I served drinks until 2.30a.m. as was my wont, got a warning, and very early one Sunday morning, after the midnight cabaret had finished and people were dancing, there was a panic phone call from the doorman to the receptionist announcing that half a dozen uniformed policemen were coming upstairs. She raced up to tell me. I dashed on to the floor, silenced the band and announced that tonight, to celebrate the fact that we had been open for two years and nine and a half months, we were, regardless of expense, presenting an additional floor show: please welcome the men from Gerald Road police station. As the assembled company began to applaud, half a dozen out-of-breath policemen (our stairs were not to be taken without a rest halfway up) crashed into the restaurant. The applause increased in volume: a second act of six men in uniform, with food and wine and coffee and cabaret and dancing, all at £2 a head; what a terrific establishment to be a member of.

The police asked members for their names and addresses; members told them not to overdo it. It was memorably chaotic. The Saturday drinking law was changed very soon after that.

And then there was the case of theft by C.R. Freud, proprietor of the Royal Court Theatre Club, London SW3, accused of stealing electricity from the Royal Borough of Chelsea and Kensington. I received a warrant, pleaded guilty.

170

When I had opened in 1952, a cowboy electrician suggested that I have a flashing light over the canopied door which served as my entrance — the only entrance when the theatre was closed. I agreed, and that light flashed invitingly throughout the night. Four years later a caring citizen noticed that the light above my entrance flashed in harmony with the zebra crossing light on the far side of the pavement. The electrician had connected me to the terminal that powered the beacon. I was an electricity thief. It was very hard to keep a straight face and when we were taken to court the case, like the prosecutor and the accused, collapsed.

I had no public relations firm to look after me — one did not have PR in those days — but I did, on one occasion when business was less than very buoyant, give a party for my members. I thought long and hard about a venue, decided that the club premises were too small for the five hundred-odd people who might come and that the noise they generated would infuriate the theatre management yet again.

There was a bar on the west-bound platform of the Circle Line at Sloane Square underground station which adjoined the theatre (train noises also infuriated the theatre, but there was less they could do about that), and I negotiated with the station bar and sent my members platform tickets and vouchers for two drinks at our party to be held from 5.30 to 6.30 on a Thursday evening.

It was a tremendous success. My guests filled the platform and every ninety seconds a train would stop and try to unload a hundred passengers into the drunken throng already there. The next day's papers had pictures and details.

Things improved: I bought better-quality wine, served classier food, increased membership to 2500, sent members newsletters every couple of months to tell them who was to be in cabaret and the destination of the next outing (we had a party of seventy-five travel to Sundew's Grand National in 1957) and all the time I was learning. If things went wrong, those things tended not to go wrong again — new things went wrong.

I was wandering through the restaurant one night and saw a man face a plate of soup which looked strangely dark. I called the waiter, asked him what he had served the man, was told, "Turtle soup." Went into the kitchen, asked chef whether he was adding gravy browning to the turtle soup. He denied this, showed me the turtle soup pan standing in the bain-marie with a bowl of sliced turtle meat and a sauceboat of decent sherry by its side. It was golden.

"Where did you get the soup for table 14?" I asked the waiter.

He showed me. It was the pan containing black coffee . . . and rather than embarrass the punter, who had laced the coffee with ground pepper and salt and was halfway though, we just worried what we would do if he asked for coffee after the meal.

One of our best customers was a Mr Grace. He looked like a Guards officer; we were too polite to ask him what he did, where he came from, how he had so much money. He would come to dinner three or four times a week, always with a different girl, always order champagne. One night he had a row with his guest, a pretty French girl who told him to leave her alone, stop putting his hand on her thigh and go back to his bloody pigeons. As she stormed out she told the receptionist that our Mr Grace took photographs in Trafalgar Square. We continued to be respectful and treat him like the Guards officer we had thought he was. Later we found out that he had been a Guards officer, but was now taking pictures of people feeding pigeons beneath Nelson's Column.

Cabaret artists were queuing up to work at the club. The policy of not serving food while the show was on, and of evicting members and guests who disturbed the act, may not have been good for trade but made the Royal Court an excellent place in which to perform. We had auditions two mornings a week — Mrs Carrington and Elsie put on special clothes to make it look as if we had an audition panel — and we listened to mainly young and inexperienced acts such as would work for £10 a week and their food and drink.

We had regulars like Rolf Harris, who began by being a sketch artist, then a couple of years later sang at the piano. The worse his show went, the longer he would stay on. There were nights when the audience sat in silence, the waiters and I were signalling to him to end the show and let us try to sell some food and drink, and the chef was shouting blue murder through the kitchen door because the soufflés were sinking . . . and still Rolf went on singing or telling stories about losing his way in Italy. The Royal Court was where he first sang "Tie

173

Me Kangaroo Down Sport" and I gave him the line "Hold My Platypus Duck, Bill".

Barry Took was another regular, Nicholas Parsons did his act, Trader Faulkner performed Spanish dances with castanets, Richard Baker sang engagingly at the piano, Aud Johansen had a stunning voice, Fenella Fielding was funny, David Frost did a dozen stints or more before he became very famous and got me a job on the late-night satirical TV show *That Was the Week That Was*. Jonathan Miller appeared in cabaret with Rory McEwen, their first public appearance. We had Dudley Moore, Peter Cook, Leslie Phillips, Peter Reeves, Bernard Hunter, Betty Marsden, Lance Percival, Thelma Ruby, Jimmy Thompson and Richard Waring. Robert Morley offered to "try out" his cabaret act before taking it to the Café de Paris. I said I would not let him do it. He was narked. I had to explain that if he appeared in my club, people would ring up, ask who was in cabaret and then not book because they had not heard of the artiste who was on — they would wait till Robert Morley returned.

My warm-up at the club got longer and I would work on a story for a week or more (few people came more than once a week) until I got it right; not too many performers get that chance. I remember having trouble with a story about a man who went into the Sahara desert with his dog Rover and, due to fallacious map reading, found himself one day without food or water, some 200 miles from the nearest mirage. In the daytime the sun burnt down at 125 degrees and at night it froze. He sat there in the sand, waiting for the

174

inevitable end and on day three, his tongue swelling with dehydration, he looked down at Rover, who was similarly inconvenienced by the elements, and a thought passed through his mind but was rejected. Not Rover, not man's best friend. On day five he killed the dog and drank his blood and ate him. And on day seven, sated, he looked down at the canine bones beginning to turn white in the noonday sun, and tears trickled down his cheek as he thought: "Rover would have liked those bones."

When Princess Margaret came, HRH's secretary, who was later Lord Plunkett, said, "If you tell anyone she was here, she will never come back." I told everyone and put it into a newsletter. People came and said, "Where did she sit?" and I would take them to an available table; some evenings the entire room was filled with people sitting where Princess Margaret had sat. She did not come again, but her visit was probably the turning point. We invented a waiting list for membership, and started evicting more and more members whom we preferred not to have in the club.

They formed a flourishing Royal Court Blackball Society which met at the Antelope pub, 200 yards from my club, and one year asked me to be guest speaker at their annual dinner. I thought of making a futile gesture ... like telling them that they could come back, all is forgiven. It would not have worked.

CHAPTER
EIGHT

In which I become accustomed to owning a night-club and look further afield.

When you get a night-club nicely organised, as I did after the first few years, the work becomes easier. You buy wine several cases at a time, because you know how much you will sell. You reduce the number of main dishes on the menu to a red meat, a white meat, duck and vegetarian. You produce puddings that people can pronounce and will eat; and if you are thinking about soups, Heinz tomato to which you can add double cream, also Lusty's turtle to which you should add sherry are good and easy and acceptable; no one really gets switched on by Soupe de Jour. These were the prawn cocktail years, and we had a really good prawn cocktail sauce: a tomato and Dijon mustard mayo sharpened with brandy, spiked with Worcester, mellowed with anchovy oil.

Mrs Carrington did the bills and orders and banking and laundry and took stock (most restaurants of our size lose about twenty-five teaspoons a week); she also had envelopes ready for newsletters. I managed to do my work in two to three morning hours and spent the afternoons at home or playing cricket. I kept wicket and batted halfway down the order for *The Stage*, West End

Theatre, Mitcham Wednesday, Wembley Thursday, the BBC and anyone else who asked; it was a very effective way of making new members.

The Stage was fun: Bill Franklyn, Harry Secombe, Kenneth Haigh, and on one occasion Wilfrid Hyde-White. A batsman came in, announced that he was a left-hander, looked around the field with care, took his guard, checked his guard, had another look around the field, asked the umpire how many balls remained in the over, nodded to announce that he was ready . . . and missed the first ball, which was straight and hit his wicket. As he walked back to the pavilion Hyde-White, who was fielding deep square leg, went up to him and said, "Excuse me, sir, how did you find out you were a left-hander?"

At Mitcham the pavilion was across the road from the pitch, and if you were really unlucky you scored a duck and got run over by a bus. I played for the Lords Taverners, notably on one occasion against the England ladies' team at the Oval. I was standing up to Ian Carmichael's bowling when a voice from the crowd shouted: "Stop looking up her skirt, you dirty old wicket-keeper."

In the winter I played hockey for Westminster Hospital (a neighbour of ours was a surgeon), and occasionally rugby for a Sunday side in Streatham, but was neither fit enough nor fast enough to be asked back. I did employ their stand-off half as a kitchen porter and quite a lot of the team turned up on the grounds that I had played for their club, so surely they could come to mine without paying a membership fee.

Roger Bannister, Chris Chataway and Chris Brasher were members, and used to change in the club before training at the Duke of York's barracks; we gave a massive Bannister party when he ran his 3-minute 59.4-second mile and some months after that Brasher, who had left Cambridge and become deputy sports editor of the *Observer*, rang to ask me whether I could do a football report. "John Arlott is ill and we need someone to go to Portsmouth and send in 450 words. Ring Fleet Street 0202, ask for 'Copy' and make sure we have it by five o'clock."

"I'm your man," I said.

On Saturday I took a train to Portsmouth, went to the United Services Club and found there was no game on. I phoned Chris and told him.

"Where are you?"

"United Services Club."

"Not *that* football, you moron! Go to Fratton Park."

I went to Fratton Park, found the Press entrance, sat in the back of the box, didn't like to ask anyone which side was which, had tea and tongue sandwiches at half-time and wrote my report: "Portsmouth, to the approval of 24,516 supporters, won this not very interesting game by the only goal . . . scored according to the man sitting in front of me by Dickinson after 37 minutes though the old boy on my left who was watching through binoculars said it was Stainsforth after 36." I mentioned the man holding up a "Prepare to meet your God" placard following the one that announced "The *Observer* is here today" and added a bit about one of the linesmen who wore very thick glasses; wondered whether players would have much confidence in his flag-waving.

The report appeared in Sunday's paper, headed "Portsmouth 1, Huddersfield Town 0 by Clement Freud". Jill was very impressed. I hoped my members would see it and come to talk about it in the bar over expensive drinks.

Chris phoned me on Monday morning. He was angry. Said I was probably the only sports journalist ever who had had a by-line over his first article.

"What's a by-line?"

"'By' Clement Freud, like we had to put over your copy — you wrote such crap, we couldn't put 'By our football correspondent'."

Brasher telephoned me a fortnight later and asked me to lunch. I thought being bawled out for a second time was overdoing it, but agreed to meet him.

"Yer know," said Chris (who started most sentences with "yer know"), "we've had quite a few letters about your football article from readers who said that if the *Observer* has got to cover sport" — in those days sport was confined to the back page, while the inside back page gave results — "the way Freud wrote it is better than the run-of-the-mill match report." Chris had spoken to the editor, and I was offered a weekly game about which to write. Five guineas plus expenses.

"And I can go on writing crap?"

"What else can you write?"

I was given games that looked as if they might be interesting, like local derbies, Stanley Matthews' return to Stoke City from Blackpool, FA cup-ties on sloping

West Country pitches, Accrington Stanley's terminal matches before bankruptcy forced them out of the League. To my embarrassment I became quite knowledgeable about football, wrote about passes being square, fifty-fifty balls, off-side traps. When we had an England goalkeeper called Hodgkinson, who was five foot seven, I wrote: "Unlike the female giraffe Hodgkinson had trouble with the high balls." This was cut from my copy by a considerate sub-editor but, embarrassingly, the phrase appeared in an article about gardening on another page. We were still in the hot metal days, and a "cut" meant excising a lump of metal type.

I won a small following of readers, some of whom came to my night-club.

Millwall were drawn to play Trowbridge in the first round of the FA Cup and it was considered "Freud's sort of game". Freud was sent. I travelled to the ground, found that there was only one phone in the Press box and went to look for alternative means of communication. Near the exit I found a house with telephone wires connected to a lonely post, rang the front door bell, explained to the householders that I was a football writer for the *Observer*, there to report on the cup-tie, and was empowered to give them 5s if they would let me make a reverse charge call to London after the game. "Final whistle is 4.40. Copy has to be in by five o'clock, so you will be without your phone for about a quarter of an hour."

They agreed.

Millwall won, and as the players came off the pitch I legged it to the house. My hosts had put the phone on a small table in their sitting room and invited the neighbours in: eight of them, sitting on chairs facing the table.

When I got through to the copy-taker I did the usual routine: "FA Cup first round football copy. Clement Freud, that's eff, are, ee, ewe, dee, from Trowbridge. New line. Trowbridge nil, Millwall four. New line. Trowbridge in Wiltshire has long been recognised as a town with a fine reputation for its pork sausages and nothing that happened over ninety minutes on their field of play this afternoon would cause one to change this assessment. Point paragraph . . . Please would you keep quiet!"

"Whaddayamean?" asked the copy-taker.

I had to explain I had not meant him; it was my audience of Trowbridge natives who were becoming restive. I learnt later that the householder had charged them 6d each to sit in on my match report. They did not like what I was saying.

Running a night-club did mean that, unlike fellow hacks who filed their copy and spent the evening in friendly hostelries, I dictated copy and raced off for the train to London. I was in Bournemouth one afternoon and when I came out of the ground there was one taxi waiting; the driver said that he had been booked to take the referee to the station. I thought the man would surely give me a lift, waited for him to come out, introduced myself and asked if I might share his cab — offered to pay the full fare.

He said, "No", got in the cab and left.

Bournemouth and Boscombe Football Club is some way from the station and when I finally got there I had missed the train I had hoped to catch, arrived in Sloane Square later than I liked, especially on a Saturday when we had full houses. By 3a.m., the last customer had gone. I was in the kitchen looking for food I could take home for Sunday lunch when it occurred to me that I had an FA year book in my office and that year books contained the names of licensed referees and their addresses. I got the man's number from Directory Enquiries and rang him at about 3.15a.m. It took a dozen rings before he answered.

"Is that Mr Corcoran?"

"Yes, yes, what is it?"

"I am the man to whom you wouldn't give a lift to the station at Bournemouth. I wanted you to know that I got home safely." I put the phone down and felt better.

I became rather good at organising trains back from distant locations. Huddersfield Town was then an important and talented side, and I cracked the London to Huddersfield journey by taking a main line train to Wakefield and a taxi. After the game there was a 5.45 fast train back to Euston, which suited me well. On one winter afternoon I reached Wakefield at 5.25 and went to the station's refreshment room.

"Cup of coffee and a ham sandwich."

"No ham sandwich." said the drone behind the counter.

"Cheese sandwich, then."

182

"No cheese sandwich."

"What have you got?"

"No sandwiches."

"I'll just have the coffee."

"No coffee."

I said I'd settle for a cup of tea, but the woman looked at her watch and said, "Too late. We close at 5.30."

I was then writing a column on English gastronomy for *US Gourmet* magazine, my journalistic career was burgeoning and one month, having written 700 of the required 750 words, I added: "But when you are done with the brilliance of London's Ritz Hotel restaurant, the charm of Betty's Tea Rooms in Harrogate, the compulsive thé dansant at Torquay's Imperial Hotel . . . then for old-world charm, imagination of menu construction, range of ingredient availability and caring service, do not miss the Refreshment Room at Wakefield Railway Station."

It was about a year before I got to Wakefield again. It was 5.30p.m., too late for tea (if they had tea), and I was sitting on a bench waiting for my train when a man in a suit asked me whether I was Mr Freud.

I told him I was.

Would I come with him to his office, just down the platform?

There he showed me a file of some fifty letters from the United States, requesting details of his establishment and making provisional bookings for distant dinners. "All down to your effing article."

Luckily my train arrived.

When the football season ended I asked if I might write about cricket, a subject on which I was even more knowledgeable. I also wrote features for the *Observer* and never missed writing about the Greyhound Derby, which was run very late on a Saturday night at the White City. They kept 180 words for my annual Greyhound Derby piece, 150 of which I wrote on the amazing Derby atmosphere and the final 30 on the result. Real journalism.

And by a huge slice of luck I found a bookmaker who had the same name as my new catering supplier in Victoria. So when I won, I cashed the bookie's cheque; and when I lost, my accountant presumed the statement from Staines and Co. was in respect of purchasing replacement teaspoons and saucepans, and claimed it against tax.

Robert Morley had become a friend; we went racing together and he came to the Royal Court, sometimes leaving the club and going on to a casino where I joined him. He called me "dear"; actually he called everyone "dear", like whenever he had a cup of tea he would say, "Best cup of tea I've ever had, dear." He was much loved.

One evening he announced that he was taking all his investments out of breweries and buying shares in espresso coffee businesses. I pointed out that there were not, as yet, espresso coffee businesses, just some avant-garde coffee bars that used the fierce Gaggia machines. By the end of the evening we had agreed that we would purchase premises for which we would each pay half and open the place as a coffee bar with an espresso machine. I would do the work and he would sit in the window, beaming at passers-by, for a minimum of an hour a week to promote trade.

We bought the Green Parrot Tea Shop and Bridge Club in Hereford Road, Bayswater. My father drew up plans to turn it into a restaurant/coffee bar, a local builder did the work and we opened with a very strong cast not that many weeks after we had first thought of the idea.

The Green Parrot became La Boîte. I cooked, Jill ran the café, actors and actresses manned the Gaggia and did the washing up. Our waitress was a very short-sighted girl called Vanessa who drove to work, left her car at least 18 inches from the pavement and was being courted by a National Service sailor who sat outside and whom we often asked in for a free coffee. The suitor, who eventually married Vanessa, later became Nigel Lawson. (Actually he was always Nigel Lawson, later became Chancellor of the Exchequer.)

Our trade at La Boîte tended to be customers from the many nearby hotels that take young foreign students on two-week trips to London. The parents pay a small sum to have their offspring housed and breakfasted; for the rest of the day they go to museums and/or search for inexpensive meals.

I remember a German girl of about eighteen who came in one evening from a hotel in the square across the road, had a coffee, asked the waiter if she might help him clear the tables, then went into the kitchen to assist the kitchen porter, who took her to bed when the place closed at 11p.m. Next day it was the porter's day off, so she helped the waiter, who took her up to his room in the afternoon. And that night she was in the kitchen chopping vegetables before leaving to go home with the chef.

She was back the next day, and the espresso machine actor taught her how to froth up the milk and how little coffee you could get away with in the making of a cappuccino. She was a good pupil and got her reward from the actor that evening in one of the staff bedrooms upstairs. I came into La Boîte the following morning to find her sitting at a table writing postcards and when she went to help someone do something I ambled over to see what she had written in German. "Dear Mother, I am the toast of London . . ." was how it began.

She would be about sixty-five now. I wonder whether she recalls that fortnight as fondly as my staff in Hereford Road?

La Boîte made money, about 15 per cent of what the Royal Court made, though working there instead of in my night-club caused the Sloane Square turnover to diminish alarmingly until I gave up command in Bayswater.

Our take at the Royal Court was approaching £1000 a week and, with food costs and staff costs each at around 30 per cent, membership subs paying rent and rates and utilities, there was around £6000 a year profit after tax, which was then sufficient to live on in some style.

Nicola went to a kindergarten called Mrs McCaffrey's where they had a daily lesson called "report". I would not have learnt of this had she not come home one afternoon and said, "All the children at Mrs McCaffrey's are praying for the boil on your bum".

It was 1957, and Jill was pregnant with Dominic. I took Nic in to work every Saturday morning, when Elsie made a fuss of her and she was despatched to cross the road (by the zebra crossing that illuminated my side door) to W.H. Smith's and buy our papers. I heard from a number of my members that this pretty five-year-old child asking for *Harold Hare's Own* comic and the *Financial Times* was a happening keenly anticipated by the staff. Jill got a job playing Sally in *Mrs Dale's Diary*, a daily soap opera on radio, and we bought a holiday house in Walberswick, the East Suffolk village where my father had had a house, as had my Aunt Anna and one of my cousins and Anna's friend Dorothy Burlingham.

We had rented houses in previous summers, and now there was one for sale for £2850. Against all Jill's better feelings I made an offer for it, and we bought Westons with an acre and a bit of garden for £2800. My father built a gallery and a circular staircase at one end of our 40-foot sitting room (which some years earlier had been a barn attached to the pair of cottages), and designed a fireplace (he was the best man for fireplaces in the land) for which we bought a copper hood from a local blacksmith. He suggested corrugated iron. I inquired whether there was anything nicer. He said, "Not at a sensible price" — and it transpired that copper did indeed cost £3 12s 6d more.

The Royal Court Theatre, noticing how successful was my business, how modest my rent, sued me for my lease on the grounds that they wished to develop the upstairs part of their building. I had numerous members who were lawyers and one of them offered to take the case. I thanked him; he was a good man, never complained about his food and steadily ordered Gévrey Chambertin with his main course, half a bottle of Château Climens with his dessert.

That's the trouble about caterers: we think that a good customer must also be good at his trade ... which is why on the advice of customers I kept buying shares in remote Romanian oil companies when I would have done really well buying Marks and Spencers or W. H. Smith. I also bought insurance policies, though these had a happier outcome. I was a soft touch. I sold my members food and drink and they sold me life insurance.

The first one said, "Do you have a policy?"

I said, "No."

He said, "That will never do", and sold me one.

The next one asked whether I had life cover.

I said, "Yes."

He said, "Let me have a look at it", and decided it was quite the wrong policy for me. "Make it paid up and buy this one."

I did; then another; then a fourth ... always celebrating the purchase with a bottle of good wine, which helped cash flow.

Thirty years later, each of these aborted policies matured and yielded wholly unexpected five-figure sums.

The house in Walberswick was a joy. When I had been a child, the journey from my parents' London house to the Suffolk seaside was 96 miles and took four hours. Now, thanks to bypasses and wider roads and the M25, it is 125 miles and takes just over two hours if you choose the time with care (early morning going there, but wear sun-glasses because the sun does tend to rise in the east; drive back late at night). Jill loved the village, rode, took the children on wondrous outings, produced plays in our barn and later, when I was in Parliament, entertained handicapped children from the constituency, giving them riding holidays and outings to the Broads and Leiston Abbey and barbecues on Walberswick beach for a fortnight each summer.

In 1959 Tim Beaumont, whose extreme wealth had caused him to buy *Time and Tide* magazine and the Liberal Party, asked whether I would become his magazine's cookery writer; I accepted. Because of my performances preceding cabaret I had done an after-dinner speech or two. My first one was at the Café Royal, went well, and Bob Monkhouse, who lived nearby in St John's Wood and had become a friend, told me he had heard good reports about it.

"What did they pay you?"

"Pay me? Well, they sent a car to fetch me and take me home and gave me dinner."

Bob said he got 60 guineas when he made speeches. (I was still paying £10 a week for a cabaret act, often involving three artistes receiving £3 6s 8d each.)

Sixty guineas was serious money. Bob said next time I was invited to speak I would be a fool to do it for free.

It was a week or two later that someone rang, said they had heard me at the Café Royal, were giving a dinner at the Hyde Park Hotel next month and wondered whether I would make a speech for the guests. "I can promise you a really pleasant evening and we will provide transport."

I mentioned that I would be pleased to do this, but had a fee.

"How much?"

"Sixty guineas."

There was a pause before he said: "For 60 guineas we could get Bob Monkhouse."

By 1960 the Royal Court Theatre Club was flourishing. Egon Ronay had written about it in his *Guide*. The stylish *Town* magazine, published by the company owned by Michael Heseltine and Clive Labovitch, gave it a plug in their "Places to Go": "Expect to pay £6 10s per head." The average spend in my club was under £3 and I wrote indignantly to the editor, who neither published my letter nor replied.

I asked someone what I could do to annoy *Town* magazine and was told, "Publish something in *Queen* magazine." So I did. Beatrix Campbell was the editor and a friend of one of my members. I sold her a series called "The Mr Smith Investigations" . . . wherein I set out to prove that if your name was Smith, and you looked pretty much like everyone else, you were made to suffer for your anonymity.

I started the series with "Mr Smith Goes to Lunch". There were then six first-class hotel/restaurants in London: the Savoy, Ritz, Berkeley, Dorchester,

190

Grosvenor House and Mayfair. Over the next week or two I booked a table for two at 1p.m. at each, dressed modestly but tidily, as did my guest, usually Jill, arrived punctually, ordered the very cheapest meal they served, asked for more rolls, more butter, an extra jug of water, more coffee, paid the bill in cash and left a threepenny bit as a tip. At 1.30p.m. my secretary telephoned the hotel where I was lunching, asked to give an urgent message to "Mr Smith what's dining in your restaurant to say important you get to the usual place quick as you can."

I chronicled the restaurant's reaction: where they placed a man not known to them and not looking like a big spender; the timing and wording of the message; the reaction to the tip, which was just shy of 1 per cent; and assessed the quality of food and service. The Ritz came out of it best, the Grosvenor House had a 10 per cent service charge so the threepenny bit was almost welcome, the Savoy treated me like a leper. The Mayfair translated my message into "You are expected to attend the customary location at your earliest convenience", which impressed me, though I did not receive it until I was on my way out at 2.25.

The article was much admired in circles where Mr Smith's real identity was known. I got a note from Lord Beaverbrook complimenting me on the idea and execution, and *Town* magazine offered me a job as their cookery writer. Meanwhile the court case to have me bounced out of my premises continued.

Mr Smith went to art galleries. I managed to borrow a very fine Renoir drawing, wrapped it in some old newspapers together with three pictures I had bought in Portobello Road market for a shilling each, and took them to Sotheby's, Christie's, Marlborough Fine Arts, Wildenstein's and Ogden's in Bond Street. I explained that I had just bought this house in Welwyn Garden City, found these paintings in the attic, my wife needed a washing machine and I kept reading in the newspapers about people finding pictures that were worth money — were any of these valuable?

I had expected all the galleries to recognise the Renoir and looked forward to them offering me £5 for the four and me saying, "How about £2 10s for two and I'll keep the one of the budgerigar and that one in the nice frame?" It wasn't like that. What was impressive was the ease with which one could walk in from the street and have someone of gravitas assess a painting; less so the fact that only one out of five galleries recognised the Renoir.

Marlborough Fine Arts, who were exhibiting Impressionists, looked at the drawing and the initials in the left-hand corner and said, "This might be a John Rothenstein done in his youth but has little merit."

Wildenstein's looked at the Renoir and said, "Someone might have thought a bit of this because that's a classy frame", then admired one of the Portobello Road paintings but would not make an offer.

The girl at Sotheby's examined the four works of art, gave me a hard look and said, "Don't think you can increase the price of that by hawking it up and down

Bond Street. I suggest you have it authenticated and we will sell it for you."

"How about the other three?"

She gave me an old-fashioned grimace.

Soon after the article appeared she became a director of Sotheby's. Janet Green her name was.

Smith's fame increased; *Queen* magazine, owned by Jocelyn Stevens, with Mark Boxer as art editor, outsold its rivals; I was offered more journalistic work. And my solicitor said the court case against my Royal Court tenancy was going badly.

Mr Smith went to detective agencies to have his wife followed. He went to three companies that advertised in the trade directory: prompt, efficient, discreet, licensed by the LCC.

"It's like this," said Smith at each of the three locations. "I live in Berkhamsted. Wife used to come to London for shopping once or twice a year, and now every Tuesday she's on the 10.23 to Euston, back on the 3.45, and I've got to know what is going on. Here's her picture."

As this was 1961 and Jill was pregnant with Emma, we used a friend of hers as "Mrs Smith". She arrived at Euston, waited at the cab rank and drove to Eaton Square. Half an hour later she emerged wearing a different dress, was driven by a man wearing a Guards tie to a Chelsea wine bar . . . where the man's older brother, wearing an Old Etonian tie, emerged with her. They drove to Stamford Bridge Greyhound Stadium and in the second race she put £100 in fivers on the No. 6 dog (she placed the bet with a bookmaker friend who was giving us back the dosh). None of the agents was on the train from Berkhamsted. The *Queen* photographer had a picture of all three of them at the station doing obvious things — tying a shoelace, blowing their nose, polishing their glasses at the cab rank while attempting to overhear the address. Only one found the Eaton Square house, though he had gone when she emerged with Date No. 1's brother on the way to the wine bar.

I telephoned all three agencies, explained that I, Smith, although pretty sure they were on the case, had information that Mrs S. was having drinks in this Chelsea wine bar.

I have a picture of a detective standing ostentatiously in a flower pot as she came out but, though they drove very slowly to Stamford Bridge, he failed to trail them.

I got the bills from each company, all saying that it seemed I was justified in my suspicions re Mrs Smith's outings but to prove this they would need to follow her over a longer period, like a month. Their bills were outrageous, one of them charging the hourly rate until 8p.m. despite "She is always back on the 3.45". All of them charged for their agent's lunch. One of them suggested that Mrs Smith appeared to be followed by other people also, which in no way facilitated surveillance.

Mr Smith booked himself into each of the then six reputable health resorts, slimmed for four days, each time from 14 stone. In between I was writing restaurant criticism for *Town* magazine and had got myself a column on the *Sunday Telegraph* financial pages thanks to their finance editor, Nigel Lawson. "What *Town* putteth into him, *Queen* taketh out," wrote Nick Tomalin as I binged for one trendy magazine, slimmed for the other.

In one of my Smith investigations I had had my fortune told by five society clairvoyants in one day . . . and while each predicted the sort of things that are likely to happen to most people, one looked deep into the entrails of a guinea-fowl (or whatever) and said, "You are about to abandon what you have been doing most of your life and take up a new occupation. You will do well."

That was the month my night-club closed and I took up journalism as a profession. What Lady Pellegrino (for it was she) did not know was that having been a caterer one remains a caterer. I go into a restaurant and my eyes sweep across the tables and I note that one of them misses a pepper-pot, a "cover" over there has no bread knife on the side plate, another needs a napkin. Regardless of where I am dining, if someone shouts "Waiter!" I move in my chair . . . before remembering that I no longer have responsibility.

Anyway, in 1962 the exposed part of me ceased to be in the restaurant business.

Early that year I was ordered to vacate my premises to enable the landlords to build an extension to their theatre's auditorium. I had a week of farewell parties, all of my old cabaret artistes came back for final performances, we sold the wine and the furniture at an auction one weekend and the English Stage Company, they who were expanding the auditorium, let my old night-club to a man called Corbett at a high rent. Corbett did not last many months and the Royal Court were shamed into translating my club into the theatre upstairs.

The week I moved out of the Royal Court, the *News of the World* employed me as a columnist at a fee twenty-five times that which I was getting for football reports. They also paid expenses.

My last "Smith" was about buying theatre seats. I went to six London theatres to buy the best seats they had. At exactly the time I was at the box office my secretary was at a ticket agency like Keith Prowse "You want the best seats, we have them", buying "two best seats" for that theatre. The article showed that agencies buy whole rows of seats in advance, and if you want a third row centre seat at the Aldwych for a performance in six months' time the theatre hasn't got it, nor will they tell you which agency has. I sent the article and the theatre tickets to *Queen* with my expense claim.

A week before the "Mr Smith Buys a Theatre Seat" article was published, Jocelyn Stevens wrote to theatres and agents stating that "Our Mr Freud inadvertently bought theatre seats from you; he now finds he cannot use them and I would be grateful for a refund."

They sent him the money. I was outraged, went to *Queen* offices, took a swipe at him, have not spoken to him since. Smith investigations had been justified on the grounds that I was a customer and had a right to criticise. Demanding the ticket money's return turned the exercise into entrapment. I felt it to be a mean and dishonourable thing to do, but that is how Stevens was seen by many others.

In 1963 Jill was pregnant with our fourth child, Matthew. I was now a journalist and decided I could write my columns as well from the Suffolk seaside as from my St John's Wood study. We moved to Walberswick, and twice a week I commuted on the 8.12 from Saxmundham.

CHAPTER
EIGHT AND A HALF

A short summary detailing me and communications.

My television career had begun in the early 1950s when Michael Jeans, who had been at Bryanston with Lucian and lived in Walberswick, became a BBC TV director and invited me to appear on a programme about "looking ahead in my profession". I spoke as a cook, predicted that the hypodermic syringe would be the utensil of the next fifty years, showed how a duck could be shot full of orange sauce and be left to macerate therein before being roasted and becoming wonderfully delicious.

That held back my TV future.

In 1960 Southern TV in Southampton had a programme director called Roy Rich, who had been director of productions at the Arts Theatre; he asked me to do a cookery show ... with a pretty girl who would sing between my cooking things, mostly so that we could wash up and clear the work surface for the next trick. Then I was briefly Anglia's football reporter, given a bicycle and pedalled back to Anglia House from Carrow Road to tell the masses how Norwich City had lost.

Television was live and recordings could not be edited. If some disaster struck, they just filmed on, and the only way you could get the cameras to stop and start again at the beginning was to say, "Fuck, fuck, fuck" until the director said, "Cut, roll the captions, cameras running, action."

Anglia gave me a show called *Health and Beauty* to host, a show replete with masseurs and acupuncturists and practitioners of alternative medicines. Pete Murray was my guest on one show, having agreed to talk about acne, which had ravaged his countenance. I introduced him by saying: "And now we come to our next spot: Mr Pete Murray . . .", and he got angry.

Live TV has always brought out the worst in me, because I talk before I think. Announcing that I was writing a show for Fanny Cradock and Lionel Blair called *Butch Casserole and the One Dance Kid* is something I would not have done had I had my time over again. Yet now and then it works. I was doing a West Country TV tasting of home-made wines, many of which had only minimal merit, and the host, seeing me look unimpressed by my glass of damson and rhubarb cordial, asked with which food I would recommend this to be drunk. I said, "Porridge." Had I thought for a week I could not have come up with a more apposite reply.

I think it was in 1962 that Southern TV had an *Advertising Magazine*: a half-hour programme devoted to advertisements, with a little entertainment in between in case the full half-hour had not been sold. I was booked to stand by in case there was a gap between the ads.

"How long will I have?"

"Probably no time at all . . . but the man who was going to promote New Zealand cheese hasn't turned up and you may have to do that. We have a rough script."

The show went out at 9.45p.m., which was not then prime time; in Southampton, from where the show was broadcast, the all-night café closed at 8.30.

At 9.15 I asked how things were going.

They said, "All right, but slow."

"How many minutes have you sold?"

"Four. You'd better rehearse your New Zealand cheese because the man hasn't shown."

I rehearsed with a 3-ounce wedge of Cheddar: "Children nowadays seem to prefer cheese to sweets — mine certainly do. Do you realise that this 3-ounce piece of New Zealand Cheddar contains twice the goodness of its own weight in spinach and yet it costs less than half? New Zealand Cheddar — hurry to your grocer." Did it half a dozen times and it all went smoothly.

The *Ad Mag* host introduced the show, told the viewer (viewers?) that Clement Freud, "whom some of you will remember from *Sweet and Sour* two years ago", was the link man, and showed the four-minute commercial. Then it was me and the cheese.

The piece of Cheddar had become rather soft under the hot lights, but I grasped it like the friend it had become and said: "Children nowadays seem to prefer cheese to sweets — mine certainly do. Do you realise that this 3-ounce . . ." at which the triangular piece of cheese had had enough. I held it by the apex, indeed went on holding the apex, as the rest of the Cheddar, now the consistency of Welsh rarebit, phlopped down to land on my Chelsea boot.

"When I say '3-ounce piece' . . .", I explained into the camera, "I referred to the original amount that I was holding. This stalagmite between my thumb and forefinger weighs a scant quarter-ounce and yet you can buy it for the price of a broad bean." I looked at the monitor, which shows what the viewer can see, and saw the picture swinging wildly from side to side. The cameraman was having hysterics. As for me, I had twenty-five minutes in which to talk about not very much to fill the half-hour. I finally got the wind-up signal, went to my dressing room and changed into my driving-home suit.

As I left the studio in Southampton, I heard the phone ring in the deserted lobby. There was no one around. I picked up the receiver and said, "Southern Television, can I help you?"

A man's voice said, "I want to complain about the *Advertising Magazine*."

A director who had been at Southern TV moved in 1963 to Tyne Tees in Newcastle and commissioned a half-hour cookery series . . . I think mostly on the basis that I worked quickly . . . and for some years *Freud on Food* went out weekly on Grampian, Channel Isles and Southern. The fact that London, Birmingham, Manchester and Bristol viewers missed it was just one of those things.

Freud on Food featured me and my elder daughter or one of her friends who acted as my commis. We arrived in Newcastle at 6p.m.; had a light meal at the Gosforth Park Hotel, went to the dogs at the local greyhound track (where I tried to limit my losses to the amount I was paid by Tyne Tees), and the next day, between 9a.m. and 12.30, recorded three half-hour shows.

A typical one would involve a three-course meal — starter, main dish and pudding. And if things went wrong, as things did, I would explain that things also go wrong in the professional kitchen; on one occasion I spent the half-hour showing how to uncurdle mayonnaise, and after another disaster what to do with a burnt saucepan (soak it, scrub it with a solution of salt and vinegar and in the end throw it away and buy another pan). The shows were fun to do; the crew was allowed to eat anything left over after each session, so they liked being on them, and there were memorable moments . . . like when I dedicated a programme to sandwiches.

The Tyne Tees buyer had purchased loaves hot from the local bakery — loaves which turned into soft dough when approached by a bread knife. At the start of the show, I sent out a member of the crew to buy a couple of supermarket sliced loaves and, as he had not returned by the beginning of the programme, we spent the half-hour preparing what might have gone into the sandwiches had we had the bread. Corned beef with tomato chutney. Egg mayonnaise and sliced hard-boiled eggs with chopped watercress. Sardines mashed with Dijon mustard, tomato purée and grated horseradish. Crumbly Lancashire cheese with thinly sliced pickled onion. With ten minutes to go and no

202

bread in sight, I made a selection of butters: with chives and lemon juice; with minced anchovy fillets; with light Dijon mustard; with chopped hard-boiled egg. When the programme was over the man arrived with the bread, and the crew had a really good time.

By then I was preparing the work surface for the next programme and changing my suit. I wore different clothes for each programme in case viewers would think I kept the same shirt on for three weeks.

My journalistic work was coming on apace. In addition to my sports writing for the *Observer*, I wrote about cookery for *Time and Tide*, food for *Punch*, light-hearted City pieces for the financial pages of the *Sunday Telegraph*, and that amazingly valuable column for the *News of the World. Woman* magazine asked me to follow six English girls to Playboy HQ in Chicago: in the course of this assignment I met Hugh Hefner, later became a Trustee of the London Playboy Club.

And I was a father of four and determined not to do what had been done to me as a child. On Sundays we might all have gone to the Zoo after lunch, but mostly it was one child and me: to a tea dance with Nicola, a backgammon tournament with Dominic, a tug-of-war competition at Alexandra Palace with Ashley, a pantomime with Emma and Matthew . . . who were (still are) very close.

CHAPTER
NINE

In which I achieve fame.

I achieved fame at 10.45p.m. on Sunday, 26 October 1964. I had covered the Tokyo Olympics for the *Sun* — the broadsheet, orange-spot-on-the-cover, pre-Murdoch successor to the *Daily Herald* — and on my last day in Tokyo received a telegram asking if I would appear on the Eamonn Andrews show the following Sunday. When I left London Eamonn had been a genial sports critic, a some-time boxing correspondent, a TV Irishman and game-show host of fluency and charm. I accepted. While I was away, he had been given the first TV talk show in Britain. I was to be the first guest on his programme.

I had had a good Olympics: the new paper had not been as switched on as some of its rivals in obtaining permits and passes, so I covered the games on such documents as happened to be in my briefcase. I recall a morning when I was denied entry to the Press car park . . . finally made it by showing the Japanese police a lease on the semi-detached house in Bayswater which Robert Morley and I had opened as a coffee bar. It had several wax seals upon it, was tied with a pink ribbon and began, as such documents tend to, with "The Commissioners of the

Church of England Estate hereinafter known as the freeholders . . ."

I also caused a minor riot in a Song Shop, a Japanese eating house and cabaret, where some five hundred waitresses knelt by their customers pouring their rice wine and filleting their fish (they throw away the fillets; the bones and the head and the tail are eaten). In order to prevent anyone creating warm understanding with a waitress, the girls were changed every ten minutes. Just as you were beginning to start to get to know one, a bell rang and they all moved four customers forward, so you got the one who had been serving four places back.

Waitresses had numbers on their kimonos . . . and after an hour of eating and drinking and flirting the whistle blew, and I had kneeling by my side waitress No. 2845.

My room number at the New Otani Hotel was, coincidentally, 2845. I showed her my Otani key tag, called the manager and claimed her. He called the police. I showed them my lease.

I went to Yokohama to cover a sailing event in which we were expecting a medal, hired a limousine at the station and was driven to a pier, which was not the sailing pier; I was mistaken for the Swedish ambassador, who was to launch a ship, who was late, who would have been the only other Caucasian there. So I launched a ship, which I had not done before and the champagne bottle did not break but bounced up and down and gave the hull occasional playful smacks. His Excellency arrived as I was blessing the ship and bought me a drink.

I spent three and a half weeks in Tokyo, had paid a month's rent in advance and, when I asked for my account, rather expected the bills for food and drink, telephone calls and laundry to be mitigated by a refund for the four days' accommodation paid up front and not used. The Otani Hotel would have none of that. Accommodation and extras were separate departments. "You don't have to leave. You can stay until Saturday." I left on Tuesday, giving copies of my paid bill and my room key to an agreeable American jazz musician/dope-peddler whom I had met in a bar. "Nice large room, useful for jam sessions," I told him.

To return to fame: by 1964 I was sort of "known" from regional TV cooking shows, sports writing for the *Observer*, my City column and my pieces in *Tatler, Time and Tide* and *Punch*; I had owned that night-club and was Sigmund's grandson, Anna's nephew, Lucian's brother.

On the morning of Monday, 27 October the milkman who had been delivering our milk every day for thirteen years rang the bell to say, "I saw you on the Eamonn Andrews show", as did the postman, who prior to this had just shoved mail through our letter-box. Jill asked him in, gave him a cup of tea, at which pastime he was joined by our dustman, who wanted to check on something I had said on the Eamonn show. Nicky phoned from her boarding school: my fame had rubbed off on her — several day girls had invited her to go and stay during half-term; Dominic, aged six, was voted captain of his class, came home with twenty-seven autograph books for me to sign; and the phone started to ring and ring, and did so incessantly for the next eight years. Going ex-directory is plum inconsiderate when you have children who might get asked to parties and outings, so the phone had remained accessible to anyone with a directory.

Being famous changed everything. My car was repaired more quickly; dry cleaners said, "You don't need a ticket — we know who you are"; restaurants started not charging me, now that for the first time I was earning serious money; we went to a cinema where the manager pursued us up the stairs to give me back the ticket money, saying he would like Jill and me to be his guests — "Always delighted to have famous people in my Odeon." I got upgraded on planes, appeared on *What's My Line, Tell the Truth, Call My Bluff, Question Time, Panorama*, cookery shows, gardening shows, chat shows, afternoon programmes and late-night phone-ins, made after-dinner speeches, opened fêtes, appeared as guest celebrity at a hundred functions: one in Liverpool may have been the highlight.

Mr Cusson, a tallish, sixtyish, reclusive member of the soap family, was retiring (to no one's disappointment) and after the final board meeting there was to be a surprise farewell party for him. He was, my agent told me, a terrific fan of mine and regardless of expense I had been booked as celebrity guest.

The Imperial Leather company's staff had been tidied up and assembled, some two hundred of them, in the hall where concerts were held and Gilbert and Sullivan operas performed. Mr Cusson, passionate about wild animals, was retiring to South Africa, so the stage was filled with replica giraffes and zebras and ostriches. Mr Cusson was walked by his fellow directors through the main aisle of the hall and escorted up some steps on to the stage, where I stepped out from behind a stuffed wildebeest to considerable applause from the audience.

I shook Mr Cusson warmly by the hand, could see from the bewildered look on his face that he had no idea who I was, but the audience cheered. Their chairman was shaking hands with the man off the telly.

Mr Cusson, realising that he ought to say something, said to me, "You're with the animals."

I said, "Absolutely not."

Mr Cusson, alarmed, asked whether I was against the animals.

I denied that also.

There was dinner, at which I was seated next to my "fan", who looked at the place card bearing my name and finally asked, "What do you do? I mean, what are you doing now?"

I did not want to tell him that I was earning my fee the hard way.

I did more prime-time shows and became a public face. If you are a film actor, people go to a cinema, pay to watch your performance, accord respect when they see you in the flesh. As a TV celebrity you appear willy-nilly on a million sets in a million homes and become part of the furniture. I was on an Eamonn show with a comedian who told jokes, which were not particularly funny, at which I did not laugh. The director spent that section of the show cutting from close-up of comedian telling joke to close-up of me looking unamused. For years after that people would come up to me and ask, "Why do you never laugh?" In fact I laugh a lot, though hardly ever at jokes told without much flair. Appear on television and the viewers of the land feel they know all about you, the way they all know about the striped curtains that hang next to the TV set showing your picture. I once did a commercial for which the client asked me to wear a cardigan and, as I possessed none, they bought me one. The following year I was voted worst-dressed man on TV — "It's those awful cardigans he always wears."

My sort of fame does not travel. After my initial visit to Chicago I became food and beverage man to the Playboy empire and on my next visit to the windy city, Hugh Hefner's public relations team got me on to the No. 1 radio show in the Mid-West, a show heard in 34 states, relayed by 297 radio stations. The host, a cigar-chewing dwarf, carried the shows and when it was my turn to come on he announced: "I have a real humdinger of a terrific guest for you now! From London in little old England, none other than Gloment Trend . . . Well, hi, Glom, how're you doing?" We talked amicably for ten minutes.

During the break there was some discussion, between the host's production team and Hefner's PR dept so at the beginning of Part Two, the dwarf said, "Welcome back, folks! I've been having you on. When I told you that my guest was Gloment Trend, it was in fact Clement Frood — so whaddya know, Clem!"

I said I preferred Glom.

The problem with being famous is that your talents are usually ignored; you are perceived merely as a marketable commodity. In that first year of fame I opened a filling station in Cardiff for a four-figure sum; there were over a thousand onlookers gathered to see me put a nozzle into a car's fuel pipe and unleash a gallon of Four Star. I over-heard a girl of about ten say to her mother, "Who's he?" to which her mother replied, "He's famous, that's what. You'll be able to tell people you saw him."

Unlike winning the pools, fame is not necessarily accompanied by fortune. I continued to work as sports columnist on the *Sun*. But now I would ring some promising boxer who had won five fights on the trot, ask if I might come and meet him to write a profile for my paper . . . and he would say yes and ring his local paper and tell them: "Clement Freud is coming to my house tomorrow. Stop by and take pictures of him and me."

And I continued to work on radio and television. Ian Messiter was a man who thought up shows. *One Minute Please*, which had gone out in the 1950s, was a half-hour radio panel game in which contestants had to speak for one minute without hesitating, repeating themselves or deviating from the subject they were given. They included the wondrously lugubrious cartoonist Gerard Hoffnung, who played the tuba, made some famous speeches at the Oxford Union and devised a symphony for household instruments like Hoover, squeegee and dustbin lid.

Messiter telephoned me in 1965 and said he would like to revive the show, which had fallen by the wayside only because whatever channel it was on had got a new controller. Did I fancy being the Hoffnung character? It would now be called *Just a Minute*. "If you want something done, ask a busy man" is the saying. I was doing half a dozen other programmes at the time. I said, "Yes, please."

Nicholas Parsons, with whom I had been to school, who had done cabaret for me at the Royal Court, of whom I was not very fond though I hugely admired his industry (there cannot be many folk in the profession who get that much work with that amount of talent), was to be chairman. Ted Ray, Cardew Robinson, George Melly, Peter Haigh, and other neighbourhood gods featured, as did a woman: first it was Aimee MacDonald, who managed to achieve hesitation, repetition and deviation in a single syllable, later Sheila Hancock and a whole host of well-known thespians and singers.

After a year the team settled down to Derek Nimmo, Peter Jones, me and one woman. Two years in, Kenneth Williams became a regular member and it all changed. No longer a word game gently contested among four performers, it was now a Williams monologue performed for a small audience of players (me, Nimmo and Jones) and a burgeoning audience, also the Kenny Williams claque: a couple of dozen fans led by Kenny's mother and aunt. The fans were mostly female, never missed a Williams performance and lived their lives through Kenny.

We broadcast from the Playhouse Theatre on the Embankment. A brand-new graduate called David Hatch, later to become Head of Broadcasting, then to reach dizzy heights in the BBC hierarchy, was our first producer. We recorded a series of six. The Controller of Light Entertainment heard them, said, "Well, yes, but no thanks." And David Hatch said, "OK. In that case I will leave the Corporation." As they had high hopes of Hatch, the show went on.

Kenny was the star; Kenny was the one whose autographs the fans at the stage door wanted. Nimmo, Jones and I would walk out quietly, and as Kenny appeared the mob closed in and Mr Williams camped it up: "Oh, my piles . . . don't push, dear, otherwise I'll never get to Great Portland Street", and he grimaced and acted haughtily and put on funny walks . . . anything not to be left alone with his own persona.

He was lonely; had two friends — Gordon Jackson and Stanley Baxter — and even these, the only ones to be invited to his flat, weren't allowed to use the lavatory, had to walk to Baker Street Station if they wanted to pee. He was erudite, read histories, sulked a lot, had an extraordinary facility for spreading alarm and despondency. Nimmo and Jones and I would be in the green room cheerily discussing cricket, politics or some fallen friend's misfortune when Kenny arrived, started to limp as if a red-hot poker had been stuck up his rectum ("If only," he would have said), went up to Peter Jones and said, "You look terrible — have you been ill?", told Nimmo he had seen his review for some programme: "Awful, my dear, I am sooo sorry", and told me he had considered asking the director if he might sit away from me (we always sat next to each other) as I put him off so, and was I sure I had had a bath this week?

Kenny would take deep dislikes to people, especially women, especially Wendy Richard. A learned forty seconds by Tim Rice on the subject of Metabolism would be interrupted by Kenny saying, "Listen to her!" He reserved his best performances and his best lines for the audience before the microphone was switched on . . . and when Nicholas went on stage to warm up the house and introduce the panel, you could hear loud backstage shouts of "Speed it up, Parsons — they want to see *me*."

Usually, when Nicholas was explaining that on tonight's panel are . . . , we would all walk on together, led by Kenny pretending to have terminal haemorrhoids. His gimmick was to ask the producer for bizarre subjects, like Theosophus III, so that he could (a) mug up on it and do a hilarious monologue and (b) inhibit us from challenging him for fear of getting the subject and having to talk about someone of whom we knew less than nothing.

Nimmo was a bit trigger-happy, would interrupt almost regardless of the entertainment value of the speaker's prose. Jones was a brilliant counter-puncher — never tried to win but was basically funnier and read the game better than any of us. His one-liners shone.

A good chairman is one who steers the game with a minimum of interruptions, encourages the contestants and makes correct decisions. Nicholas is a performer;

as chairman he misses the opportunity to perform, nevertheless feels that what the audience has come for is a Nicholas Parsons twenty seconds of gibberish that sounds like French; a Parsons interruption of a homily in a Scots accent; and over and over, telling listeners that he receives letters from all over the world, which is why he had better explain what Clement Freud really meant when he said . . . which is the certain way to kill humour.

In the early 1970s Ian Messiter thought it would be fun to alternate the chair. In turn Derek, Peter, Kenny and I became chairman, and noticed that we got a 15 per cent higher fee than as contestants. When it was my turn to be arbiter, Nicholas buzzed his buzzer and said, "Could you just explain: if the word on the card is in the singular, can you use it in the hyphenated form more than once?"

He had been chairman for ten years.

Having written about food, broadcast thereon, done food on television and in demonstration halls, I had over the years been asked to do commercials but declined. I felt it to be dishonourable to write about food for magazines while plugging specific items on television. "Take a pound of butter" sounds unimpressive coming from a man who, during the commercial break, advises the use of Stork margarine. I turned down Green Giant sweet corn, processed cheese, PG Tips and Kenco coffee. I got plenty of offers. "This is J. Walter Thompson. We wondered whether you might be interested in . . ." was as far as I let them go.

214

Then a man called from Collett Dickinson Pierce. "Do you like dogs?"

"Not other people's dogs, I don't."

"Do you eat dog food?"

"Not knowingly."

"In that case, would you do a dog food commercial?"

I said that while I saw no reason not to, I would (a) be very expensive and (b) want to speak my, rather than the copywriter's, words.

Mr Tim Warriner, a dapper Australian, saw nothing wrong with that; explained that the theme would be "You are the famous cook/gourmet who appreciates this or that amazing dish, while the dog (and you can choose a dog that looks like you or that you can look like) is hooked on product."

"What is the product?"

"It's called Minced Morsels."

I apologised for wasting his time: "Minced Morsels is not something I am prepared to say on television."

Warriner suggested that someone else could say Minced Morsels, do the "hard sell". "What do you mean by 'a lot of money'?"

I said, "What the Prime Minister gets."

We left it there.

It took him an hour and a half to ring back and say, "The deal is on." You do the dog food commercial, write your own words, not name the product, get paid what the Prime Minister is paid.

We met, got on rather well. Warriner was an account executive and read the scripts the agency had worked on in a Clement Freud accent, made them sound more like me than I could have done.

The Quaker Oats people made Minced Morsels; no one I knew had heard of Minced Morsels. What harm could it do, and might it not help us send four children, plus Ashley who was a nephew and had adopted us, to their expensive private schools? I asked Jill what she thought. She thought what the Prime Minister gets on top of what I was earning would be helpful . . . "But you don't like dogs."

For £45,000 I am prepared to sit next to a dog.

Tim Warriner and I chose a dog, were torn between a bloodhound and a basset hound, had me sit beside a number of brutes with a mirror behind the camera while I imitated his expression (which was quite like mine) and his stance. We finally picked a basset hound who smelt unpleasantly of dog and was managed by a woman who gave forth a similar odour.

And we agreed a first script. We were going to call the dog Henry. He would wear a bandage around his ear and sit beside me at a dinner table. "As today is the second anniversary of Henry's operation, I thought we would celebrate. I bought a pound of Aberdeen Angus steak, marinated it in 1961 Château Beychevelle, dusted it in flour, simmered it in butter and added some double cream. And he hated it. Said he wanted this stuff."

I held up a packet as the hard-sell voice said: "Minced Morsels."

I had 26.5 seconds for my part.

We filmed at a studio in Wandsworth. The set was dressed and lit, the table was laid, a platform was built on which the dog would sit so that his head came up to the height of my head. I went to make-up, as did the dog. We met some time later under the fierce lights. A coordinator had prepared my plate with the steak, fine wine and a good-looking claret glass. The director looked at us through the lens, then the client looked through the lens, finally the cameraman took over. Action.

"Today is the second anniversary of Henry's . . ."

I was looking at the mirror behind the camera so that I could move if Henry moved. Henry was handsomely trained, hardly moved at all, but five seconds into the script the heat caused him to have so massive an erection that between suave me in a dinner jacket and soulful Henry wearing an ear bandage there came into picture an entirely gynormous, red and glistening penis.

"Cut," said the director, rather unnecessarily.

The studio gaped at the erection in amazement. The client shook her head in disbelief, the men from the agency sat and stared, and the woman who had brought the dog said, "I thought that might happen and have brought some bitches who look very similar."

We went out to the local pub had a drink, came back and started over again. A number of bitches had been assembled, all of them Henry-like if you did not look down, and we selected one and got her in place and the clapper-boy said, "Minced Morsel commercial Take Two."

I always hoped that Denis Norden in his TV Bloomers programme would find Take One. It would have to be shown after 9p.m.

There were a number of reasons why we went to Take 41. Henry had to sit still; I had to hit my allotted time. What tended to happen was that I got spot on 26.5 seconds and Henry barked or sniffed or played doggo; Henry behaved impeccably and I over-ran, under-ran or fluffed a line. Occasionally, we both did it perfectly and a helicopter flew overhead to Battersea heliport.

The commercial went out a few nights later; then again, then again and again; three, four, five times each night. Packets of Minced Morsels stared at one from supermarket shelves. Rumour had it that the sales director of Kennomeat shot himself, Chum reduced its price, Spillers advertised for new personnel for their PR department. Minced Morsels became brand leader and wherever I went people who did not bark at me asked after Henry's health.

I continued to write football; on a good day only 750 people came up to me and said, "How's your dog?", expecting me to fall about with mirth.

On the credit side, I received a letter which I treasured:

"Dear Mr Freud

"Your address was given to me by a person in high place." (For the record, it was in the telephone directory.)

This dog food you say is good, is not so very good; it smells bad and it don't go too well with green banana chips. I felt you should know."

At around that time Harold Wilson gave himself a very large pay rise and, as my fee was geared to his salary, I became wealthier.

The commercials went on and on. Tim and I thought up new Henry situations and directors fell over themselves to lend their names to them: Dick Lester, Terence Donovan, Brian Duffy. "I went on holiday to Provence and wrote to Henry about a place that serves wonderful Bouillabaisse. He sent me a postcard about a tin he had bought in Tunbridge Wells" . . .

"Chunky Meat," said the hard-sell voice; at some point during the campaign the product had changed its name. Sales soared.

The commercial made me virtually unemployable. *Panorama*, game shows, quiz shows, talk shows, even children's shows could manage without featuring someone of whom 99 per cent of viewers said, "Where's his dog?" I grew a beard to avoid immediate recognition. It hardly helped.

Henry's owners did well: Henry or one of her brothers/sisters opened garden parties and fêtes, became celebrity guests at functions, received hundreds of letters asking for paw-prints. I became paranoiac, very hard to live with, accepted every invitation to work in foreign countries where I could be me rather than the two-legged half of a dog food commercial.

Which is why, in 1970, I agreed to go to Australia and New Zealand to be chairman of the judging panel that selected the winner of the Great Australian Bake-off. Eight weeks; two TV Bake-off shows a day. A minder, a driver, all the food I could eat and accommodation at the best hotels in Perth, Sydney, Brisbane, Adelaide, Melbourne, Auckland and Wellington.

Australian Women's Weekly sent a columnist to interview me so that the new continent would have knowledge of the celebrity who was to be amongst them and select the 1970 top Oz baker. He was a no-nonsense, chain-smoking man, followed me around for a couple of days and wrote that "Freud does just about everything there is to do, except train budgerigars", which information was widely carried in Antipodean papers.

I arrived in Australia at a time when hating the English was trendy. Princess Margaret had been and upset folk by being Princess Margaret; and Jimmy Edwards had done some gigs and said "fuck" on stage, was expelled as a consequence. They were just about ready for someone else to take umbrage at.

I arrived in Perth, was sprayed with disinfectant and as I got off the plane was mobbed by a reporter at the bottom of the plane's steps.

"How do you like Australia?"

"It's a bit soon to say."

"So far?"

"So far I've been sprayed with disinfectant."

I made the front page of the Perth newspaper: "'Far from expressing pleasure on his first visit to Australia, English celeb cook Clement Freud whinges about agricultural hygiene' by our own correspondent, see

Page Three." Page Three had a picture of me coming off the plane, looking like someone who had been up all night in a plane.

In Sydney I received a proper reception and was introduced to my hosts, the sponsors of the Great Australian Bake-off: they were the chief executives from Spilsbury flour, the Australian Milk Marketing Board, Australian butter and Oz sugar. Somehow, no one had told me that flour, milk, sugar and butter had to be ingredients in every recipe submitted to the competition's judges.

I was allotted a minder ... a tall, laid back, fifty-year-old fatso who was to meet me outside the VIP lounge at 11.45. I waited and he arrived half an hour late, shook my hand and said, "Mr Frood. OK with you if I call you Sigmund?" By 12.20 I was minderless, my own man. Moved into the Wentworth Hotel where the hall porter had worked at the London Savoy and became a friend.

Australian Women's Weekly sent people to quiz me at regular intervals and their PR dept had me booked on talk shows, game shows, discussion shows; on my first night they had arranged a Channel Nine interview with Dr Twinkle, a therapist who had recently achieved notoriety by publishing in the *Morning Herald* a guide to which suburbs of Sydney were the best for sex. Intercourse in Rose Bay was hardly worth crossing the Harbour Bridge for; in Woolloomooroo it was quick and basic; at Kings Cross 58 per cent of women were desperate for it and Double Bay was for folk into unobvious positions.

On his show, Dr Twinkle said I could call him Twink.
I thanked him.

He asked how I had found Australian women.

I told him that I had been in the city since lunchtime and the women looked pleasantly attractive, the ones who did not have skin cancer.

"But what are they like between the sheets?"

"I arrived at lunchtime."

"Mr Freud, are you trying to tell me that a good-looking man like you, with the name of Freud, has spent ten hours in Sydney without pulling a woman?"

I replied that I had not "tried to tell him anything".

He would not let go. "Did you see the first part of the programme, the one in which I spoke to the girl who had multiple orgasms?"

"No."

"But you are mad at yourself for missing her? Hang around and I have three virgins who serve table in a harbour bar and a woman taxi driver with a breast implant coming next. Does that turn you on?"

I was tired. I did not see the conversation as one from which emergence with honour was likely, so I said: "Twink, let me tell you something. In England many men take sexual pleasures with women beneath their social station. As it must be difficult to find anyone beneath the social station of an Australian, you could be missing out on a lot of fun."

The switchboard lit up like a Christmas tree as women rang in to complain; the next day some two hundred battle-axes stood outside the Wentworth Hotel

222

with "Freud Go Home" notices held high. Half of my appearances were cancelled. *Australian Women's Weekly* wept.

The Bake-off heats were televised every afternoon in front of invited audiences. On my judging panel I had a French cabaret artiste of what the French call *un certain âge*, an ex-pat wine merchant who had been at Framlingham, the public school in Suffolk, which he held in high regard and was president of the Old Framlinghamians in Oz. Also a Julian Clary-like minor TV personality called Bernard King, pronounced Ber*nard*.

Contestants cooked. We tasted. The French artiste sang. Each day we had a winner who would move forward into the next round. Flour, sugar, butter and milk make for a sort of sameness, and after the heats Bernard, the pride of Framlingham and I would go to a restaurant and eat steak tartare or Kentucky fried chicken.

It was not a time of which Australia was proud; the old gag of "What is the difference between Australia and yoghurt? Only one of them has culture" was applicable in 1970. In the theatre, film industry, radio, television, even in journalism the achievers' ambition was to get noticed, and take a job in Britain or the USA. So high achievers left Australia and what remained were the ones who did not care.

I worked for seven weeks with crap camera crews, dictated my articles to crap copy-takers, and got interviewed by hosts who had either failed to make it, or were off next week to seek their fortunes in Los

Angeles/London/New York. My employers, the flour/ milk/butter/sugar people, gave dinner parties for me; and the French artiste, who only got four out of ten for holding drink, fell over on an afternoon TV show and was repatriated. We did Sydney, Melbourne, Adelaide, Brisbane. An hour and a half every afternoon on television, dinners and promotions and chat shows in the evening. After my experience with Dr Twink I was the man they liked to hate, which got me a twice-weekly newspaper column which was syndicated around the continent so people could hate me for my writing also.

I wrote about laundries that starched my underpants, devoted a few hundred words to taxis that pulled up outside hotels and had drivers announce where they were going rather than ask people standing outside the hotel where they wanted to go. "We call that mode of transport a bus", I wrote. Oz taxi drivers do not let you get in the back, not if you are alone, so you sit with them in the front while they talk at you and smoke at you. They do not accept tips; on the contrary: the meter shows ten and a half and they say, "give me ten".

It was a triff year for immigration in Australia and every new influx of Europeans meant promotion for those who had already been in the country for a month. This was especially so in restaurants. The man who served you last week is now the maître d'. The man who cooked your good dinner the week before has been elected to Parliament. The manager, at the time you first went to the place, is in jail. I went to one restaurant, looked at the menu, ordered a Châteaubriand

224

Sauce Béarnaise, got a hamburger with a bowl of Heinz salad cream.

"This is not a Châteaubriand and that is not Sauce Béarnaise," I told the waiter.

"How long have you been in this country mate?" was his reply.

In a bar I ordered a pint of lager; got a pint glass, two-thirds full of froth. "This isn't a pint," said I.

"It's what we call a pint," said the barman.

In my second week in Sydney the hotel operator told me I had a phone call from a man who would not give his name, but sounded English: should she put him through? I said, "Yes."

The man said, "You know who I am?"

"Not yet, I don't. Tell me."

"I'm the one who gets more publicity than you at home." He had a cockney undertone to his Australian accent, sounded depressed. "I wouldn't mind meeting you as long as you come alone," he said. "I need someone for a chat, someone who won't sell me down the line".

I asked if his initials were RB. He said maybe, and if I wanted to find out for sure, go to the coffee shop at the south end of Bondi beach and if I didn't come alone, he wouldn't be there.

Sad that the only really interesting thing that happened to me in Sydney could not feature in my syndicated column. Biggsy by this time was being bled by just about everyone he met and was waiting for a passage to some place where they might leave him alone without having to pay bundles of cash every time someone identified him. I offered him a job on my judging panel. The show was now attracting so few viewers, I told him he would be safe; he declined. We talked about London and Esmeralda's Club, which the Krays had run in the 1950s off Knightsbridge, not far from my night-club. He left Australia for South America some days later and I realised that being frightened of recognition is even less fun than being recognised.

I wrote a "Mr Smith"-type article for the *Melbourne Age*. The personal columns of most papers were swollen with advertisements from dating agencies who could provide, at short notice, female companions for dinners, dances and friendships, especially for out-of-town visitors to Melbourne who might otherwise be lonely. Credit cards accepted. So one evening I asked the hotel to lay up a table for six in my sitting room and rang five agencies explaining that I was in Melbourne for a few days, was lonely, had seen their ad. and could they send me someone with whom to have dinner.

"Would someone petite, late thirties with dark hair be suitable?" asked a woman with a Greek accent who was clearly an owner/driver. I said, "So long as she has a Greek accent," and she giggled. (When she arrived she was in her very late thirties, like fifty, had perhaps aged since our phone call.)

Four other agencies were pleased to supply escorts and at 8p.m. they began to be ushered into my sitting room by the portering staff. The petite Greek came first; then two rather bored girls in their early twenties; next a battle-axe who took a look at the table for six and the other three hookers, asked whether I was some sort of pervert.

Twenty minutes after the appointed time, when we were getting to the end of the salted peanuts, there came a knock on the door. I went to open it and one of the prettiest, warmest, sexiest, youngest, most sparsely dressed redheads I have ever encountered gave me a warm smile, came into the room, saw the four hookers and flcd down the passage.

The evening was deeply boring: the four tarts drank the *Melbourne Age* wine and swapped anecdotes. I regretted the foolishness of the exercise and wondered about the one who got away.

I described her in depth in my newspaper column, offered to put her on my judging panel, but never heard from her again. The agency who had sent her could not help; explained that she was from a pool which supplied escorts when their own were all engaged.

When I arrived in Adelaide, a camera crew were at the airport to greet me. I came down the steps of the plane and a woman held a microphone into my face and said, "Mr Freud, you've rubbished Sydney and trashed Melbourne. Which of the two did you really like better?"

I said, "It's like asking someone to compare leprosy with syphilis".

The item went out on every newscast in the land and I was hated again. "Bring Back Jimmy Edwards" was a placard that greeted me when I left my hotel the following morning.

Bobo Faulkner, wife of Trader Faulkner who had been a Royal Court cabaret artiste, hosted a Saturday night talk show in Adelaide, invited me on it, asked me questions about my grandmother, which no one had thought of doing before, and on Sunday took me for lunch to a famous mud crab restaurant. Some eighty of us sat in a courtyard and every ten minutes or so a man with a bucket would come in from the kitchen and distribute a dozen freshly boiled crabs to the next dozen customers.

When I got mine, it had missed the pot; it was dead but raw . . . and I had to wait for ten minutes before the man came out with his new haul, held my peace until he had served them, called him over and said:

"This mud crab is raw."

He gave a fleeting glance at the crab, turned to me and said, "No one else has complained."

I used that as a title for a book about the restaurant business.

(There was one occasion when I had nearly said that myself; I did "cook-ins" at the Belfast Festival, when I performed in the ramped university physics laboratory theatre to an audience who watched me cook as they ate what I had cooked for them earlier that day. On the last Saturday of my week in Belfast (a young Delia Smith was in my team of helpers) I did three performances for full houses of 140 people — an early, timely and late lunch — and had prepared 450 portions of everything on the menu: a Greek chicken and lemon soup; boiled salmon, new potatoes and asparagus hollandaise; apple crumble. The university kitchen where I worked had a 50-gallon stockpot and I made the soup by simmering overnight thirty boiling chickens, cut up; thirty lemons, halved; 5 kilos of onions and herbs and salt and pepper. The stockpot had a tap and we had gallon jugs. For service we beat six large eggs with half a pint of double cream into each jug and whisked as we opened the tap and added the simmering broth through a sieve.

At the third lunch I asked, as I had at the previous ones, whether everyone had been content with their meal and a man said, "I thought the soup was a bit over-lemony"; I thought about saying, "Four hundred and nineteen people did not share that view", but let it go, apologised, explained that lemony was very much a matter of taste. After service I went into the kitchen to congratulate the team and see how the portions had held out, looked into the stockpot and found that, while the chickens had been removed for staff lunches, the lemons had been left in and the last jug was a secondary stock sifted through sixty lemon-halves that had settled around the tap.)

After my experience with the mud crab I left for Brisbane on Friday evening, booked into my hotel and went straight to see Tom Graveney, who was captain-manager of Queenland's cricket team and had become a friend while I was covering an England tour in the West Indies for the *Sun* and BBC. We played squash and he gave me nets over the weekend, until I no longer felt like a battery chicken nurtured on a diet of flour, milk, butter and sugar. I returned to my Brisbane hotel at four in the afternoon, ready for my

5.30p.m. Bake-off programme, to find the hotel surrounded by TV vans, each representing one of the four stations that competed against each other from the hill above the city.

Oh good, I said to myself; another famous nobody has arrived and will make the headlines. I was wrong. They were waiting for me. I had been invited by Clem Jones, the mayor of Brisbane, to a luncheon in the town hall where I was to be guest of honour, make a speech and give awards to trainee cooks ... and had not turned up. To them it was like not turning up for an investiture. Microphones were thrust in my face.

"Why weren't you there?"

"I wasn't asked."

"You were."

"I wasn't."

"Where were you?"

"Playing squash."

"Don't you like Clem Jones?"

"I don't know Clem Jones, though his first name sounds nice."

"Supercilious Brit Cook Humiliates Mayor ... Squash More Important Than Lunch at City Hall ... Another Arrogant Pom Shows His True Colours" were the evening paper headlines, taken up by radio, TV and the dailies.

That night I had been booked to do a stand-up half-hour at a veterans' club — who pay serious money, like fifty times what I paid my cabaret artistes for a week. I appeared on the stage and upwards of a thousand people booed; I looked at my watch after a

230

few minutes of standing there being abused and having the odd egg and tomato thrown at me (where do customers get eggs and tomatoes? Do they put them in their pockets when setting out for an evening at the club, just in case? What do they do with them if they like the show?) and finally, when the noise had subsided a bit, I took the microphone and spoke.

"Ladies and gentlemen of Brisbane, I am really sorry that you have seen fit to greet me in this unfriendly manner. Not only do I have considerable affection for your city, but my wife's people come from near here'and as I saw the audience relax and settle down to be entertained, I added "New Delhi".

They were angrier than before, also sorry that they had thrown all the things they had, were now devoid of ammunition, forced to resort to booing.

My masters, the CEOs of the sponsoring companies in Queenland, reluctantly took me to dinner, whinged about my high fee and the bad publicity, and I offered to do the Queensland week for nothing if England lost the Test Match at Perth, double my fee if they won. They accepted. Cowdrey's team won. Now there were not too many folk in Australia who loved me.

CHAPTER
TEN

In which I recall my short career as a thin man.

I was working for the *Sun*, long before it shrank in size and depicted parts of girls one does not see in Marylebone High Street. One day I wrote about an amateur rider (who claimed 7lb) and warned readers to be wary of supporting his mounts as he tended to carry overweight. "What a disgrace to burden your horse with a stone more than the handicapper has allotted it; there should be a law against it," I opined.

Some time later the sports editor said, "You've got a horse. Why don't you ride him? Save money on jockeys and it'll make a good piece." I explained that (a) I didn't ride, had not done so since prepuberty, and (b) though Charles II competed in the Newmarket Town Plate at 14stone 4lb, people of my build were not now accommodated by the Racing Calendar.

"Lose weight and learn to ride," he said.

I lost thirty pounds. Having sat next to Jimmy Lindley on a flight to Washington for the International race, I rang him and asked whether he might give me race-riding lessons. He agreed. The following Tuesday and again on the Thursday he came to the stable where I had horses. I rode round and round a field and he kept shouting, "Stop looking like a fucking policeman." I learnt to stick my bum in the air and lower my shoulders, something you seldom see mounted constables do.

I asked my trainer if he would recommend me as a jockey, and he wrote a note that stated: "C. Freud is not much worse than some of the amateurs riding today." I sent the note with my application to ride to the secretary to the stewards of the Irish Turf Club; by return I received a note asking me to present myself for inspection at 11a.m. the following Friday.

I flew to Dublin, made my way to the Merrion Square office and was called into a room in which half a dozen elderly men sat behind a table. They stared at me for a while, one of them remarking that I looked rather better on television — an observation to which I have still not found a good answer. It was the senior steward, Major Victor McCalmont, who kicked off proceedings.

"How long have you been riding, Mr Freud?" he asked amiably.

I was able to tell him exactly: "I started on Tuesday of last week — early on, around 7.30a.m."

He looked perplexed, had a quick whisper with his colleagues and came up with Question No. 2: "Have you done any speed work?"

I assured him that it had nearly all been speed work: I would get on a horse and the horse galloped away. I added that if the stewards thought I was the sort of swine who pulled his horse to prevent it from winning, they could rest easy.

There was a longish pause before one of the men said, "Give him a licence — what harm can he do?"

I was told that I could ride in amateur races and was warned not to make a nuisance of myself ringing owners and trainers at all hours asking for rides. I promised not to.

A dear man called Jo Hehir, who was a patron of my trainer, offered me a ride on his horse Saxon King on the last Saturday of the month.

"I am afraid I am unlikely to be much use as a jockey," I told him.

"The horse is not much use either, so you'll get on fine together," said Mr Hehir and poured us each a large glass of Bushmills.

I lost more weight, rode out two lots a day for whoever would have me, and read *The Theory and Practice of Flat Race Riding* by John Hislop. This is an invaluable volume, containing much excellent advice and some dubious statements such as "Settle a horse on the gallops by sitting quietly with a long rein". The first time I tried this, it took me a mile and three-quarters to pull the brute to a trot. There is an interesting paragraph dealing with starters. "Jockeys who consistently refer to starters as ham-fisted deaf-mutes are unlikely to get the best breaks when the field is sent on its way. Also, some starters have an aversion to jocks shouting 'not yet, sir' at them."

I started my riding career in a bumper at Naas. "What if the horse bolts on the way to the start?" I asked the trainer.

"Aim him at the other horses; they are gregarious beasts," he said.

It all went swimmingly. Adrenalin flowed, I started well, and my bottom never touched the saddle. Coming into the home turn on the first circuit, Mr J.R. Cox, the best and reputedly most expensive amateur jockey in the British Isles, rode up beside me and asked me whether I was enjoying it. He took hold of my horse's head and pushed him into the lead, so that I was first passing the stands.

I hadn't realised that jockeys could hear the commentary and the shouts of the punters and the bookmakers. I was so taken with this that I forgot to steer, until I heard a man shout: "Open the gates, he's coming in!"

Saxon King and I tired after twelve furlongs: I had been afraid that I would not be able to pull up after the finish: not a bit of it. Two miles of fierce galloping had both of us ready to call it an afternoon. I walked him to the enclosure, got off and found I was too weak to remove the saddle to weigh in, which is not essential when you finish fifteenth.

I rode a few more times in Ireland and at Leicester and Bath. Why did they dope-test the horse, I wondered, when it was I who was up to the gills with amphetamines and diuretics in order to make under 12 stone, which God had never intended as my weight. I was not always finishing fifteenth. One year I had a 50 per cent strike-rate; regrettably the amateur riders' table required a minimum of five wins and I had only won once, so my name did not figure.

My greatest race was an affair which started in late May 1971, when I ran my five-year-old horse Winter Fair in the Hugh Fraser Amateur Riders' Stakes at Hamilton Park — to which the Scottish industrialist had contributed £1000 in prize money. In the parade ring prior to the event, modestly attired in Fraser tartan silks, stood the generous sponsor and I, recalling the halcyon days of yore, flung a metaphorical glove into the mud of Hamilton Park (the going was described as soft) and challenged the second baronet to a race.

"Done," he said, pronouncing the word as men do north of the border.

"A thousand pounds a side?" I asked.

"A thousand pounds it is," said he.

"Mile and a half . . . classic distance?"

He nodded.

"Shall we say 12stone 7lb?"

We shook hands.

I returned my hand in the general direction of my fourteen-stone frame and told Toby Balding, my trainer, what I had done. He received the information with limited amusement.

For the record my horse, ridden by that peerless rider Mr Philip Mitchell, won the race. And some yards beyond the finishing post Sir Hugh, who was in penultimate position, dismounted from his steed in what is regarded as an unorthodox manner, i.e. sideways, at considerable speed, picking himself gingerly from the turf and moving crabwise towards the weighing room, while an honest lad was despatched to reclaim the horse. I mention this not in the spirit of what the Teuts call *Schadenfreude*, which means joy at someone else's misfortunes, but to put paid to vile rumours that I had waited till Sir Hugh had fallen from his horse before issuing my challenge.

The announcement of the match, carried quietly in a number of minority publications, caused a clutch of clerks of courses to inquire whether we might, perchance, care to hold the contest at their tracks; and in the fullness of time we settled on Haydock Park, 30 September. The choice was made for a number of good reasons: Haydock was roughly equidistant between London and Glasgow — my home and his; the 30 September programme featured a ladies' race, so that the pure academic seriousness of the occasion was already impaired; there had never before been a "match" at Haydock, but when racing started there at the end of the eighteenth century the first event was for horses carrying 14stone 4lb, proving that the terrain was suitable for feats of weight-carrying.

Moreover, late September would afford my horse the chance to frolic in a field for a month — something my trainer termed "letting it down" and I considered a rare extravagance at 20 guineas a week — before he would be "wound up" with the match in mind. For Sir Hugh, it meant a summer holiday and time to look round for a better horse. "You're nay goin' to hold me to riding that animal?" he asked.

I shook my head in sorrow. We agreed that, whatever horse he bought, we would take the official Time-form ratings for the respective mounts, burden the better nag with 12 stone 7lb and let the lesser animal carry the lesser weight according to handicap.

There remained for me a number of small problems — like riding at 12 stone 7lb entails weighing around 11 stone 13lb, the remaining poundage being taken up by saddle, stirrups, boots, breeches, shirt, girths and other attributes without which equestrian propriety would be offended. Thus, around 30lb of C. Freud would have to go again.

Mid-August saw me firmly inside the 14-stone barrier. Admittedly, forty-five days in which to lose 28lb presented a steeper graph than did the original 36lb in four months, but I was playing Real Tennis at Lords, walking, swimming and having odd games of golf, cricket and tennis.

By 15 August, in Hampshire Winter Fair had finished a month of road work and was doing some fastish ten-furlong spins on the gallops. In London I embarked on the Grapefuit Diet, an amazing method by which you eat up to twelve fried eggs and twelve slices of bacon for breakfast, lace your coffee with cream and provided you precede every meal with half a fresh grapefruit, you lose 10lb in ten days. There were a number of don'ts like no other fruit, no starches, no corn oil or margarine, no sugar, no sweet wines — simply as much fat and protein as you can gobble, with half upon half of catalytic grapefruit.

It seemed to me that such a diet should be taken seriously, away from the temptation of thin toast cunningly slipped beneath your caviar, so I accepted an invitation to stay on a Chinese junk in Majorca, took with me the diet sheet and explained to my hostess that it was in a grand cause: when I won Sir Hugh's £1000 I would buy her something lovely at Harrods. She told me she did not remember ever seeing a grapefruit on Majorca, though in fairness she had not really looked. Together we looked. We scoured the fruit shops and greengrocers, supermarkets and harbour warehouses of the island and after each bout of shops we sat down and had a glass of wine and planned our next move. In six days I put on 5lb in weight and on the last day I lost 4lb; returning to London I preceded each meal with half a grapefruit, did exactly as I was told and, after five days, where the blurb promised that there would be a sudden 5lb weight loss, the scales flickered to show a decrease of 1½lb — 24lb to lose in thirty-two days.

I lost 11lb in four days. I was alone in London while my family was summering in Suffolk, and, with amphetamine pills prescribed by a doctor who advised against them but said that they would do no lasting harm, I lost my appetite and gained uncommon energy. So I spent days jumping up and down, playing Real Tennis wearing a polythene vest between two jerseys over a sweatshirt and managed to drink sufficiently small quantities of white wine to make the weight loss realistic.

Down to 12 stone 12lb, I booked myself into Grayshott Hall Health Hydro in Hampshire, where the osteopath put me on the scales and said, "We'll feed you a bit — 12 stone 12lb is on the thin side for you."

"Hot water," I said hungrily, "with an occasional grape."

He wished me luck.

My timetable was wake up at 5.30a.m. and drive to Toby Balding. Ride at 7a.m. and then again at 9a.m.; then drive back to Grayshott. Gravitate between sauna and massage parlour and sitz-bath and gymnasium (where there was a static bicycle) until 3p.m. collapse. Watch television and go to sleep as soon after 11p.m. as was consistent with the foul taste of hunger and dehydration on my palate. I left Grayshott weighing 12 stone 5lb; used a belt to support my trousers and took up residence with my trainer, whose wife decided to go to Scotland — swearing that the journey had nothing to do with my arrival.

Sir Hugh and I met at the beginning of September. I gave him several large whiskies, and we sent in our joint challenges to the Keeper of Matchbook at Weatherby's in Portman Square. As there have already been eight "matches" since the war, the man cannot afford to sleep for more than 364½ days in the year. We also gave a small press conference in the discotheque of the Playboy Club, to which we invited racing correspondents and Diary editors.

After the first case of champagne we announced the match, and answered questions which were of the what do you weigh/who will win variety until a man asked Sir Hugh (whose properties had that week been valued at £125 million) what he would do with the money if he won.

"Give it to the Injured Jockeys Fund," said the knight.

"How about you?" asked the journalist.

240

"Keep it," I said, giving my colleagues of the Press the first quotable quote.

"On reflection," I added, "and bearing in mind the champagne I have dispensed, together with the fried prawns, devilled chicken livers and barbecued spare ribs, I would prefer you not to mention this in your papers."

They smiled the way I used to smile.

On Tuesday, 19 September, weighing 12 stone 11b, I had a preliminary outing; a well-behaved racehorse, Tsarzen by name, the property of Mr Robert Marmor, was entered in an amateur 1½ mile race at Leicester and I was permitted to ride. The weight it was allocated was 11 stone 71b and, in view of having ridden fewer than five winners under any recognised rule of racing, I was to claim a further 5lb. After a morning of fierce squash following a day of no food or drink, I had the sort of tongue which any respectable doctor would have advised me not to put back in my mouth. Notwithstanding, in the words of the great P. O'Sullivan, "Freud put up the equivalent overweight of twenty-two one-pound tins of dogfood" — a statement that hurt my pride, even while it delighted my masters who produced those fine canine products which permitted me to appear on television.

The race helped me greatly. I got into the swing of jockeys' changing-room talk, learnt a number of four-letter words the existence of which I had only suspected and gleaned from the valet that you put nylon tights on your legs, dust these with talcum, whereafter you can slide your riding boots on and off with a minimum of strain. I also came to grips with goggles, found that the chinstrap of a crash helmet fitted over my beard in such a way that I looked like every other clean-shaven jockey and I had my first experience of starting stalls. Tsarzen and I were led into one labelled 7, the door slammed behind us and the honest horse moved so that my leg was squashed against one side. Having watched dressage in the Olympics I tried a few ploys to make him move six inches to the left, like beating him fiercely with my whip, also pushing him with all my weight; Tsarzen remained comfortably where he was.

In the stall next to me, the man said he could not remember a jockey ever leaving a leg or part thereof in the stall; nevertheless I decided to take my imprisoned leg from the horse's side and place it forward near its mouth. So there I sat. Right leg in horse's mouth. Left hanging down. Both hands on the reins, which were doubled over the withers while my two thumbs gripped the mane as per instructions. The theory here is that a horse might jump out of the gate with such celerity that, unless you hold on to it, only one of you completes the course.

I wondered about shouting, "Just a minute, sir," decided against it and saw the white flag go up, after which the stalls opened with a rare crack. We emerged, and by the time I had got my right foot back by the horse's side we were lying comfortably in fourteenth place, the other thirteen runners kicking lavish clumps of mud into my face. Leicester is a right-handed course and one races far from the close scrutiny of the crowd

242

until reaching the four-furlong straight; I rode a stirring finish, during which I passed a number of horses who were by then going backwards and came in eighth. The next day's *Sporting Life* noted that "Tsarzen dwelt [official word for starting slowly with jockey's foot in horse's mouth] and made some late progress."

As a result of the race my confidence was immeasurably strengthened; also I went out to dinner and put on 8lb in weight.

Two days later, riding Winter Fair for the first time, the horse bolted with me at the end of the gallops. Not unduly worried, I steered him down a seven-furlong straight; he had already worked a mile and a quarter, which had exhausted me and must have tired him, but I found that the harder I pulled the horse, the faster he went.

At the end of the gallop was a high hedge trimmed with barbed wire — and as Winter Fair was making straight for it there seemed little else to do but haul fiercely at the right rein with such strength as remained. This made the horse turn, fall and slide into the barbed wire, in which his legs became desperately entangled. I did what I could to ease the situation and finally he kicked out, disentangled himself at the cost of a fair amount of flesh and blood and cantered away. I removed myself as best I could, and by the time the horse was caught it was clear to those assembled that I had broken some ribs, bruised an elbow and was lame in my right ankle.

An hour later the vet came. Winter Fair had been cleaned up magnificently with iodine that blended into the deep chestnut of his skin; when I asked the vet what were the chances of his racing on Saturday week, he opined that they seemed a damned sight better than mine.

In the afternoon I went to Ascot to do a television interview about the forthcoming match and heard (a) that a lady called Jean Cooper was a smashing physio when it came to ribs, ankles and elbows; (b) that Hugh Fraser had sprained an ankle. News of my adversary's ankle was exaggerated, but I owe a great deal to Miss Cooper. Having ascertained that my sixth rib was broken in two places, she got me into a sound if in-pain state; and on the following Monday evening I drove up north to ride the Haydock course.

Two things happened on that Monday night. I was caught speeding on the M6. Park Ward Continentals with their hoods up have a notoriously small rear window, and what I diagnosed as a white jeep behind me turned out — at 92 miles an hour — to be a police Range Rover. Later, at the Midland Hotel, Manchester, I pushed myself out of the bath and with an audible crack such healing as my rib had achieved went by the board. I spent a night of acute pain and at 6a.m. drove to Haydock like the hunchback of Notre Dame.

The course over which the match was to be held is left-handed — an oval of just over a mile and a half so that our start was in front of the stands, 60 yards beyond the finishing post. I walked the course with the groundsman, who explained that you stuck to the rails until you got to the BREW TEN advertisement hoarding, then made for the chestnut tree on the far side of the back straight, going to the inner by the mile starting gate and keeping there round the home turn, whereafter you made your best way home down the five-furlong straight.

At 9a.m. George Owen, a kindly northern trainer, arrived with his stable jockey and a mare upon which I was to ride round. After some difficulty mounting I found that a walk and a gallop were bearable speeds for my strapped ribs, so we walked to the start and galloped round the course. My plan was for the other horse to take the lead while I came at him in the home straight, riding a fantastic finish to win by a neck.

In fact Mr R. Crank, George Owen's jockey, went so slowly that my mare zoomed past him and in the home straight he surged past me and there was no way I could get back on terms. In desperation, and remembering Winter Fair's reaction to being hard pulled and ordered to stop, I took a firm tug at the bridle and shouted "Whoa." Mr Owen's mare slowed obediently, so that I lost five lengths and experienced great pain in my ribs. However, I had learnt the right way to steer a horse round Haydock, got a feeling for the speed one would go in a two-horse race and thought that if I could ride within twelve hours of re-breaking a rib I would be absolutely fine in four days' time, especially if I took care not to get out of baths quickly.

Meanwhile, news from Winter Fair was that he was making a great recovery. His initial stiffness had gone and, according to his trainer, he was fit to jump out of his multi-punctured skin. On Thursday, 28 September I drove to Newmarket, where Toby was witnessing the sales and we spent an hour discussing tactics.

On form, I had the better horse — though the enemy had an advantage of 10lb in weight. Winter Fair had won over 1½ miles on the flat; Star Award, Sir Hugh's three-year-old, had won a couple of races over a mile, come fourth over ten furlongs carrying 8½stone — so there was no reason to believe that he would rocket down the final straight with an extra 50lb on his back.

The danger would be that if I went too slowly the three-year-old might do me for finishing speed and, if I raced off at breakneck speed and my horse blew up, Sir Hugh might just be able to bide his time and come in with a late run. The bookmakers had made my horse favourite at 1–2. If we were both experienced jockeys, mine would win and there seemed no reason why, as we were both thoroughly inexperienced jockeys, the result should be significantly different except "racing is a funny game".

I drove back to London, and by the time I left for Manchester on Friday evening I had recorded four deathless episodes of *Just a Minute* and gone to a wine tasting at which I spat out more wine than any taster has ever before expectorated. I had also spent a fair amount of time rereading *The Theory and Practice of Flat Race Riding*.

After dinner with the Baldings and my elder daughter in the French Restaurant at the Midland, two friends and I went to a club called the Cossack. Basically, this seemed to work in the following way: you stood outside and rang the bell and in God's good time the manager, with a half-smoked cigar wedged between his teeth, unbolted and unlocked the door. The opening was narrow, and the only way of getting past him was to take the active end of his cigar in your mouth and perform a quick pirouette. "Clem," he shouted, "great to see you. Got a cough? Never mind." I introduced my friends, he blew smoke in their faces and pushed us forward. The place was dark and full: men were square and middle-aged; girls young and acquisitive. If I understood correctly, the scene was that you danced with whom you liked — with the exception of the middle-aged square men — and if you had any proposal to put to your partner, the sum of £5 paid to the management gave you the right to go outside, get your face slapped and come back. But I probably got it wrong.

A waitress called Marie blew gently into my ear and I ordered two bottles of champagne. Two girls came with the champagne and left with the empties. And Cigar Face kept bringing along people to whom he introduced me as Clem — all of whom promised to back me the next day.

Back at the hotel I took two Mandrax pills, one Tuinal, two laxatives, an iron pill and a salt tablet, and asked for an 8a.m. call. I woke at 5.30a.m., then again at 6.46a.m., when I took the two diuretic tablets that Toby had acquired for me. Before the Leicester race I had taken one and it had been almost entirely ineffective. With two, the yield was as follows: 7.35a.m., fifteen fluid ounces; 7.58, ten; 8.16, nine; 8.39, ten; 8.58, three; 9.15, two.

In view of the previous night's dinner and champagne I decided to while away an hour in a sauna and found one, open twenty-four hours a day, which gave me 5s discount for being a member of Equity. I tried to get a further discount as a member of the National Union of Journalists, but discounts, like contemporary prison sentences, seem to run concurrently rather than cumulatively. The sauna had a door which was so stiff that I was as apprehensive about getting locked in as I was about damaging my ribs trying to get out; forty-five minutes at 100 degrees resulted in a loss of 2lb. The scales registered 11 stone 9½lb; short of amputating a limb, which would not significantly have helped my equestrian thrust, I had done what I could.

At 11a.m. Toby and Caroline Balding and I drove to Haydock Park and as we approached the owners' and trainers' car park my wife and three younger children landed on the course in a Piper Aztec plane. Then I heaved my bag containing saddle, boots, breeches etc. into the weighing room and walked the course with my trainer, "Emma, Dominic and Matthew in attendance", as they say in Court Circulars.

We noticed that the going, officially described as "hard", was well covered with odd patches in the back straight where the previous day's racing had left a wide path of hoofprints; these could only be avoided by going far into the centre of the track, or by sticking so close to the rail that the chances of your left leg remaining attached to your body would have been poor. Walking the home turn there was all of 300 yards in which one changed from south-east to north-west, but riding it at 35 miles an hour one would be likely to be carried off the rails — in which case, Haydock specialists said, you are better making straight for the finishing line than going back to the rails.

We returned to the stands at noon, I gave Julian Wilson of the BBC a quick one minute of voice to be put over the television coverage of my horse being led out on to the course prior to the race at 1.15p.m. and, with time galloping on, I made for the weighing room. Halfway down the near-side wall is an aperture that leads to the jockeys' changing room and as I made to go in I was stopped. The man explained that the changing room was for jockeys only. He knew who I was — "Goodness, yes, wife's a great fan of yours . . . but not in here you don't come".

"He's riding," said a man behind me.

"He doesn't come in here," said the man.

"He's Clement Freud," said the valet from within, waving my riding boots.

"I know that," said the clerk of the scales.

The man finally withdrew, I was reunited with my riding gear and received valeting of an incredibly high order: the man in question steadily held trouser legs or jacket sleeves at the angle at which they most appropriately slid over the limb in question.

It was now 12.40, thirty-five minutes to go. I was dressed: bandages, tights, breeches, boots, silk blouse, stock, crash helmet, saddle cloth, saddle, breast plate, surcingle, number cloth — got on the scales and weighed 12 stone 2½lb, 4½lb, less than I need have weighed. I could have had two roast grouse, bread sauce, breadcrumbs, game chips and a magnum of Château Palmer 1955 . . .

They gave me a leather belt with slots for lead weights and fed lead into it until the pointer hovered on 175lb. Then, on reflection, I asked them to take out a weight and had a cup of tea. Toby and I went into the trainers' luncheon room and as my tea arrived Toby asked whether I had had my salt tablet that day. I said no.

"Very important, salt," said my trainer. "When you are dehydrated, it stops you getting cramp."

"I am dehydrated," I said.

He got a teaspoon, filled it with salt and I swallowed it, washing the stuff down with tea and feeling as sick as I have ever felt.

Had there been a bookmaker around, my odds might well have lengthened to 4–6; instead they contracted to 4–9 with Fraser at 6–4 against, though I learnt later that such support as the tycoon had came less from the people with faith in him or in tycoonery than from those confident that 6–4 against represented fair value when it came to a real live gourmet remaining on a moving horse for twelve furlongs.

The fact that I have not yet mentioned my adversary on this great day is due neither to egocentricity nor forgetfulness, for Sir Hugh Fraser had failed to show. Even my idea that he was being barred from entering the course by some further representative from Rent-a-moron turned out to be false when it was learnt that he had flown over the course at noon but his pilot had refused to land because of cross-winds. He was diverted to Liverpool and Sir Hugh was currently gnashing his teeth in a taxi somewhere along the M6.

If what had passed to date was comedy, the next twenty minutes belonged to high farce. Here was Haydock Racecourse on a glorious September afternoon with seventeen thousand people in attendance. Also, a television audience estimated at 8 million. Over in the paddock two horses walked quietly around the ring, watched by humanity ten deep. Outside the weighing room, and lining the route to the paddock, was a crowd that would not have disgraced Newmarket on Guineas Day. In the weighing room I sat and waited, as did the Clerk of the Course, the stewards, the stipendiaries, the starter, the course commentator, and the valet deputed to help the absent Fraser arms into the waiting tartan sleeves.

Officially, lips were sealed — with the odds against the Jockey Club ever giving their consent to another televised match lengthening minute by minute. Unofficially, I was approached by all manner of men with all kinds of helpful suggestions. Would I, for instance, care to claim the race, issue another challenge and race at the end of racing, like after the last race? I said no. Would I mind waiting a little longer — like till Sir Hugh arrived? I said that would be a very good idea.

It was 1.10p.m. On the television set in the weighing room, the BBC commentator was explaining that there could well be a delay and over now to the baths at Aberafon for some wrestling . . . and at 1.17p.m. there was a stirring in the multitudes and a buzzing and a

251

cheering — and Sir Hugh arrived, wreathed in smoke, cigarettes protruding from every orifice. The air was thick with Celtic apologia: "Hoots, och the noo, sorry, ye ken I've wrecked it all . . ."

"We waited," I said. "Get changed."

Jackets, shirts and pants flew, boots were kicked off and in the course of three minutes Sir Hugh was clothed and weighed and lit another cigarette and threw it away. Escorted by two policemen we walked into the paddock amidst many a cry of "Hurrah," "Yippee," "At last," and the inevitable "Where's your dog?" The stewards stood in hollow square; Winter Fair's connections, consisting of Jill and my children and the Baldings, occupied pride of place; some way distant stood Sir Hugh's trainer and a factotum who looked as if he had come straight from Harrods, where, I seem to recall, you can get absolutely anything.

With our arrival and the stewards beaming with relief, there was one further delay. Star Award, having been taken away to be tacked up with the saddle with which his owner-rider had weighed himself, took a few minutes to return to the paddock, so that Winter Fair completed his forty-seventh circuit alone. Sir Hugh lit a quick cigarette, but after that it was not unlike when they brought the good news from Ghent to Aix. We sprang to the stirrups, were led out. The starter omitted to have a roll call but did explain that he would raise his flag and drop it — which he did, almost immediately, around which time I galloped, Hugh galloped and the relieved crowd, noticing in passing that it was 1.29p.m., shouted "God's speed," "Cor, look at them," also "Where's your dog?"

Having been drawn outside my opponent, I made for the rails ahead of him and steered, as planned, on the rails, across the course by the BREW TEN sign and back again to the mile gate, round the far turn into the straight, which carried me wide and into the home straight with the crowd cheering and the commentator, whom I heard very clearly, saying that I was in the lead — which I realised — and that Fraser was second, which he, too, must have observed. In that order did we pass the finishing post, the official distance two and a half lengths and such fears as I had about being unable to pull up and have to compete in a ladies' race (which was due to start at 1.45p.m.) were quickly dispelled. The horse behaved immaculately. As for my weight, it was 11 stone 8½lb stripped at 1p.m. on Saturday, 30 September.

Around 2a.m. that night I went to bed, a 12 stone 12lb ex-jockey. It was the drink that did it: when you are thoroughly dehydrated, a pint of lemonade can put on 7lb; as for a magnum of Château Petrus . . .

Some time ago I went to a Hall of Fame celebration in New York where the greats of basketball were nominated for lifetime achievement. A man of seventy made an acceptance speech, during which he said, "The older we get, the better we were." On reflection, some thirty years on, I don't think I was much good in the saddle, but I did have fun.

A silver-framed picture of me riding Winter Fair to victory at Haydock stands on my desk. As it was taken sideways on I have to explain to people that it was I who was riding — though really you can tell because I look a bit like a policeman.

CHAPTER
ELEVEN

In which I suffer in the cause of journalism.

Journalists write about what other people do; John Anstey's idea was that I was to do things and write about them.

Anstey was a gentleman editor, surrounded himself with very pretty secretaries who rarely allowed you to speak to him and brought out a successful weekly *Telegraph* magazine. He asked me to go to Lincoln, Nebraska for a week and write about Middle America, where drugs, vice, political scandals, heists, kidnaps and shoot-outs were as rare as they are in Lincoln, UK. My article was to show that there was another, better side to the USA. We agreed a fee; he secured me first-class plane tickets and I was met by the head of the local TV station, accommodated at the best hotel and made much of.

Lincoln is where Johnny Carson, Dick Cavett and other famous US communicators came from: trouble about Lincoln, it is a town from which you come. No one goes there. People leave Lincoln in droves; at the airport the departure lounge is many times the size of the arrivals hall. It is the insurance capital of America and for the record has the longest street in the USA: O street runs from Lincoln to Omaha, 50 miles north, and if you fancy a six-figure house number, O Street is your street.

I was accorded the freedom of the town, invited to watch the Corn-huskers (University of Nebraska's American football team, coached by Bob Devianney, the winningest coach in US college football) from the president's box, taken to luncheons in city clubs and played golf on courses that prided themselves on being 100 per cent Wasp. I went through a drive-in café and ate a fishwich, was guest speaker at a university debate attended by 485 eager students, 476 of whom told me that they loved my accent and asked how long was I staying.

The editor of the local newspaper gave a dinner in my honour. He provided drinks, guests brought food. The temperature was in the eighties, everyone wore suits and collars and ties and a local politician came up to me and said, "I know you are here for an English magazine to write about us. Well, in Nebraska we play it straight down the line, wouldn't want you to make anyone think otherwise."

I told him that I had come to that conclusion myself.

About two and a half bottles of vodka later this same man came up to me, pointed to a largeish woman who looked as if her hair had been sprayed with quick-setting cement, and said: "Mr Freud, sir, you see that woman over there — the one in the bronze dress?"

I told him it would not be easy to miss her.

"Well, sir, she fucks like a rattlesnake."

I said, "But surely, in Lincoln, Nebraska people play it straight down the line."

256

He said, "Take her to Omaha and she fucks like a rattlesnake."

I left that conversation out of my *Telegraph* magazine article, but Anstey and *Telegraph* readers liked what I wrote and I was offered a series about doing things.

"Like what?"

"Like fly."

"I don't fly."

"Learn."

I learnt, wrote. They took pictures.

I drove to a flying school in Denham, 20 miles west of London, and took lessons for which the *Telegraph* paid; it took only a few hours to master the craft, for anyone can fly. Trouble is that not too many people can take off and hardly anyone is able to land.

I was the exception. With an instructor sitting beside me, I convinced myself that if he could do it, so could I. We flew a small Cessna, took off into the wind, achieving an on-the-ground speed of whatever miles an hour it says in the manual before gently tugging at the joystick and lifting the plane from the ground into the air.

After that there was nothing to it, except for other planes which I never managed to see but my instructor did. There was a screen in front of the pilot's seat on which moving dots were other planes. "Aircraft at eleven o' clock," said my guru. I was at that time wearing a digital watch and "eleven o'clock" was meaningless, "in front of you slightly to the left, a thousand feet higher than us" made sense. I took avoiding action.

Once up in the air, the whole world was my oyster and I had ear-phones so that I could listen in to the control towers, which one received by dialling their wavelengths, which one found by consulting a piece of paper; during consultations the sage on my right pointed out that there were aircraft at five o'clock, also nine o'clock, and I told him to ensure we did not hit them while I went on looking up wavelengths on my instruction leaflet.

I flew to, well over, just about everywhere: Chalfont St Peter, Chalfont St Giles, Beaconsfield, Farnham Common, Rickmansworth, Winchmore Hill and one afternoon nearly made it to High Wycombe, only the lesson ran out.

"Watch me land," said my mentor.

I watched him. It was a matter of getting 150 feet altitude over the hedge and then reducing the power to slow the machine and pushing forward the joystick to lose height, with a reassuring voice from the control tower in your ear telling you to do a bit more of this, less of that.

After six lessons, the instructor let me land the plane myself. This I did several times, first hitting the runway quite hard, bouncing back into the air and hitting it less hard, bouncing not as high and then keeping it on the ground and only just not running out of landing field; had I done that at Heathrow, it would have been a doddle. Subsequent landings were less eventful.

After a couple of weeks I applied for a private pilot's licence (which you need in order to fly unaccompanied) and the great day came for my solo flight. I was in good shape, confident. Jill came along, was apprehensive. The *Telegraph* photographer pretended he did not want me to crash, but you could see that a scoop of my demise would have been substantially more profitable than pictures of me getting into a plane, disappearing and coming back.

My solo flight was to take the familiar route to Chalfont St Giles, achieving a height of 3000 feet, turning clockwise and coming back in over Denham Green to land on the strip from which I had taken off. I had had a medical. The doctor tickled the sole of my foot and nodded appreciatively as my toe twitched. He checked my eyesight and my hearing and hit my knee with a hammer to gauge reactions. "You can fly," he said, signing a form.

"Anyone can fly," I told him. "Will I be able to land?"

He wished me luck, said he hadn't lost anyone that month.

It all went according to plan. The Cessna took off while six anxious people stood by the control tower willing me on. Fifteen minutes later I returned and saw Jill wave, bit my lip, went through the landing procedure, checked the indicator panel, passed over the hedge at the requisite height and hit the runway hard, but not excessively hard, taxied to my people who were relieved.

"What did you think of the landing?" I asked the instructor.

"If you can walk away from it, it's a landing," he said.

Anstey was pleased with the article, gave the picture of me holding up my pilot's licence the front page, then sent me to Switzerland to learn to ski. I broke my ankle, mainly because of my odious ski-instructor but to the huge satisfaction of my photographer. "Great!" he kept saying as I lay writhing around in the snow. "Now look up and to your left . . . now smile . . . now try to touch your ankle."

A blood-wagon arrived to take me down the mountain the driver, having first had to carry out an emergency operation to get my Visa card out of my trouser pocket.

It got the front page of the magazine . . . as did my next piece about driving a Formula Three car at Brand's Hatch.

People were now writing in suggesting madcap schemes, and I became a film extra in *Macbeth* directed by Roman Polanski. If you saw the movie and did not see me, do not blame yourself, for I saw the film twice and was unable to pick me out in the background scene in which I was hanged while Macbeth was otherwise engaged. It took three days not being visible in that scene, and I had to go to North Wales where the film was shot and get a wig and have make-up and step into a heavy harness to which the hanging rope, which looked as if it had encircled my neck, was attached. Four of us were hanged: the chief executive of *Playboy*, (Playboy Inc. financed the film), occupied the gallows next to mine and could not be seen in the film either, and we ate and drank and played backgammon into the night, at one time playing for a pot worth thirty-five times my daily rate as an extra.

I went down the Cresta Run in St Moritz, having had to wait two days, as novice Cresta runners have to, in order to make my first descent; two days in Cresta kit, wondering when they might call your name, sweating with apprehension each time they say "Next one down will be Mr ...", then a mixture of relief and disappointment. The Cresta is a steep, icy, winding track; you lie face down on a heavy iron skeleton which you push, jump upon, grip the front with padded, gloved hand and rake for all you are worth with the spikes in your boots to stop the skeleton from going too fast and zooming over the ice-covered bank on the many turns. Your nose is barely a foot from the ice, which accentuates the feeling of speed.

On my first run I raked so hard that I feared I might be the first contestant not to reach the finishing line, returned a time so pathetic that the time-keeper announced, "Here's one for the ladies", meaning that panic-induced strength in the lower leg might be an acceptable attribute to what is called après-Cresta.

I went down three more times — the third time, to the delight of my photographer, parting company with the skeleton at Shuttlecock Bend, which gains you admission to the Shuttlecock Club, which allows you to buy a Shuttlecock Club tie, as a consequence of which people come up to tell you they did not know you played badminton. I called the article "The Ultimate Laxative". Picture of me on skeleton made the cover.

Having facilitated my adventures in the air and on land, the *Telegraph* magazine agreed to let me tackle the sea also. In New York I had appeared on *The David Frost Show*. Another guest on the programme was Robin Knox-Johnston, who had sailed single-handed around the world, come back, divorced his wife, sailed round the world again and remarried her. Frost, in the best tradition of TV hosts, did not meet his guests before the show and disappeared afterwards (with Johnny Carson, on whose show I was a regular guest, one knew where he drank, so could join him in the Irish bar on Sixth Avenue if keen to remain in his company). Frost was driven away in his limo and Robin and I went to a bar, drank a bit, got on rather well and decided that, with his sailing and my writing, we could enter for the Cape Town-Rio race next January and make the trip self-financing.

Did I sail?

"No, but I have met a lot of people who were overtly stupider than me who did, so it can't be difficult."

"Can you read a sextant?"

"Of course I can't, but I can learn."

That autumn Robin bought a 69-foot Nickerson boat, called her *Ocean Spirit* and sailed from Malta to Cape Town. We spoke on the phone quite often. The plan was that the *Telegraph* magazine would pay up front for weekly progress reports and a big article with pictures. Robin would get five friends whom he could trust to help sail, advertise for a sailing doctor and sell six berths for £400 each to people who wanted to come along and were fit enough to pull ropes, though they don't call them ropes on board a ship (boats are called ships).

We discussed the merits of asking a woman, ideally a deaf and dumb nymphomaniac who could do the washing up, decided against.

I flew to Cape Town soon after Christmas. The boat was empty, wholly unfurnished, though there was a lavatory, which is called the "heads", with a bowl which you "rode" and a flush which had to be pulled backwards and forwards from your crouching position. To flush it was like riding a horse in a tight finish. Next to the heads was a space which Robin told me would become my kitchen, which on a ship is called a galley. I was to furnish it. It is typical of sailing mentality that lavatories and kitchens should be housed close together in the least desirable part of the ship. What they consider important are sails, then bunks.

Cape Town workers were excellent and very inexpensive: we put in a sink and a stove and I built a freezer of corrugated iron, the size of a large coffin, which would house layers of dry ice wrapped in newspaper and meat and fish and vegetables and butter and eggs and sausages and fruit in plastic bags, then more dry ice, more food, more ice, more food and so forth. Each layer to last about six days, food at the bottom less desirable than that at the top. Our journey would take between twenty-five and forty days, depending on winds, and if it took much longer than that we had cases of sardines and spam and biscuits and cod liver oil.

Cape Town thirty years ago was politically odious; the workman who was building my kitchen was black and not allowed to come into my hotel, though as a special favour reception rang and told me that there was someone outside the front door who wanted to talk to me.

"Ask him to come up," I said.

"Ach, man, he's black and the hotel's white," said the receptionist, who was "coloured".

We found a doctor who was a keen sailor; Leslie, Billy, Jerry and Andrew had all sailed with Robin before and were quality men . . . and we sold passages to six local men, four of them from Mozambique, who paid willingly. I spent days in Cape Town markets buying food; the local papers ran stories about this gourmet ship that had a real chef who also rode racehorses; a wine merchant gave us lots of wine of such poor quality that I sent it back, with deep apologies; someone sold that news item to a gossip columnist, after which every other wine merchant in Cape Town sent us wine for sampling. We filled up with Eddie Barlow's Nederberg wines. Barlow a distinguished cricketer, with whom I had played for the Lords Taverners, was delighted when I accepted twenty-five cases . . . two-thirds of a bottle a man a day.

Journalists from women's magazines came to see the galley . . . none of them telling me that half the cupboards whose shelves I was gradually filling with provisions would empty their contents on to the floor the first time we tacked, nor that the other half would follow when we tacked the other way. Tacking . . . also port, starboard, leeward and windward, are sailing expressions used on boats. I mean ships.

For the last week before we sailed I would wake up during the night, write "cinnamon" on the pad by my bed, then sleep again. My great fear was that I would forget something really important, like matches or dishcloths, and I spent many hours going through every stage of catering for fourteen people three times a day for up to forty days. Six days into the South Atlantic was not going to be a good time to realise we had no tin opener, corkscrew, loo paper or marmalade.

On the evening before the start of the first Cape Town-Rio race there were parties. The fourteen of us took our last look at women, gritted our teeth and prepared for the journey.

We started in a Force 8 gale. *Ocean Spirit* literally flew out of Cape Town harbour. Our marker to port, the last patch of African land we saw, was Robin Island; none of us, in fact hardly anyone anywhere, knew that this was where Nelson Mandela was imprisoned. We did not see another ship until we arrived at Rio four weeks later. The flotilla of 70 vessels was scattered by the winds, had to report their positions daily to the mother ship, the SS *Tafelberg*, and we plotted the positions of our opponents, found we were sailing south of most of them and were making good progress.

What pleased me particularly was that, as we sailed out of Cape Town into waves that were 10 feet high, four of my sailing colleagues were throwing up as if there was money in the pastime — and I felt fine. That was when I found out about the contents of my kitchen cupboards . . . and was pleased that I had enough string to construct barriers for the shelf fronts.

Three hours out of port I had crown of lamb, redcurrant jelly, mint sauce and roast potatoes ready for the crew, came on deck, announced dinner. They said, "Fuck off and help pull up the spinnaker." There was between me and them a substantial conflict of interest.

Traditionally, sailors don't cook. At the beginning of a voyage they draw lots for who works the galley and the one with the short straw does so with the clear understanding that the first man to complain about the food takes over. Hence the crew who sat down for dinner, each to a plate of soup.

"What do you think of it?" asked the reluctant cook.

"Tastes like piss," said the captain, "but I like it."

In Cape Town I had seen the other ships victualled with rice and dried peas and pasta, frozen chicken thighs and tins of meat "n" veg, 7lb jars of jam, margarine, baked beans, Marmite, long life bread.

Not us. We baked our own bread daily . . . we were stocked like an up-market food store. I mixed the flour and yeast and water and salt, put it to rise in a greased basin covered by a cloth, and the midnight watch knocked it down and put it back in a warm place (everywhere was a warm place in February in the South Atlantic) for the 4a.m. watch to knock down a second time, adding some chopped walnuts and currants I had left out. At 5.30 I would shape the re-risen dough and bake the loaves for 7a.m. breakfast.

We had best butter and jams of quality; on high days and holidays Eggs Benedict, otherwise scrambled eggs

266

with fillets of smoked had-dock; good tea and coffee and a brand of long life milk which did not affect the taste of the beverages.

I had asked Robin about weight and been told it was no problem. Cape Town to Rio was "downhill" and in view of the expected winds, we would need some ballast in the hold.

"What sort of ballast?"

Robin said, "Water. Buy drums and fill them up."

I told him he was insane. So *Ocean Spirit*'s "ballast", thanks to a session with the Cape Town ship's chandlers, consisted of fifteen cases of Johnnie Walker Black Label whisky, available duty-free at a few shillings a bottle, readily saleable at twenty-five times that price in Brazil. Moreover, I pointed out to my captain, wooden cases tightly strapped together don't roll around like drums of water.

"Suppose they search us?"

My belief was that if we came first, there would be too many photographers on board for the harbour police to expose themselves as anything but the nice people they wanted us to believe them to be.

"And if we don't win?"

"We'll get the doctor to certify us as a ship bearing a contagious crew . . . beri-beri or trench mouth . . . that'll deter them from a search."

For the first week we sailed over 200 miles a day, ate and drank and worked and slept, and there was no laundry problem because no one wore any clothes — not even I, not even when I fried chips.

My failure was jelly. I had brought a few dozen packets of Rowntree's fruit jelly, to each of which you add a pint of water and a few slices of peach plus a splash of port. I made a 3-pint pot one evening and by the next morning it had not set. I dissolved two more packets in a minimum of hot water, added it to the languid liquidescence in the pot and gave it another day. Nothing. I refused to submit. By day six the contents of the pot was slimy to the touch, but still fluid; It was the constant rolling of the ship that stopped it setting. I may have been the first man ever to discover that and considered writing to Rowntree's advising them to put a warning on the packages: "Not suitable for use on boats".

My success was new potatoes boiled in seawater; food just doesn't get any better than that. Seawater has exactly the right amount of salt to make potatoes wonderful. We drank our daily ration of wine, which I kept cool by trailing bottles behind the ship. Robin found me doing that, told me off for slowing us down. "Won't slow us down as much as drinking warm white wine," I said.

The six southern Africans who had paid for their passages were a disappointment: couldn't wash up; didn't know how to scrub a floor or make a bed. We had not thought of that. Billy, who was a senior army officer, and Jeremy, who owned a large hotel in Malta, were the best kitchen porters I ever had. The southern Africans explained that they had had no experience of life without servants.

And we had trouble with the doctor: an excellent sailor, he was not so much a well-qualified doctor as a frustrated surgeon. We were scared to go to him with ailments as he began consultations by scrubbing scalpels and disinfecting the table on which he examined us. Having sustained a slight knife wound when *Ocean Spirit* hit a wave while I was filleting venison, I went to the doc for a plaster. He looked at the finger and decided amputating the tip would be the most positive treatment — certainly stop it from going septic, which we did not want, did we? Was I allergic to a local anaesthetic?

I said yes and considered myself lucky I had not got cystitis.

Ten days out of Cape Town, making wonderful time, probably leading the flotilla though sailing south of it, we were becalmed. Just like that. I remember spitting into the sea from the galley porthole and seeing my globule of saliva in the same place the following morning. We listened to weather reports, tuned in to the SS *Tafelberg* bulletin to glean whether any other contestants were moving (they weren't) and realised that we would not now be able to win. The race was a handicap, each ship handicapped on size, and if we didn't move for three days, which we did not, we lost 600 miles which we might have covered whereas a small ship would lose a fraction of that; it's the luck of ocean racing against other classes.

For a day we tried to appease the wind gods; hoisted a nicely roast chicken up to the top of the mainsail, sacrificed a bottle of whisky . . . throwing it overboard with appropriate incantations. Nothing. The wind resumed when it was ready to resume.

We fell out with one another and then fell in again. Every member of the crew put on weight, which is unusual, they said; and I, who had decided to take no sleeping pills on the trip, failed to sleep, lay there on my bunk wishing I had brought a bucketful of Mandrax. When you take pills, you don't dream. Now, when I was not sleeping, I had only to close my eyes to have hallucinations — dreams, I suppose, but so unconvincing that if I did not like them I could open my eyes and start over again. A body needs rest, not sleep. I might have discussed this with the doc, but worried he might give me a lobotomy.

We continued to make good progress, appeared to be ahead of the flotilla, although Eric Tabarly, a sailor all sailors feared, had announced radio failure a week previously and could have been anywhere.

Our first sight of land, two weeks or so after leaving Cape Town, was St Helena, where Napoleon had been imprisoned, and where the term "Hello Sailor" came from. The French Emperor had agreed with his incarcerators that he would be allowed to go to the island's beach each day for one hour of exercise; as a consequence, after luncheon (maybe just lunch) he would summon his guard and say: "*A l'eau; c'est l'heure*." Not many people know that.

Jill and I had arranged to meet in Rio. As I did not know when I would be there, I asked her to listen to the news and fly out when it seemed likely that we would arrive. On her second day in Rio she went to the harbour, met some journalists who said they had heard that a ship had been sighted by a spotter plane and was invited to go along with them while they discovered whether this was a contestant or a fishing vessel. Some 15 miles from the finishing line, then, *Ocean Spirit* encountered the first ship it had seen for twenty-six days and at the helm stood my Jill, waving wildly. It was very moving. *Ocean Spirit* was the first to cross the line, to win what is called "line honours"; on handicap a boat that arrived a couple of weeks later was declared overall winner.

We were feted in the city in which Mardi Gras was about to be celebrated. The British ambassador gave a party for us, sadly not inviting any other guests, so that apart from Jill there were His Excellency, Mrs Excellenc, and the fourteen of us who had actually seen enough of each other and had eaten and drunk quite as well on board as we were now eating and drinking in the embassy.

On the day of our arrival I appeared on local television, a programme I would like to have seen. A TV company researcher had come to the harbour, identified *Ocean Spirit* and called to one of the crew that TV Rio 7 wanted to interview the chef. The crew member, one of the southern Africans, called me. TV Rio 7 inquired whether I was the chef.

"I suppose so," I replied, and was whisked away to the studio.

The Peter Sissons of Brazil asked, "You are the chef of the *Ocean Spirit* which has come first in this prestigious inaugural Cape Town — Rio race?

"Yes."

"What were your thoughts when you left Cape Town in a Force 8 gale? Did you think you would win?"

"I was worrying about whether or not to serve courgettes with the lamb."

"The flotilla sailed to your north. What persuaded you that a southerly course would be advantageous?"

I told him about the jelly.

"And your men — they were obedient, did what they were told?"

"They ate what they were given, mostly," was my response.

The conversation went on for a while, long after I had realised that "chef" in Brazil is the man in charge: probably ended when my interviewer realises that "chef" in English is someone who cooks.

We sold the Black Label at a good price, had a happy time at the carnival, flew home to London and our children and, apart from a summer afternoon at Oulton on the Norfolk Broads, I have not sailed since.

The Cape Town — Rio race reminded me of how much I enjoyed competing. In 1969 the *Daily Mail* announced a transatlantic air race to commemorate the fiftieth anniversary of Alcock and Brown's historic flight. It was in 1919, eight years before Lindbergh famously flew from New York to Paris in the *Spirit of St Louis*, that they became the first men to fly the Atlantic. They took off from Newfoundland, landed in Ireland; the journey took 16 hours 27 minutes in a Vickers Vimy plane and both men were given knighthoods. Alcock died of injuries received in a plane crash later that year — he was twenty-seven. Brown, a Scot, lived on, became manager of an engineering company.

Quite why the starting post for the 1969 race was the top of London's Post Office Tower, the finish Floor 86 of New York's Empire State Building, is anyone's guess, likely to have something to do with sponsorship. To broaden the appeal of the affair there was a passenger category, open to anyone making their way from one eyrie to the other using commercial airlines. Aer Lingus of Ireland sponsored the £5000 first prize — then equal to what I was paid for 250 instalments of *Just a Minute* — and as their rules demanded a stop-over at Shannon, where not too many non-Aer Lingus New York-bound planes stopped, this was probably done to make the prize self-financing. It seemed my sort of contest. I sent off for the full rules.

In London, the top of the Tower was then a Butlin-owned revolving restaurant that was losing money: waiters tended to mislay their customers who had spun 90 degrees between giving their order and chef fashioning their soup. For the air race there was to be a desk with a time stamp for competitors' cards. A similar machine to be installed at the top of the Empire State Building, and the winner would be the one whose card showed the fastest journey.

The check-in time at Heathrow was ten minutes before take-off, so one had to work out the London journey times backwards. On arrival at Kennedy you went for the winning line hell for leather, bearing in mind immigration, customs and Manhattan traffic. I was at the time visiting New York a couple of times a month, sometimes oftener, and thought that would give me an edge. The page on my passport that bore date-stamps over my US visa was so full that if I could by-pass immigration no one could prove that I had not been through.

Aer Lingus announced that during the week of the competition their planes would fly at Mach .95, which is fast, which made Lingus the airline to fly. I also worked out, as did every other serious contestant, that Sundays were the days to fly: fewer planes get "held" over the airport on Sundays, immigration queues are shorter, traffic into the city is lighter. Sunday it would have to be.

Thus, all contestants who had done their homework would have the same in-the-air time, the successful competitor being the one who made the fastest journey from Kennedy to Empire State, having completed the PO Tower to Heathrow journey and made the 11.50 deadline with breakneck speed. Flying was actually irrelevant. Poor Alcock. Poor Brown.

I had a year to work on this, a year in which I got to know the Tower and the Empire State Building on Sundays. I decided that my fastest route in London was to go by motorbike to the nearest point on the Thames where I could "park" a helicopter, discovered how to bike from Heathrow heliport to Aer Lingus check-in, missing stop lights. Gordon White of Hanson's loaned me a Bell Ranger chopper and crew. I hired a grain barge which would be moored off the Embankment, by the Savoy Hotel, on which it could sit. My elder daughter, who was then going out with second-hand car dealers mostly called Roger, knew a coven of ace motorcyclists who could out-perform their peers and I accepted an after-dinner speech for the Metropolitan Police annual dinner in return for a little help with the traffic lights in Gower Street which had to be my route to the river.

They asked for an approximate time.

I explained that this was not a matter of approximation: "I will be there at 11.27.55, and a nod around Trafalgar Square at 11.29.10 would be hugely helpful."

There was much else. My son Dominic's school were recruited to occupy the zebra crossing on the Embankment, so that when I came along eastbound, my driver could make a fast unimpeded U-turn to where the grain barge was moored. Elder daughter Nic rounded up three sirens to be dressed provocatively and start sexually molesting the time-keepers at Lingus check-in in the event of my being a minute late. Nic's friends were eager to help, suggested taking off their bras as a further distraction. I declined the offer.

That was the plan this end. At Kennedy I was going to allow my fellow contestants to storm out of the plane and race for immigration while I donned white overalls, ambled out, got picked up by a tame American Airlines motor car and driven to the Kennedy heliport. I had booked a chopper to fly to 30th Street and an ambulance to take me on from there: a private ambulance which was not allowed to hoot its horn but, under NY law, could flash its lights and have men standing on the running board shouting: "Make way!"

To foil my main adversaries, the highly organised entries from the Royal Marines, Parachute Regiment and Association of British Travel Agents, I had contingency plans to do with sabotaging the Empire State Building lifts.

The doorman at the *Sun* volunteered to be my "heavy".

"Why do I need a heavy?"

"Keep an eye on you — make it hard for the others."

A crucial part of winning is to ensure that the others lose. There is a story about a three-horse race: favourite at even money, second favourite 5–4, outsider at 4–1. Man backed the outsider, which won. When he went to collect his winnings the bookmaker said, "You are very lucky."

"I'm not lucky," said the man.

"You're bloody lucky," said the bookmaker. "I own that outsider."

"I'm not lucky," said the punter. "I own the other two."

In the *Daily Mail* London to New York Air Race, to give the event its full title, I planned to leave the top of the Tower at 11.25 for an 11.50 check-in at Heathrow's Aer Lingus desk. Reach the bottom of the tower: 11.27. Grain barge on the embankment: 11.35. Heathrow heliport and jump on bike: 11.46.

Came the day, my team met at the Post Office Tower for breakfast and champagne at 9.45a.m. There were my heavy, the motorbike men, grain barge man, helicopter crew; Jill, who was to stop the traffic-guiding boys back and forth across the zebra crossing by the river; Jill's sister to stand by; Nic and her girls; my son Dominic and his friend Dominic Faulder, for I had decided to go for the second prize also and keep that in the family; the *Sun* photographer and my osteopath — I had broken my ankle some weeks before and was still limping.

At 10.45 they went off to their destinations, leaving me with my heavy who was to ensure that the Post Office Tower lift would be awaiting me so that I could get an 11.25 time stamp and be in the street two minutes later. My heavy overdid this: hi-jacked the lift at 11.21 when it contained half a dozen contestants, so that when he let it go at 11.25 (a) the six were v. angry with my heavy, (b) they mostly missed their connections and (c) it gave me a four-minute benefit over those who did make check-in.

The trip to the Embankment went smoothly; lights green along Gower Street; nice policeman nodded us through at Trafalgar Square into Northumberland Avenue; Jill's sister waved a red handkerchief as we hit the Embankment so that the queue on the zebra could begin its inexorable crossing and my bike and Dominic's skidded into U-turns. We jumped down the steps, into the helicopter whose engineer held on to me, tugged me in; by the time my feet were inside the machine, we had passed Big Ben.

When I had left the top of the Tower there were only two contestants still to go, both with twin-engined helicopters which are allowed to fly over built-up areas.

As we came in to land at Heathrow heliport there were three bikes revving up, waiting to whizz us to check-in — mine, Dominic's and the Royal Marine's. I heard the controller over the pilot's headphones tell the twin-engined chopper to slide in behind the Bell Ranger (ours), and as we landed Dominic jumped on his bike and I made this fearful mistake: nerves, I suppose. Tugged the helicopter engineer out of the chopper, pushed him on to the back of the Marine's motorbike, jumped on the back of mine and we all zoomed off . . . leaving the Marine abandoned. We made the check-in with nearly sixty seconds to spare, which was long enough to get a hug from Nic and her sirens but not to commiserate with the Marine officer who was hopping up and down with anxiety, also hopping mad.

The next six hours were uneventful, though one man came up and asked me how to get through immigration with minimum delay.

"Tell the US officer that you are English, to take his finger out and get on with it," I advised.

My friend Tom Sutton, ex-head of J. Walter Thompson in London, now in New York, was marvellously helpful. He organised the American Airlines car and the helicopter, found me my ambulance and got hold of a Marine brigadier's uniform so that when the Marine swept into the Empire State Building ahead of the rest of us, he would be able to say, "Well done, Carruthers, use this lift", which had been programmed to stop for ten minutes between floors 45 and 46.

I phoned Tom from our stop in Shannon, told him that Carruthers' challenge had ended but the Parachute

Regiment's 2nd Lieutenant Askham was a danger. Tom said he would change the cap badge, do whatever had to be done.

We made excellent time across the Atlantic flying at Mach 95 (you break the sound barrier at Mach 1), and on the plane they drew lots to determine the order of exit. My number was in the fifties. I disappeared into an aft lavatory, came out in white overalls and sunglasses and a hat, ambled out five minutes after the rush.

Dominic was on the tarmac. We were driven to the heliport, flown to 30th Street and ambulanced to Sixth Avenue, noticing with some concern that the Association of British Travel Agents' competitor, who had gone down with me in the Post Office Tower lift, was now sitting on the pillion of a motorbike that was travelling in our slipstream.

The Empire State Building on a Sunday afternoon is not a buzzy place. Tom in his uniform gave me a formal nod and a thumbs-up — he had got someone in his demon lift, just hoped it was the right man. ABTA man and Dominic and I ran for the fast lift which made it nonstop to the 70th floor and all three of us made it, though ABTA man — who was twice my size and four times Dominic's — tried to keep us out, took a dominant part in the ascent, scowling and muttering. Sixteen floors to go.

I managed to press the 84th floor button without ABTA man seeing me, and as the doors opened he raced out and I pressed the "Close doors" button. Sadly, he realised his mistake, came crashing back into the elevator and, by virtue of his size and my limp, beat me to the time-stamp machine when we reached our destined level; he stood in front of it, glared at me, waited, then finally put in his card, got his stamp and slouched off. I stuck in my card, Dominic his. Had ABTA man stamped his card, then stopped me from stamping mine for a few minutes, he would have won.

I won. Dominic was third. The Parachute Regiment officer appeared later, said he would kill whoever had sabotaged the lift and the ABTA man said he would get me disqualified. Tom and Dominic and I celebrated, phoned home the good news and went out to dinner. Some months later, at the presentation of awards by Prince Philip, Dominic and his friend accepted the prize for me.

At the time I was on a lecture tour in Oregon. I had discovered lecture tours: was handsomely paid to speak about "The Influence of the *Mayflower* on US Cookery" for forty-five minutes, then answer questions, all of which were the same, none dealing with my speech:

"Did you know your grandfather?"

It was marginally preferable to being asked about the bloodhound.

CHAPTER
TWELVE

In which, having run what I thought was the best club in London, I join what Dickens called the best club in London.

When your face becomes public, people recognise it without necessarily being able to place it. "I'm sure we know each other; I'm from Pontefract" is not unusual. There is a lot of: "You're famous; remind me who you are", and if you say, "Clement Freud" you are as likely to get "Oh, no, you're not" as "I bet you wish you were". I find "Are you who I think you are?" a pathetic greeting, though a woman once approached me with the words "Are you who I think I am?", which was not without charm. A clergyman came up to me in a train in Yorkshire, told me I was the first famous person he had ever met. I said, kindly I thought, "You must have lived a very sheltered life", and tears came into his eyes and I had to go to the buffet car and buy him a cup of tea.

When you have appeared on TV a lot, people feel they know you. I was connected with cookery, dog food, children's TV, panel games and not laughing. Non-viewers had read me in national newspapers and magazines; non-viewers, non-readers recognised my voice from Radio 3 and 4 and sports commentaries and

Just a Minute and a Saturday evening programme in which I talked about the week, interviewed personalities, played records requested by listeners, gave racing tips and on one occasion did the shipping forecast.

My voice, apparently, did not lend itself to hard news such as that; after I had told listeners that there was "a terrifically strong wind from the south-east and do please be careful, especially in Sea Areas Fisher, Dogger and German Bight, wherever they may be", word came from on high that I was never to do the shipping forecast again. Apparently I had not been believed: navigators had thought, "That's Freud being funny" and crashed into each other all over the North Sea where the wind had been as strong as I had said.

In 1973 I did a three-week lecture tour on the west coast of the USA, was doing *Just a Minute* on Radio 4, TV shows like *Call My Bluff* and *Tell the Truth*, also guest appearances on shows with Bob Monkhouse, Frankie Howerd, David Frost, David Jacobs, Ernie Wise Derek Nimmo and Les Dawson; I made frequent and well-paid after-dinner speeches, was a panellist on a talent show called *New Faces* in which we discovered Showwaddywaddy, was writing cookery and sport and City and humour, playing cricket for the Lords Taverners and enjoying my wife and growing family. Fame had made me difficult. I could not stand being near tobacco smoke, loathed the taste and smell of garlic, had become paranoid about Dr Scholl sandals. If there is something wrong with a person's feet it should be between them and their lower extremities; I wanted to be uninvolved. My commercial had been shown for years and years, world without end . . . and people who did not poke me in the ribs saying, "It's him" asked after the health of my dog.

Remembering what my father had said about the unsuitability of Stephen, Lucian or myself for his own profession, I kept an eye on my children's achievements to see whether I might not have spawned a great chef or hotelier or hack. Nicky was into horses and boys, Dominic into banking and stockbroking and backgammon; Emma was always going to be an actress and Matthew was unpredictable: I thought he would either end up in prison . . . gave him a hessian suit with black arrows for his fourteenth birthday . . . or run the world. At the age of ten he bought two dozen white mice for £1, went to our local fair and sold them for 25p each to children who, within ten minutes, came back to say, "Mum won't let me keep this mouse — will you take it back?" Refund was not a word in my youngest son's vocabulary. When he was eighteen I thought he had found his vocation: he learnt to roller-skate, bought a hideous brown fur skin and went around delivering Gorillagrams. I sometimes saw him skating along Hyde Park Carriage Drive and gave him a lift . . . though it was not always Matthew inside the skin.

In 1973 it was clearly time for their father to do something else.

My friend Tim Beaumont had bought the Liberal Party. I was a huge admirer of Jo Grimond, the leader before the then incumbent, Jeremy Thorpe, who was also an acquaintance and a favourite man to sit near at dinner parties. While in the Army in Germany in 1945,

I had got two weeks' leave to campaign (against the Conservative Party, especially at Woodford where Churchill was seeking re-election) and my credentials as a Liberal were impeccable. My father had voted Liberal: "They have no policies either, but tend to be nicer people." Every caterer should be a Liberal, for it upsets no customers and absolves you from succinct promises — not that political promises are binding, but site valuation rating annoys few, unlike restoration of the death penalty.

Tim Beaumont's father had been a Conservative MP, left Tim a trust which was not, like other trusts, invested in War Loan 3½ but was dangerously chancey, with shares in speculative companies like Marks and Spencers, ICI and *Daily Mail*. So when Tim left Oxford to become deputy assistant chaplain to the Bishop of Hong Kong and vicar of Kowloon, home of Sam the tailor who makes my inexpensive suits, he was oozing money from every orifice. Back in England he bought *Time and Tide*, a weekly magazine for which I had become cookery correspondent, and a stunning house in Mayfair, which, on my first visit, I thought to be a Club and asked whether Tim Beaumont was on the premises. When the Liberals were staring bankruptcy in the face he saved them and, by a curious coincidence, became Lord Beaumont of Whitley.

He moved to an amazing house in Hampstead, in the gardens of which he gave Liberal parties where I took over the barbecue. He also persuaded me to give a dinner party for the Liberals in my house in Suffolk, which was a great success. We had a terrine that I made from hare and venison with juniper berries and marjoram set in a jelly of dry Madeira; home-baked walnut bread with it. Then sides of wild salmon with asparagus hollandaise and new potato and chive salad, followed by an alcoholic fruit jelly and a brilliant matured Cheddar from a Mr Green who is master of his trade around Wells in Somerset. Much wine. No fuss. Eighty people, three waiters, and people stayed to help with the washing up.

Tim took me to a Liberal Assembly in Scotland and Nigel Lawson, my ex-waitress's husband, now editor of the *Spectator*, commissioned me to write a *Which?*-type assessment of the three party conferences. I gave the Liberals 7½ out of 10.

In the spring of 1973 I read of the death of Sir Harry Legge-Bourke, MP for the Isle of Ely and the only man who in the post-war election of 1945 had won a seat for the Conservatives from a sitting Lib or Lab member. He had been an honourable if silent MP, famously remembered for being banned from the Palace of Westminster for four days in his first Parliament. Prime Minister Attlee had been talking at the despatch box when from the back benches Major Legge-Bourke had thrown a penny towards the PM, managed to get it to bounce off the despatch box and hit Attlee in the chest. He called out: "Change the bloody record." This was thought to have been his longest utterance in the House to date. He was led away by the Serjeant at Arms and the people in the Isle thought their man a hell of a guy and voted for him ever after.

The Isle of Ely is 450 square miles of flatlands and wetlands. Highest mountain 128 feet above sea level; central and most populated town March, a railway town; second largest town Wisbech, which is fruit-growing; there are also Chatteris, the capital of carrots; Whittlesey, which has brickworks; and Ely, a very small cathedral city.

Conservative for twenty-eight years, it had never returned a member from the Left. At the 1970 election the sitting member had won by some ten thousand votes in a straight fight against Labour; in 1966 a Liberal had stood and done pathetically. That was the history.

Ted Heath, inventor of the three-day week, was Prime Minister. Harold Wilson, who had lost the 1970 election narrowly, mostly because it was just after England's failure to hold on to the World Cup and the pipe smoker had identified himself with the England team who were to bring the trophy back to a Downing Street reception, was not a notable commander of the Opposition. I thought the seat was winnable.

In 1970 the Liberals had returned only six members to Westminster, all for central constituencies as Jo Grimond explained to me: Orkney and Shetland, centre of the oil industry; Inverness, centre of northern Scotland; Roxburgh, Selkirk and Peebles, centre of the Borders; Montgomery, centre of Welsh sheep farming; North Devon, centre of the West Country holiday trade; and North Cornwall, centre of tin mining. Since 1970 Cyril Smith had won Rochdale, and Graham Tope had been successful in Sutton and Cheam.

Liberals were on the up, if you could call having eight out of 650 MPs "on the up". Let us examine my experience of Westminster and the constituency I hoped to represent.

I had been to the House of Commons once, for an article in the *Daily Telegraph* on "How to Lobby Your MP". My member had been Wavell Wakefield, whose election address was wondrously simple: "WAVELL WAKEFIELD. YOUR CONSERVATIVE CANDIDATE. CAPTAINED MIDDLESEX, THE RAF, ENGLAND AND THE BARBARIANS AT RUGBY. NEED YOU LOOK FURTHER?" He stormed into the House with solid majorities at every election, as would have the pillar-box outside where we lived, had it been painted blue.

I had gone to Westminster, filled in a card with his name on it and after an hour and a bit he limped into the lobby and said, "Mr Frood".

I shook his hand, asked him how he was.

He said, "Fine, except for my legs."

"No national problems?"

Sir Wavell said there were none.

We looked at each other and he suggested I might like to have a ticket for the gallery. One was found and I was rather impressed that, from where I was placed, I could only see one side of the House — the Conservative side. Wakefield, I decided, was brighter than he looked.

Nor did I know the Isle of Ely very well, though I had driven through the southern parts of it on my way from Walberswick to the Boxing Day race meeting at Huntingdon.

I was in New York when I saw Sir Harry's obituary and telephoned Jeremy Thorpe, asked whether he might put a word in for me as the Lib candidate. He said that if he as much as mentioned a name, the local Liberals would consider that to be unwarranted interference from headquarters and ignore that person as a consequence.

"What shall I do, then?"

"Write to the chairman of the Isle of Ely Liberal Association, that's what."

The chairman's name was Russell, a fifty-plus-year-old probation officer who wore a wig and had a Greek wife. I wrote to him, he telephoned me back, we agreed a time for an interview. I was met at Ely Station by a girl who said, "Are you nervous?" (I said, "No", for I was not), and got taken to the Russell house where Mrs Russell had baked some really good cakes and there were four Liberals including the president, a carrot grower of the old school who was also president of the Salvation Army.

They asked how long I had been a Liberal. I replied that I had only ever been a Liberal and was forty-nine years old. The president asked whether I thought I would be able to represent minorities ... like Methodists. I told him that when it came to minorities I could outperform most.

Mr Russell said that the reason they were not asking me more questions was that they knew all about me. The girl, who opined that I really had not been nervous, "not like the other two who have come for interviews", drove me back to Ely Station. I wrote to Mr Russell, thanking him for seeing me, pointing out that if I did get selected as Liberal candidate I would be happy to pay my own election costs — money, currently, was in reasonable supply — and told Tim that my toe was on the ladder. Tim said that if I was selected, he would come and help.

During the next week I was back in New York and Mr Russell was succeeded as chairman by Mr Burall, a high-powered printer who employed busloads of men and women and had cornered the market in printing labels for horticulturalists. People spoke well of him. He telephoned me on my return and asked whether I might come to the selection meeting for the Liberal candidate on Sunday evening, at the Griffin Hotel in March, like at 7p.m. when there would be two other candidates. I was to speak for some fifteen minutes on any aspect of Liberal policy that I wished and then be prepared to answer questions.

I agreed. On that Sunday I drove to Cambridgeshire after lunch to do a reconnaisance.

The first thing you notice is that it is flat; that on Sundays the district is full of fishermen from Sheffield competition-fishing on the canals which are called drains, as in the 30 Foot and the 40 Foot, and were designed by the Dutch whose engineers drained the Fen in the sixteenth century; before that you needed webbed feet to get around. William the Conqueror did not "take" the Isle of Ely until fifteen years into his reign because his men had no wellingtons.

The local people are quiet, private: if there is someone in a bank they queue outside, not wanting to be thought to transgress on others' financial business; and when they retire they call it straightening up, as in no longer bending over your spade. It is the land of Ethelred and Oliver Cromwell, which is why streets and pubs and housing estates and churches are named St Ethelreda, Cromwell College, Oliver Place, et al.

The majority of incomers to the Isle were people who had got into financial trouble in the prosperous South of England, had been told by their bank managers that the way to fiscal salvation was to sell up and buy a cheap house in North Cambridgeshire. Houses were cheap then.

When I went to my first interview I was standing on the platform at Cambridge and heard the announcement: "Ely Manea March". On that Sunday I drove into the Fen to find Manea, a remote village between the cathedral city and the shunting yard town, had a cup of tea in a café there and chatted to a local man.

"Not a lot going on today," I said.

"Not ever. Where you from?"

"London."

He was impressed; had been to London twice, wouldn't want to go again, but travel was something he couldn't get enough of.

"Have you been out of England?"

"No, but I've been to Yorkshire."

I heard a story about a Fenman who had a truck and took loads of whatever to wherever. One day someone asked him if he'd take a load of wood to London.

"Yes," said the Fenman. "Where's London?"

They told him to drive towards Peterborough and then turn left — "can't miss it, not with all those tall buildings".

He was loaded up with wood and set off; took a turn to the left before Peterborough, drove south, saw all those big buildings after about an hour, lowered his window and asked a man standing on the pavement, "Is this London?"

"You want to go on a bit," said the man. "This is Luton."

So the man with the wood drove on, found some more large buildings and traffic lights and policemen, all things there aren't a lot of in the Fen, lowered his window and said to a man on the pavement, "Is this London?"

"It's Watford," said the man. "You want to drive on a bit."

And finally the Fenman found himself on the Embankment, St Paul's Cathedral behind him, the river and the National Theatre in front, and he lowered his window and said to a man on the pavement, "Is this London?"

"Yes," said the man.

"Where d'ye want the wood?"

I was beginning to get on the wavelength of the Isle: laid back, partisan, awkward, hospitable. At 6p.m. I drove into Chatteris, asked at a hotel if I might have a bath and change into a suit, and they were kind and helpful and I arrived at the Griffin in March at the appointed hour. I was to be the second candidate to appear before the selectors, was asked to wait with the third while they quizzed the first. There was, they explained, a delay.

I drank a small glass of whisky, asked the barman how many people were in the large room.

He said there had been eight for quite a long time, "but now there are some more, from the old people's home across the road, I think, so now there'll be a better audience than there might have been. Do you sing?"

I said not; not often, not tonight anyway.

He wished me luck in whatever I was doing.

I was called into the room after about an hour. Mr Burall asked me to give my name, "as if we did not know who you are", then discuss the aspect of Liberal policy as requested.

"Clement Freud," I said. "I am grateful to you for interviewing me. It does not seem to me of much consequence to tell others who share your politics what it is that attracts us to particular policies . . . so I want to tell you why I think you should select me to stand at the by-election. This is what they call a safe Conservative seat, has been for fifty years but for the time Jimmy de Rothschild bought it for the Liberals in 1935.

"Today there is either a Liberal come-back . . . look at Rochdale, and Sutton and Cheam . . . or such disenchantment with the Government of the day and the yapping Opposition that people would vote for anyone untainted by Heath conservatism or Wilson socialism.

"The Tories have selected their man, a Londoner, a political adviser to the Prime Minister's office at Downing Street; and Labour, who have never held this seat, chose their candidate last week — neither of them East Anglians like me. The writ for the election is expected to be moved when Parliament reassembles after the summer recess. But I believe that, when the Conservatives learn this will be a three-party affair and that a reasonably well-known person is standing for the Liberals, they will want to prevent us from gathering momentum and call an immediate election, possibly moving the writ this Thursday for a by-election three weeks later.

"Were that to happen, and I think it will, the fact that people know me, albeit for other than political achievements, is going to make it much easier for me to get votes. I have travelled around the Isle today and people in the Fen know who I am. If selected I will not have to explain that I am called Clement, have the honour to be the Liberal candidate at the by-election, because it will be all over the papers.

"Fellow Liberals," I continued (Conservatives called their supporters "Ladies and gentlemen", Labour called them "Brothers"), "please select me. I have been successful in a number of fields, I would like to become a Member of Parliament, your Member of Parliament, and work for you to the very best of my ability.

"I am now ready to take any questions."

There were no questions. I had been in for a scarce five minutes.

I thanked my audience for hearing me out and, as I left, Mr Burall was telling them that Clement Freud might be well known on television and radio and among comedians and bloodhounds but this was serious politics and "our candidate must be a serious politican who will devote his time to us and the Liberal cause".

As I was within earshot and had little to lose I went back into the room. "Mr Chairman," I said, "I heard what you said, not because I was eavesdropping but because the walls of the hotel are thin . . . I want to make quite sure that it is understood that, if selected, I will take this job more seriously than I have ever taken anything in my life", and went back to the sitting-out room.

Candidate No.3 left for his interview. I waited for forty-five minutes, decided to call it a night, drove back to London.

Jill, who was in William Douglas Home's *Dame of Sark* in the West End, but not on Sundays, was waiting up for me.

"How did it go?"

"It didn't," I said.

"Do you want to tell me about it?"

"I'd rather have a hot whisky and aspirin."

Mr Burall, decent chap that he was, telephoned me the next morning. "You didn't wait for the vote last night."

"I saw the writing on the wall."

"Would you be surprised to learn that you were selected?"

"Amazed. How did they vote?"

"You got it by 13 votes to 8. Candidate No. 1 decided not to push her nomination, so it was between you and Penwarden."

Not being a noisy person I gave a silent whoop and tried not to think about the eight people who were at the Griffin before reinforcement of troops from the old people's home across the road. But the thought crossed my mind that I might just be the first candidate of a political party not to have been endorsed by the chairman, vice-chairman, president, political adviser, treasurer, secretary, and the canvassing officers for the south and north of the constituency.

If someone were to ask me what was the defining week of my life, that first week of July 1973 would be right up there. On the Sunday I was interviewed by the Isle of Ely Liberal Association and drove home, believing I had failed. On the Monday the chairman of the said Association rang to tell me I had been selected. On the Thursday the Leader of the House of Commons moved the writ for the by-election for 26 July (I was in New York at the time), so on Friday, 6 July I came back. On the Saturday I went to an estate agent in March and asked him to find me an office; he said I was to leave it to him, I had come to the right person and good luck.

I went to a caff for a cup of tea and the woman behind the counter welcomed me, we chatted, and when I told her about my need for an office she said, "Until you find one you can use the shed at the end of the drive." She showed it to me. It was a broom cupboard of a place, about 8 foot by 10. Knowing a bit about politics I went out and bought a kettle, a carton of PG teabags, a pint of milk, eight mugs and a box of assorted biscuits, borrowed a table and two chairs. And I then adjourned to March marketplace and shook hands with people, explaining that I was the Liberal candidate and hearing them say, "I know, it was in the local paper. Good luck." I drove on to Wisbech, where I met David Burall and Paul Coulten, his vice-chairman. We went to Wisbech market where they introduced me to people; I bought haslet at a pork butcher's in the marketplace and when I had eaten a few slices on the hoof, as it were, bought strawberries from a barrow.

"Local strawberries," said the woman.

"Wouldn't eat any other," I said, and she wished me good luck. "Read about what you're doing in the local paper."

David Burall gave me a copy of the electoral register, which was massive (sixty-nine thousand names); he and his wife were going on holiday that night and offered me the use of their house. I accepted. Drove back to London via March, where I called on the estate agent.

"Any luck with an office for me?"

"Expect to hear any time now," he said.

I gave him my London phone number, told him he could ring me at any time of day or night.

Liberal Party HQ provided me with an agent called Terry, who was quiet and efficient and could start on Monday. I told him about the shed/shack with the kettle and that by Tuesday we would almost certainly have a proper office. Had dinner with Tim Beaumont,

296

who said that he could take a couple of weeks off (off being a millionaire), and I thanked him warmly and spent the weekend cancelling appointments and ringing friends, asking them to come to the Isle of Ely to help me if they had time to spare.

"Where's the Isle of Ely?" was the general response.

"Just up the A1 — get there in an hour."

It took an hour and a half on a good day. I was beginning to behave like a real politician.

Inheriting a constituency is like being given a sackful of assorted Christmas presents; you begin by saying, "Thank you, this is just what I wanted", and then you rummage. The Isle started north of Cambridge and stretched to the Lincolnshire border; the eastern boundary was Norfolk. To the west, I stopped 6 miles short of Peterborough in a village called Thorney. There was a lot of rummaging to do. In Thorney we had a Liberal councillor, whom I met, who was Liberal the way Attila the Hun was Liberal. In the 450 square miles there were thirty villages and many hamlets; there would be ninety-one polling stations, which meant that on election day, when candidates are expected to shake hands with the staff at each, I would have ten minutes per station, not counting time taken to cover the 160 miles criss-crossing north-east Cambridgeshire.

On Monday morning I was back at the estate agent in March ("No joy yet, but it's in hand"); met Terry in the broom cupboard, had a telephone installed there and found willing helpers with front rooms and telephones in Ely, Chatteris, Wisbech and Whittlesey. On Tuesday I discovered Littleport, which was agricultural and had some four thousand voters. I hadn't realised it was mine. That first week was spent organising posters (David Burall's company did that quickly and brilliantly) and hiring halls throughout the Isle for evening meetings, of which Terry and Tim decided I should have three a night.

We leafleted every house in the neighbourhood of the meeting hall with details of when and where I would address them and giving phone numbers of my various "offices", should they have any reason to want to contact me. Burall's printed orange and black posters that announced: "MEETING TONIGHT" and we filled in the time and place.

The bandwagon grew. Publicans, pensioners, schoolmasters, window cleaners, housewives and their children, small farmers whose grandparents had benefited from Lloyd George's "two acres of land and a cow" legislation after the First World War, probation officers alerted by Tom Russell of Ely, all came out of the woodwork, arrived at the shed/shack in March or rang Terry and offered help. Driving around the constituency, it was hard not to notice that every field, most lamp-posts and hedges and all large houses were going to vote Conservative: blue "Vote Stevens CONSERVATIVE" posters proliferated.

It was on Tuesday afternoon, sixteen days before polling day, that I learnt that the March estate agent, he who was finding me an office, was in fact chairman of the local Tory Party; Terry said he was happy in the broom cupboard, so we bought some more mugs. Terry said that smallness was actually helpful — when people

298

came in to offer help, they were given a quick cup of tea and instantly despatched with a local register to canvas; "If it's too comfortable, they stay and chat." The broom cupboard was not comfortable. As the summer of 1973 was warm and sunny we put up desks in the passage that led to it. Our posters arrived on D-Day minus 14, as did car stickers and rosettes, and we did our best to give them away and persuade people to put them in their windows. Having an orange and black car sticker on your windscreen was like belonging to an exclusive club. You saw it from afar and waved, knowing it was going to be a friend.

Five days into canvassing I was at a filling station, buying two gallons of petrol (that way I could patronise lots of filling stations and have chats with their owners and staff), when I saw a car with a "Freud Liberal" sticker whose driver I did not know. He came up to me; I said, "I'm sorry, I can't remember your name", and he said, "We haven't met, but good luck."

I was incredibly chuffed, drove past a hundred blue posters decorating fields and hedges and felt I was in with a chance. Someone had come out; nearly two weeks to go, and there might well be others.

Terry and Tim in the broom cupboard now managed my life. We had a press conference at 9a.m., having met at 8 to agree the agenda, discuss Liberal education policy, announce the numbers who had come to last night's meetings, respond to newspaper reports about my rival candidates, which parliamentary dignitaries would come and visit . . . Thorpe, Pardoe, Steel and Smith were scheduled, 50 per cent of the entire party at

Westminster . . . and then I would perform factory visits, school visits, old people's homes visits, afternoon canvasses joining teams in towns and villages. They would knock and ask whether the householder would like to meet me and I would be there to shake their hand and ask them to vote.

I never asked anyone to vote for me, for that seemed an intrusion. "You will vote, won't you? None of the candidates would be pleased to win on a really small turnout." Had I been more experienced, I might have said that this election is nationally meaningless but I am older than the other candidates, will look after you better and if you don't like what I do, kick me out at the next election. Instead I outlined site valuation rating, proportional representation ("What would that do?" . . . "Get more Liberals into the House of Commons" . . . "Then what?" . . . "Haven't worked that out yet").

I was lucky fighting a by-election when I did, for neither Tory nor Labour had much going for them. As for us Liberals, our main attraction was that we were neither Labour nor Conservative.

Each evening I held three meetings: 7p.m., 8p.m. and 9p.m. In different locations, none more than 10 miles from the last. At the first meeting the local chairman — anyone locally who had been unearthed by the canvassers, otherwise Tim Beaumont or David Burall — would introduce me. Then I spoke, answered questions and, while the chairman summed up and asked people who had come to the meeting to help canvass, put up posters, distribute stickers, write

300

envelopes for the election address, I was off to the next meeting where the chairman was treading water awaiting my arrival. Then on to the final meeting followed by drinks in the local pub — one drink per pub so that no one could accuse me of favouritism.

In my first week of meetings I talked a bit about making life better for the Third World, accepting Vietnamese refugees, saving public money by merging embassies (what is the point of having one in each of Luxembourg, Liechtenstein and Andorra?) and de-privatising Water Authorities. Big Yawns. So I sounded off about regional excellence: in Doddington there was a woman who made wonderful horseradish cream, and stressed the importance of the Community, based on the cornerstones of the school, the church, the shop and the pub, all of which had to be fought for. Hands off our primary schools, long live small shopkeepers, relax our licensing laws. That worked, as did my faith in the encouragement of regional accents, rather than teach everyone to talk like newsreaders.

I did not realise about meetings; their strength is that you hold them, that there are posters in the street and announcements in the local papers that you will be there. Those who actually attend are either supporters who applaud anything you say, however foolish, or enemies who sit sullenly silent and then bombard you with prearranged, complicated questions. The National Farmers' Union, a deeply Conservative institution, felt that returning a Tory was essential to their wellbeing and stalked me. At every meeting there would be representatives wearing blue rosettes, waiting for me to finish so that they could start.

"Mr Freud, if you were elected to Parliament, what would you do about the quota for sugar beet?" (The fact was that if I got to Parliament, the Conservatives would still have their majority and the answer was "nothing".)

"Do you grow sugar beet?" I asked one such questioner.

"Yes, sir."

"Do you grow much sugar beet?"

"Few hundred acres."

"Well, what I would urge a Liberal Government to do is compulsorily purchase sugar beet crops from farmers stupid enough to ask MPs for their advice."

I learnt a lot from meetings. Never hold them in primary schools because the chairs are too small for comfort. When people sit in the back rows, as political audiences try to, make your speech from the first row that is unoccupied. Do your homework about the town or village and blind them with your knowledge of their problems, their history, their achievements ("Very proud to be in the village that got into the semi-final of the Cambridgeshire Hospitals Cup last year").

I found that saying, "I don't know, but if you vote for me and I get into Parliament I shall find out" actually worked . . . although in the Tory manual of fighting elections they tell candidates "not to emulate Freud in admissions of ignorance". And jokes, which are discouraged on the hustings, are helpful. In the railway town of March I was asked how I thought I could represent their interests, "you knowing fuck all squared about railways", and I replied, "Let me remind you that I come from a railway family. My grandfather was Signalman Freud." Even the ranks of ASLEF could scarce forbear a smile.

And I learnt from canvassing: talk to people on the doorstep; when they ask you in for a cup of tea, it is because they have been told by their political master that the more enemy candidates' time they take up, the better their own man will do.

Learn the electoral register so that you know not only the names of the people in the house you canvass, but that of their neighbours. Registers give dates of birth of those about to reach voting age. Make use of that. "Will Theresa three doors down invite you to her party next month?"

What tends to happen is that you knock on the door and the house-holder leaps out of the chair in which you saw him/her sit and hides under the settee. I used to take that as an indication that they were not keen to be canvassed and I believe you get more support going away than pushing your luck. I had with me small printed sheets stating, "I called on you to discuss the forthcoming election and I am sorry I missed you", which I topped and tailed on the doorstep before pushing the completed missive through the letter-box for the voter to read after getting up from under the settee.

Ten days before polling day most Sunday papers had reports from the Ely by-election and on Monday morning Tim Beaumont phoned me from London to say bad news; Ladbroke's had opened a book on the event and the Libs were 33–1 against. I thanked him, phoned Ladbroke's, and two minutes later rang Tim and told him I was now 8–1.

The *Daily Telegraph* opined the following morning that "In the Isle of Ely the clever money appears to be going on Freud." In fact it was the Freud money that had gone on Freud, but it made people aware that the election was not the absolutely foregone certainty it had been forecast to be. "I welcome the jocular irrelevance of Mr Freud's candidature," the Tory chosen to step into Sir Harry Legge-Bourke's safe seat had announced at the time of my selection.

This might be a good time to profile my opponents: John Stevens, Conservative, 1-8 with Ladbroke's (put down £8 to get £9 back) was thirty-five, a stockbroker, former assistant to Ted Heath, a paradigmatic machine man who had stood against Roy Jenkins in the 1970 general election. He was a young politician of the old school. "What would you do about roads in the Isle?" someone asked him at a meeting in the village of Sutton.

He replied, "That's a very good question, because I have a son who rides a tricycle and when I come to live here, as I hope to very soon, my son will be nearly old enough to ride a bicycle. I am therefore highly interested in roads and am pleased to be able to reassure the questioner on that point."

There were a reputed ten thousand members of the Isle's Conservative clubs and only two communities with populations over five hundred did not have a local branch.

Barry Young — an attractive, bearded, one-time Labour organiser in Bury St Edmunds and prior to that in Buckingham — was currently a rep for a pharmaceutical firm who had given him unpaid leave of absence to fight the election. He was honest, sincere, intelligent, articulate and would have made an excellent MP. There were five Labour clubs in the Isle, but while Stevens stayed with Tory supporters Young, who was quoted at 4–1 (invest one pound, get a fiver back), had brought a caravan which he parked in a supporter's field in which he slept. He blamed the Heath Government for most ills and promised that a Labour administration would bring in food subsidies and be helpful in renegotiating sugar beet agreements when they came up for review.

Prior to the election, I had sailed across the Channel with Ted Heath and played golf in the Scilly Isles with Harold Wilson, been supportive rather than passionate about the Liberals, had not realised that on the ground there are Conservative supporters as egregiously odious as they turned out to be. Call on a Labour household and they say, "Sorry, I vote Labour" and will listen when you explain that, if they want to get rid of the Conservatives, only a Liberal vote will make this happen. Conservatives slam the door in your face — if they open it in the first place. We had loudspeaker vans which we used to publicise meetings; Conservatives followed these vans and drowned our message with better-class speaker equipment. In some ways it was rewarding to be taken sufficiently seriously for overt beastliness, but this was a balmy English summer and while I poked fun at my opponents they replied with vitriol.

I explained at a morning press conference that on the previous afternoon I had witnessed Stevens calling to his wife in an upstairs window in Wisbech (Stevens' speeches tended to conform to a similar pattern): "Roneo, Roneo, wherefore art thou . . .?" Stevens replied at his own morning conference that "Mr Freud is cheapening the country's political tradition and indulging in un-British personal criticism." Fancy that: criticism of a politician, whatever next?

In the last week of the campaign there was hardly a newspaper that did not have on-the-spot reports from the Isle of Ely. The *Economist* wrote, "It is difficult to see how with such organisation and a near ten thousand majority at the last election Mr Stevens can fail to win, but Freud is moving up."

Terry told me that the Fen village of Manea had sent a man to fetch two hundred "Vote Clement Freud Liberal" posters. He had pointed out that this was one for every other house, and the man had said, "That's right." When depressed, after driving through roads flanked by blue posters, I would drive east and luxuriate in the sight of Manea bathed in the glow of orange and black. I tried to canvass there. "Go elsewhere," said a householder, "You'll get the votes in Manea. It's the other places that need persuading."

My big guns arrived in the final week. Cyril Smith, of booming voice and vast political experience, emerged from a car only just big enough to take him and wowed the electorate. David Steel was more contained but entirely persuasive about the need for the party at Westminster to be strengthened by this good man from this great constituency with its historical Liberal connections. John Pardoe, our Treasury spokesman, came and waxed eloquent about Liberty, Fraternity and Equality to some 250 Chatteris voters who would otherwise have watched television. And Jeremy Thorpe did two meetings: a massive one in Wisbech and an amazing one at the Maltings in Ely where five hundred people jostled to get in and he finished with the words: "If you elect Clement Freud no one in Britain is going to ask, 'Who is the Member of Parliament for the Isle of Ely?' " He was cheered into the night.

My elder daughter had an on-going relationship with *Playboy*'s travel editor and, while with him in the United States, had been persuaded to pose naked with two large black gentlemen. A magazine whose name escapes me had published this under the heading of "FREUDIAN DREAM" and a March Conservative, presumably a subscriber, went canvassing, showing voters the pictures, asking them; "Would you want an MP whose daughter appears in pornographic publications?" Two decent Tories telephoned me to apologise for this: it certainly did nothing to promote Mr Stevens, the enemy of un-British personal criticism.

Nor did Anglia Television's Friday-before-the-election political programme help their cause. The TV company had invited the three candidates, each with six supporters, to come to the Norwich studio. The programme's anchorman would pick a supporter of his choice to ask a question — either of his man or of one of the others — and get the other candidates to comment. In the half-hour there was to be time for four questions from each party, and before transmission we sat in a local hostelry debating what questions to put and to whom.

A Conservative supporter chosen by the anchorman asked me about sugar beet, which was silly because by then I knew about sugar beet, quotas, profitability, et al. Halfway through, a Whittlesey supporter of mine was requested to put his question: he asked Mr Stevens what, if he were elected, he would do about MAGPAS.

Stevens was on the button. Very much in favour; a supporter; under-funded at the moment but he would do his best to get Government to reconsider support.

Asked to comment, I risked such political future as I might have had, turned to Stevens and said, "You are a liar. You don't support MAGPAS. You don't know what MAGPAS is. You are wholly bogus."

Stevens lost his calm. "Of course I know what it is." His face turned pale.

Me: "What?"

He: "It's one of those agricultural organisations."

Me: "It is the Mid-Anglian General Practitioners' Accident Service."

My supporters cheered. The Labour Party supporters cheered. The audience cheered.

On the drive home I asked Dr Pulvertaft, the originator of the question, how many voters would have watched the programme. He said, "All of them, and the ones who did not will be told." He was right.

On the following Monday Ladbroke's marked me down 6–1, Stevens 1–3.

"What would you have answered?" asked a journalist at the morning press conference.

"I would have said, 'I don't know', which you have been accusing me of saying to most questions."

I drove through the towns and villages of the Isle and now people waved. I went into shops and pubs and folk came up and shook my hand. Canvass returns swung our way: "won't votes" became "won't says"; "don't knows" now let themselves be registered as possible Liberals, and over and over again canvassers reported that Conservatives had told them, "I wish Freud were a Conservative — I'd vote for him then."

In the *New Statesman* Alan Watkins wrote of the campaign that there were two good messengers without a policy and a good policy needing a messenger. Stevens had been imposed on the Isle by Central Office . . . a plum bad choice to have a smooth identikit Tory carpet-bagger to succeed a bluff, honest gentleman farmer who never made a speech but that he pulled a piece of paper out of his pocket, announced that "I've just made a few notes" and read it. The previous Member's appeal was that he was "different", the way Fen people are "different". Stevens was like all the other politicians. I made much of that: explained at meetings that he wore a campaign button bearing his photograph so that he would remember what he looked like.

He looked increasingly apprehensive and on one occasion, watching his supporters rushing him around Ely market in a camouflage jacket, I came by with my loudspeaker van and announced that, camouflage jacket or not, I could see him. "The disguise doesn't work, the way Tory policies don't work."

At my selection interview — it seemed a hundred years ago but was actually three weeks as we entered the final campaigning days — what I had promised about being recognised and welcomed became abundantly evident. In the *Statesman* Watkins wrote: "Mr Freud is the image made flesh. Small boys ask for his autograph, mothers hold their infants aloft so that they can get a better view of him and men thrust themselves forward to shake his hand and wish him the best of luck. He has no difficulty in drawing audiences of 150 in small villages while Mr Stevens draws 50, Mr Young half that figure." Watkins also opined that, if the election had been one week earlier, Stevens would have walked it; now he was not so sure.

On the Saturday before polling day there had been a Liberal Regional Assembly in Cambridge and I went over, spoke to them about my by-election and promised that, if any of them came across to help canvass, I would, if they wished, come to their constituencies and help during the next election. Some twenty of them came and were invaluable, teaching my home-grown canvassers a thing or two. Nancy Seear, later leader of the Liberals in the House of Lords, deserves particular praise: she was able to go into an empty house and emerge, two minutes later, with three Liberal converts.

On the eve of polling day we had a rally: all helpers assembled, I made a (for me) rousing speech based on Henry V before Agincourt and Terry distributed the paperwork for the thirty-eight committee rooms which would monitor our vote and send out cars to pick up those who had not voted but had promised to do so. We also had three hundred volunteers, including Jill and all my children and relatives and friends, to shove leaflets stating "Good morning it is election day. Don't forget to vote and thank you for being so kind to the Liberal candidate" through people's letter-boxes between 4.30a.m. and 6.30a.m.; we warned the distributors to do so quietly and try not to disturb the dog.

A friend with a Range Rover came to chauffeur me and we started on the Lincolnshire border at Tydd St Gyles at 7a.m. — handshakes for officers in the polling station, ensure that they had tea and sandwiches, thank you and goodbye. Ninety stations to go. By noon I was convinced that I was going to win. Three weeks after I had been greeted with embarrassment and silence, there was hardly a pedestrian who did not wave at my battle bus or stick up their thumbs in goodwill gestures. The law states that party posters must not be displayed outside polling stations lest someone who sets out to vote for one candidate sees another hopeful's poster and puts their cross against that name instead. There was much phoning of agents to report transgressions; otherwise things went smoothly. We had been able to man all but six of the stations to take names and numbers from voters' poll cards, so we could compare these with the list of those who had pledged support.

The Conservatives manned every station, Labour about half. The three tellers would stand outside and, while the Conservative shook hands with his rep. and went in to make thank you noises, I made a point of shaking Labour and Tory tellers' hands before according my Liberal teller a slightly protracted contact. By 8p.m. we were beginning on our third sweep of houses, announcing that there was not long to go and our cars would take people there and bring them back.

At my meetings I had told audiences that, when it came to election day, they might do better being taken to the poll in a Conservative car: usually more comfortable, there are more of them and they are newer than ours; you don't have to tell them which way you voted. As it happened, by 9a.m. we had some two hundred cars appear from around the land, their drivers come to help: "Give us a sticker for the windscreen and tell us what you would like us to do and where."

It was like the small ships sailing to Dunkirk.

The count for the Isle of Ely by-election took place in a hall in March and was scheduled to start at 10a.m. on Friday, 27 July . . . which was coincidentally the day the House of Commons rose for their three months' summer recess. (This had been helpful, in that I was able to tell voters that Labour's Barry Young was fighting the election from his own pocket and victory for him would condemn him to penury as the Westminster fees office did not reopen until October.

"You wouldn't want that to happen to a nice man like him.")

John Pardoe had been deputed to come to March for the count, to hold my hand and answer difficult questions on why the Liberal challenge had failed. He was to arrive at Huntingdon Station, some 20 miles from March, at 11.05.

I drove to Huntingdon to meet him. He was perplexed. "Why aren't you at the count?"

"Wanted to make sure you got here safely."

"How bad is it?"

"Bad for the Conservative, worse for Labour."

He did not believe me. Told me to say, whatever happened, that this was a good result for us Libs and gives us a solid platform for the general election.

"But I won," I told him.

He looked at me as doctors look at dying patients who invite them to come to Christmas dinner.

There was a massive crowd outside the March hall, mostly Liberal supporters because the majority of Conservatives, by virtue of their standing in the community, had gained access to the count. Barry Young looked depressed. Stevens looked terrible. Sixty council clerks were emptying the ballot boxes and counting the voting slips and as they sorted them into piles for each candidate, the three parties' tellers were checking the distribution. On the tall centre table were the piles of candidates' ballot papers and mine was slightly, but significantly, taller than Stevens', substantially taller than Young's.

Pardoe shook his head in puzzlement. "I didn't believe you, but you're right."

Jill looked at the wholly dejected Stevens and said, "I didn't realise how much he needed this victory. Perhaps we should have let him win. Look at him." Stevens was close to tears.

The High Sheriff, who was acting as returning officer, ambled across to me, having spent the previous hours chatting to the Tory cluster, and said, "Freud, how do you pronounce your middle name?"

I told him to go forth and multiply, not using those actual words, adding that he had had three weeks to ascertain that, could have spent time on the pronunciation of archangels' names instead of sticking ever more "VOTE STEVENS CONSERVATIVE" posters on his house.

At noon, from outside the hall there came screams of delight and shouts of joy. The result of the other by-election, that at Ripon, had been announced: a Liberal win. "Make it ten! Make it ten!" they chanted. Double figures for our Westminster representation, which had been six at the general election in 1970, was a result beyond the dreams of optimists.

We made it ten.

The High Sheriff cleared his throat and announced the vote to have been as follows: Mr Clement Raphael Freud 17,390 . . . Mr John Stevens 15,920 . . . and no one could hear Barry Young's tally of 12,153 for the din made by my supporters, who had been let into the hall. "I therefore declare Mr Clement Raphael Freud to be the duly elected Member of Parliament for the constituency of the Isle of Ely."

I shook hands with my two opponents before being besieged by orange and black kisses, while Pardoe faced the TV cameras explaining Liberal policies: "Liberty, Fraternity, not to mention Equality . . ."

I had spent three weeks concentrating on winning, hardly remembering what I was trying to win. I got up earlier than my rivals, went to bed later, shook more hands, made more speeches, gained more column inches of newsprint than Stevens and Young without giving thought to what I would do if I won. There is no connection between fighting a campaign and running a country. It makes as much sense as giving office of state to the person who wins the underwater breast-stroke competition at the baths.

On that Friday afternoon of euphoria, posing for a thousand pictures, hugging and being hugged, exchanging congratulations with supporters and bursting into laughter with joy and disbelief (also having some thoughts about what would happen at the Maltings in Ely which the Conservatives had booked for a celebration party that evening) it began to hit home: campaigning is fun; representing is serious. As the House of Commons closed for summer hols two hours after my result was announced, I would have three months of being an MP without having a base, an office, or a seat on a green bench from which to speak.

Unlike other contests in which I had competed, this had not been for a one-off silver cup or a holiday in the

Canary Islands, but for a position that would affect the rest of my life. Other Freuds had been nominated for Nobel and Turner prizes, received honorary doctorates, academic awards, freedoms of cities, Companionships of Honour. This Freud had been elected to Parliament to represent seventy thousand citizens.

"Why aren't you looking happier?" asked Jill. Good question; It suddenly occurred to me that after nine years of fame, I now had something solid about which to be famous . . . and cheered up no end. I put on my happy look.

After an hour of sipping lukewarm victory champagne, jumping up and down, doing yet more hugging and being hugged, agreeing to host an all-night party at the Griffin Hotel, it was decided to have a celebratory motorcade around the Isle. I was to stand in the back of an open pick-up van with Matthew, aged nine, by my side, whizzing along the open roads, dawdling and waving as we passed through towns and villages.

At Wimblington, a few miles along the Chatteris road from March, there were fifty cars behind us, blaring horns, flashing headlights into the afternoon sun. By the time we reached Doddington, two miles on, we had been awarded a police escort. People waved and cheered, we waved back and Matthew said, "I think you are now the most important person in the whole world."

Deep down, just for a brief moment, I was tempted to agree with him. Remembering my role of father, I modified his opinion to "one of the most important in the Isle of Ely". Seeing his disappointment, I added, "which is one of the most important places in the whole world."

INDEX

Bernard, Jeffrey 34, 69
Berry, Sir Gerald 146, 147
Biggs, Ronald 225
Bonaparte, Princess Marie 26, 106, 92
as bookmaker 120-1
boxing 23, 38
Brasher, Chris 176-7
Braunton, Saunton Sands Hotel 114-23
British Railways catering 141-3
Brown, A.H. 118-20
Bullitt, US ambassador 27
Burall, David (constituency chairman) 288, 292-6 *passim*, 299

C
Café Royal 65, 189
Call My Bluff 205, 282-3
Campari, selling 141-3
Campbell, Beatrix 190
Campbell, Patrick 165
Cannes, casino 107-9; Martinez Hotel 97-114
Carrington, Mrs (secretary) 163, 175, 176
Carson, Johnny 26, 255, 261
as celebrity guest 205-6, 227-8
Chancery, David 66
Chataway, Chris 176
Chuck (gambler) 109
Churchill, Winston 130, 284
class 56
Clunes, Alec 134

Coates, Michael and Caty 105, 113
Coffee Ann 46, 65
Coghill, Neville 38
cooking 45-6, 56-7, 151, 157, 163, 165, 198, 203, 227, 265-7, 284
Cooper, Dinks and Toe 33-4
Cooper, Jean (physio) 242-4
Cossack Club, Manchester 246-7
Cox, J.R. (amateur jockey) 235
Crank, R. (jockey) 244
cricket 21-2, 136, 140, 175-6, 184, 227, 283
Cusson, Mr 205-6

D
Daily Telegraph 285, 303
dancing 17, 51
Dartington Hall 10-20
Dawson, George 102-3
Dawson, Les 283
Dawson, Tony 136
demobilisation 91
Denny's outfitters 39, 58
Dersztay, Count Anton von 51-3
Desert Island Discs 16
dogs 26, 150 ; dog food commercial 215-19, 283
Dorchester Hotel 37-46, 51-64, 94, 116, 157; chefs 43-4; kitchen 42-6, 53-8; waiters 58-60
Douglas, Norman 49
drink 13, 100

shipping forecast 282
Silk, D.R.W. 163
Sizewell inquiry 30
skating 53
skiing 260
Sloane Square station 119
Smid, Monsieur (head waiter) 58, 61, 117
Smith, Cyril 285, 299, 306
Smith, Delia 227
Smith, Reggie 140
Southern TV 198; *Advertising Magazine* 200-1
Southwold 30, 31; Harbour Inn 33, 34; Summer Theatre 138
Spender, Stephen and Natasha 37, 121
Sporting Life 242
St Paul's 23
Stage, The 136, 175
Stais, Johnny 134
stand-up performance 228
Star Award (horse) 246, 250
Steel, David 37, 299, 306
Stevens, Jocelyn 193, 196
Stevens, John (Tory candidate) 303-14 *passim*
Sun 203-4, 208, 232
Sunday Telegraph 194, 203
Sutton, Tom 279, 280
Swing, Sally 14

T
Tatler 205
Ted (gopher) 131, 132
Telegraph magazine 255-63 *passim*

Tell the Truth 205, 283
Terry (agent) 296, 298, 306, 311
theft of electricity 172
Thomas, Dylan 139
Thorpe, Jeremy 283, 286, 299, 305
Time 95
Time and Tide 189, 203, 205, 284
tobogganing, Cresta Run 260-1
Tokyo 204-5
Tomalin, Nick 194
Took, Barry 175
Town 190, 191, 194
Trocadero 130
Tsarzen (horse) 240-2
TV career 195-203, 206, 223 271-2, 281; commercials 206, 215-19, 283
Twinkle, Dr 221-3 *passim*
Tyne Tees TV 201-3

U
USA 206-8, 255-6, 279, 280, 282
US Gourmet 180

V
Van, Mr (head waiter) 60, 61, 117
Vanessa (waitress) 188, 284
Venezia restaurant 86-8, 114, 128
Victoria 117
Vienna 25-7

W

waiters 57-60, 156 *see also individual entries*; pay-table 119; tips 60

Walberswick 28-36, 103, 189, 196; Anchor inn 30, 31, 34; Bell inn 30, 31, 34; ferry 52; Gannon Room 33; house 188, 189, 196

Wakefield Refreshment Room 180-2

Wakefield, Wavell 285-6

Walls, Tom 35

War, First World 5, 25, 33, 80-1; Second 28, 37, 42, 47, 130

Warriner, Tim 215-17 *passim*

Watkins, Alan 309

Weeks, Major 69, 72

West Country TV 200

What's My Line? 205

Wheeler, Tony 97

White, Gordon 274

Whitehead, Sergeant 85-8

Wilkinson, Mr (customer) 109-11

Williams, Kenneth 210-12

Williams, Mr (staff manager, Dorchester) 116-17

Williams, Sir William 124

Wilson, Harold 217, 285, 304

Wilson, Julian 248

Winter Fair (horse) 235-7, 244-5, 250-1

Wise, Ernie 283

Woman 203

Wontner, Sir Hugh 151

Y

Yokohama 204

Young, Barry (Labour candidate) 304, 309, 312

ISIS publish a wide range of books in large print, from fiction to biography. Any suggestions for books you would like to see in large print or audio are always welcome. Please send to the Editorial department at:

ISIS Publishing Ltd.
7 Centremead
Osney Mead
Oxford OX2 0ES
(01865) 250 333

A full list of titles is available free of charge from:
Ulverscroft large print books

(UK)
The Green
Bradgate Road, Anstey
Leicester LE7 7FU
Tel: (0116) 236 4325

(Australia)
P.O Box 953
Crows Nest
NSW 1585
Tel: (02) 9436 2622

(USA)
1881 Ridge Road
P.O Box 1230, West Seneca,
N.Y. 14224-1230
Tel: (716) 674 4270

(Canada)
P.O Box 80038
Burlington
Ontario L7L 6B1
Tel: (905) 637 8734

(New Zealand)
P.O Box 456
Feilding
Tel: (06) 323 6828

Details of **ISIS** complete and unabridged audio books are also available from these offices. Alternatively, contact your local library for details of their collection of **ISIS** large print and unabridged audio books.